THE GOLDEN TRIANGLE

THE GOLDEN TRIANGLE

Inside Southeast Asia's Drug Trade

KO-LIN CHIN

Cornell University Press
Ithaca and London

Copyright © 2009 by Cornell University

First published 2009 by Cornell University Press
First printing, Cornell Paperbacks, 2009

Printed in the United States of America

Library of Congress Cataloging-in-Publication Data

Chin, Ko-lin.
  The Golden Triangle : inside Southeast Asia's drug trade/
Ko-lin Chin.
     p. cm.
  Includes bibliographical references and index.
  ISBN 978-0-8014-4666-5 (cloth : alk.paper) — ISBN 978-0-8014-
7521-4 (pbk. : alk. paper)
  1. Drug traffic—Burma—Shan State. 2. Drug traffic—Golden
Triangle (Southeast Asia) 3. Wa (Burmese people)—
Commerce. I. Title
  HV5840.B93C55 2009
  363.4509591—dc22   2008036071

Cornell University Press strives to use environmentally responsible suppliers and materials to the fullest extent possible in the publishing of its books. Such materials include vegetable-based, low-VOC inks and acid-free papers that are recycled, totally chlorine-free, or partly composed of nonwood fibers. For further information, visit our website at www.cornellpress.cornell.edu.

Cloth printing   10 9 8 7 6 5 4 3 2 1
Paperback printing   10 9 8 7 6 5 4 3 2 1

For my parents
and
In memory of my grandmother and Wei Xiang

Contents

Acknowledgments   ix

Introduction: Into the Thick of It   1

1. The Golden Triangle and Burma   8

2. The Wa   17

3. The Opium Trade   47

4. Heroin Production and Trafficking   86

5. The Methamphetamine Business   127

6. Drug Use   155

7. Drug Control   187

8. The Business and Politics of Drugs   220

Appendix: Names in Pinyin Romanization
      and Other Spellings   243

Notes   245

Bibliography   259

Index   275

Acknowledgments

Many people have contributed to this research project and I very much appreciate their assistance and support. First and foremost, I would like to thank Larry Chung, executive director of the International Foundation for the Peaceful Elimination of Opium Crops. Without Larry's relentless efforts in helping me overcome a variety of obstacles along the way, this project would never have been initiated or completed.

A courageous woman in northern Thailand and an equally stalwart man in southwest China assisted me on the occasions when I was trying to clandestinely cross the border into the Wa area of Burma. They also aided me in locating key informants to be interviewed in the border areas. They took great risks in helping me, and I can never thank them enough for their assistance. I can only thank them anonymously because their identities should not be revealed.

I would also like to thank all the people who played a key role in helping me collect data in the Wa area. I am most grateful to members of my research team: Wei Xiang, Chen Wei, Chen Lifan, Ai Ying, Wei Xiaolan, Zhao Liqing (Yixi), Xiao Qinghong, Li Xiuqiong, and Ting Xiao. I was fortunate to have recruited an exceptional group of interviewers and research assistants who were not only completely dedicated to the project but were pleasant companions and fun to work with. Two weeks after

I had completed data collection and left the Wa State, I was shocked and deeply saddened to learn that Wei Xiang, the lead interviewer, had been hit by a car while riding her motorcycle in Bangkang. She was taken to a local hospital, but died a few hours later. She was only twenty-two. This book is partly dedicated to her.

I also wish to thank the Wa leaders, in particular Bao Youxiang, Xiao Mingliang, Zhou Dafu, Wang Keqiang, Chen Longsheng, and Yan Shengbing, for helping me in many ways; their support was critical to the successful completion of this research project. During my stay in the Wa area, the leaders kept their promise not to interfere in my activities in any way. Moreover, they gave me complete freedom in the recruitment of research assistants and interviewers, the selection of research subjects and sites, and the development of interview questionnaires. All my requests for assistance were responded to promptly and efficiently by the Wa leaders. Their level of cooperation far exceeded my expectations.

I am also extremely grateful to three anonymous reviewers for their careful reading of early versions of this manuscript and their detailed suggestions as to how it could be improved.

Huan Gao of California State University, Stanislaus, and Galma Jahic of Istanbul Bilgi University were my research assistants for this project in the United States when they were PhD students at Rutgers University. They were instrumental in helping me manage and analyze the data set. They were meticulous and efficient, and invaluable colleagues in this undertaking.

This manuscript was carefully edited by Judy Mellecker, and I thank her very much for spending so many painstaking hours figuring out what I was trying to say and helping me say it correctly and clearly. In addition to editing the manuscript, Judy provided me many good suggestions on how to improve the structure of the manuscript. I also thank John Raymond for his excellent work in copyediting the manuscript and suggesting ways to improve it.

I wish to thank Peter Wissoker, my editor at Cornell University Press, for his patience and understanding in working with me. Peter played a key role in helping me transform a lengthy manuscript into one that I believe is more concise and better focused. Susan Specter, the manuscript editor, was extremely helpful in the process of transforming a daunting amount of material into a book. I also thank Rutgers Cartography for preparing the maps included in the text.

It is hardly necessary to absolve others from responsibility for the views set forth, but I do so anyway, to resolve any doubt that those acknowledged necessarily share my assessments of the problems. Support for this research was provided by Grant SES-0095929 from the National Science Foundation. The opinions in this book are mine and do not necessarily reflect the policies or views of the National Science Foundation.

THE GOLDEN TRIANGLE

INTRODUCTION

INTO THE THICK OF IT

Burma is the second largest opium-producing country in the world after Afghanistan.[1] Within Burma, most of the opium is grown in the Wa area of northeastern Shan State.[2] Very few people have had access to the Wa area. The sale of opium, as well as the heroin and methamphetamine that is also produced there, enriches a small minority of merchants. But it also goes to fund the growth of the nascent Wa State, supporting the building of infrastructure and state institutions.

Most people know very little about the everyday people that produce and distribute drugs. This book explores the drug trade in Burma. It is based on face-to-face interviews with a large number of opium growers, drug producers and dealers, drug users, and Wa leaders in the Wa area, as well as interviews with key informants along the Thai-Burma border and law enforcement authorities in the United States and several Asian countries.

The Wa area is located in the Shan State of Burma. Divided into the Northern Wa State and the Southern Wa State, it has a population of approximately six hundred thousand people, including the Wa, Lahu, Shan, Chinese, and other ethnic groups.[3] There are an additional 350,000 Wa people on the Chinese side of the border, primarily in the counties of Cangyuan, Ximeng, Lancang, and Gengma of Yunnan Province (Luo 1995).[4] This Mon-Khmer, animist ethnic group is essentially an agrarian people. Over the past two decades the drug trade has remained one of the few viable businesses in this traditionally very poor area, and it is the most reliable means for Wa leaders to raise the money they need for state building.

This has led many in the area to grow opium as their primary crop. Leaders among the Wa tend to see business and politics as tightly intertwined, often blurring the distinction between private and public interests. Wa leaders, who are involved in the drug trade both as private entrepreneurs and as state agents, see themselves as having a responsibility to raise large amounts of cash for the central and local governments. These Wa leaders consider themselves conscientious political leaders—state builders trying to promote the well-being of their people—rather than drug lords. Although these businessmen/politicians and their families live a lavish lifestyle, they also pour large amounts of money into public works projects such as schools, roads, and power plants.

The triangular relationship that binds together people involved in illegal activities, legitimate business entrepreneurs, and corrupt politicians is neither new nor unique to the Golden Triangle. In Italy, Russia, Colombia, Mexico, Nigeria, Taiwan, and many other locales where Mafia and other organized crime groups flourish, there have been highly developed links between gangsters, businessmen, and politicians (Stille 1995; Thoumi 1995; Shelley 1997; Zaitch 2002; Chin 2003; Chepesiuk 2003; Godson 2003).[5] What distinguishes the Wa case is that this cycling of money also flows back into the public sector. In this book I show how these practices take place on a daily basis, bringing readers into the everyday lives of drug producers, drug merchants, the farmers who supply them, and the users who are the local consumers of these homegrown products.

The Regional Context

To understand the local political economy of the drug trade in Burma one must also see it in the context of its neighbors. The drug industry in the Shan State of Burma is made possible by corrupt agreements between Wa leaders and Chinese "businessmen" and between leaders in Rangoon (Yangon) and Beijing. Wa leaders need someone who can teach them how to make money, and Chinese businessmen, mostly from the adjacent Yunnan Province of China, need a place where they can wheel and deal freely, even if they have to pay their host (Wa leaders) a share of their earnings. The Rangoon authorities need to make peace with the Wa so that they can concentrate on the opposing political forces in Rangoon, Aung San Suu Kyi and the National League for Democracy or NLD. The Wa leadership's willingness to act as a buffer against Thai armed forces in the southern part of Shan State also appeases the Rangoon government. For the Chinese authorities in Beijing, establishing a good relationship with Rangoon is probably much more important than suppressing the Wa drug trade (and embarrassing Burmese officials). China is eager to exploit Burma's natural resources and is developing a transportation corridor along the Mekong to improve economic development in the mostly underdeveloped southwestern part of the country. In sum, politics and economic development supersede drug enforcement, and corrupt exchanges between state actors and drug merchants are made possible by the unique geopolitics of Southeast Asia in the new millennium. China is determined to develop a strong economy and, to do so, it needs vast amounts of natural resources to fuel its growth. Burma is not only rich in natural resources, it is also one of the few countries in Southeast Asia that is more closely allied to China than the United States. Regardless of how much the authorities in Beijing dislike the Rangoon regime and their drug-producing ethnic minorities in the border area, they are careful not to allow Burma to become a U.S. ally, fearing they would lose the ability to exploit the country's natural resources and its strategic position as a gateway to the Bay of Bengal.

After Burma gained independence from the British government in 1948, the Communist Party of Burma (CPB) became a major force in the resistance against the newly formed government in Rangoon. In the war against the Rangoon government, the Burman-dominated CPB leadership relied primarily on armed groups in the border areas for muscle; these groups included the Shan, the Kokang, the Kachin, and especially the Wa. During that period, the Wa leadership came largely from the top ranks of the military resistance against the Burmese army (Lintner 1990). After the Wa dissociated themselves from the CPB in 1989, they were eager to establish their own identity and improve living conditions in their region. After decades of war and destruction, the Wa area was one of the least developed places in the world. For Wa leaders, who were deeply influenced by the reform and open door policy in China, their number-one priority was state building, and state building required a large amount of capital. Consequently, opium, which had been cultivated in the area probably since the 1830s, became a major source of tax revenue for the Wa leadership. In the early 1990s, as both legitimate and illegitimate cross-border trade between Burma and China began to flourish, many entrepreneurs from China began to look for business opportunities in the Wa region and other newly established special regions.[6] With the arrival of the Chinese, heroin production began to take off: it became much easier to import precursor chemicals from China into Burma and to export the finished product from Burma to the international market, especially China. The surrender of Khun Sa, one of the most powerful drug lords in the Golden Triangle, to the Burmese authorities in 1996 was also a key factor in the movement of heroin production from the Thai-Burma border in the south, where Khun Sa's forces had operated, to the China-Burma border in the north.

When Thai authorities began to crack down on methamphetamine production in their own country, Chinese entrepreneurs in Thailand, Burma, and China took advantage of the situation and began to mass produce methamphetamine in the Wa area to meet the enormous demand in Thailand. The development of the methamphetamine trade was ideal for the Wa regime: In 1996, Wa leaders promised that they would end the cultivation of opium and heroin production by 2005. Not only did it help the Wa leaders achieve their promise, but by refraining from feeding China's drug market with heroin from the Wa area, it avoided antagonizing the Chinese government. Wa leaders were fully aware that their prospects for economic development rested mostly on a good relationship with China. For the Wa leaders, supplying Thais with methamphetamine tablets was a lesser evil than supplying heroin to the Chinese. Besides, the production and distribution of methamphetamine was much easier to manage than the production and distribution of heroin. However, after the Wa regime began to manufacture methamphetamine tablets in the mid-1990s, they never stopped their involvement in the opium and heroin businesses.

On the Ground

The research for this project was carried out primarily in 2001, with subsequent trips to Asia to collect additional information from law enforcement authorities and key informants in the Thai-Burma area. Very few people have had access to the Wa area, and the ones who did have access mostly did not speak or write Chinese, the language most likely to be used by Wa leaders and people in the drug trade.

I worked with a group of local Wa students whom I trained before going out into the field. We took three trips to the remote areas and were able to interview three hundred opium farmers. The interviews were conducted face-to-face in the Wa language. The interviewers wrote down the answers in Chinese on a standardized questionnaire that also was in Chinese. We also conducted interviews with fifty-two drug users in Bangkang, including twenty-five opium users, twenty-five methamphetamine users, and two heroin users. Either the heroin users were the most difficult type of drug user to locate or there were simply not many heroin users in the Wa area.

Besides drug users, we also conducted interviews with people who were involved in the drug business, including traders, producers, and traffickers. These subjects were extremely hard to locate, simply because no one in the Wa would openly admit that he or she was involved in the drug business, even though most of the rich and powerful people in the area were involved in it and everyone knows who is involved. We interviewed thirty-five drug businesspeople, most of them opium traders, followed by methamphetamine producers and distributors. Locating heroin producers or dealers was, like finding heroin users, the most challenging. These thirty-five subjects were willing to talk to us mainly because most of them were family members, relatives, or neighbors of my interviewers.[7]

Besides opium farmers, drug users, and drug entrepreneurs, I also interviewed twenty-one Wa leaders. Interviews with Wa leaders were not as rewarding as I had anticipated, mainly because most of them were not as open and candid as I wanted them to be. Luckily, however, several Wa leaders were willing to tell me at great length about the drug problem there, and I conducted multiple interviews with these leaders.

In sum, I stayed in the Wa Hills from February 10, 2001, to May 18, 2001, and conducted three hundred interviews with opium growers, fifty-two interviews with drug users, thirty-five interviews with drug producers/dealers, twenty-one interviews with Wa leaders, and ten interviews with key informants. Altogether, 418 interviews were conducted. Between 2002 and 2005, I also interviewed twenty law enforcement authorities in Burma, Thailand, Taiwan, and China. I conducted the interviews face-to-face, aided by an interview guide. The interviews were conducted informally in a restaurant or a teahouse, and the subjects were mostly people I knew or had been referred to by their close friends or colleagues. As a result, they were relatively open and candid during the interviews. I visited Burma in July 2002, October 2004, and August 2006 to interview law enforcement officials and key informants in Rangoon, Mandalay, and Muse.

I also asked three Wa women to conduct ethnographic fieldwork in a Wa village for about three months. The purpose was to collect qualitative data on the everyday life of Wa farmers by living near them and working with them. It was very demanding work, but they were able to collect invaluable field data for me, even though they were not professional ethnographers and had never lived in a remote village before.

Conducting a study of this magnitude on a sensitive topic in a difficult terrain like the Wa Hills was a major challenge. Even though we conducted more than four hundred formal and informal interviews with people from diverse backgrounds and locations, the findings should be considered exploratory and should be interpreted with caution because of the inherent limitations in the use of personal contacts as well as in the snowball sampling technique we used. For example, we interviewed a small number of opium farmers in a village in Nandeng Special District across the border from China in Burma. We knew that this particular village, occupied mainly by Chinese, was not representative of the entire district because the region was occupied by many other ethnic groups, each with its own pattern of opium cultivation. Opium yields could differ dramatically from village to village. Also, the study could be considered limited in scope, because the research team did not visit Southern Wa State or interview anyone from the area. Although it is not a major opium producing area, the Thai media has reported that it is a center of methamphetamine production and trafficking.

In any study like this there will not be complete rapport or trust between the researcher and his subjects, in this case the Wa leaders and the drug entrepreneurs. Even though the Wa leaders allowed me virtually total freedom to conduct this study in their territory, they did not completely trust me nor were they always truthful when I interviewed them. Some Wa leaders were skeptical of who I was and what I was doing there. It was only natural for them not to reveal too much about the drug trade in their area. Drug producers and traffickers are, by definition, suspicious people. However, the fact that my interviewers were, in most cases, the relatives or friends of the drug entrepreneurs we interviewed gave me confidence that the data was relatively reliable and valid. Wa leaders also became more cooperative after they noticed that I worked hard every day; my busy schedule and lack of involvement in the many diversions available (drinking, drugs, gambling) convinced the Wa leaders that I was serious about my research project.[8]

In this book I offer an inside look at one of the global centers of opium and methamphetamine production, and at the importance of a nexus made up of the organized criminality embodied by the drug trade, state building, and a group of individuals who are simultaneously local political leaders, drug entrepreneurs, and members of heavily armed militias. Throughout I will return to questions about how this political-economic configuration developed, what motivates its participants, and how it shapes life in the Wa areas of Burma.

The people involved in the drug trade, and their motives for being involved, are often misunderstood. Outside observers may see them as being motivated by greed or by a desire to escape their poverty. What we fail to see is that the drug trade can be, in certain parts of the world, a legitimate and logical endeavor for many people to simultaneously improve their living conditions and build a state. Moreover, because the drug trade is an important part of the politics of Southeast Asia, and deeply embedded in one of the most isolated and war torn countries in the world, it is not possible to permanently eliminate the drug problem without solving the political and economic problems that are responsible for the development of the drug trade in the first place.

CHAPTER ONE

THE GOLDEN TRIANGLE AND BURMA

One of the world's major opium cultivation and heroin producing areas
is the Golden Triangle, a 150,000-square-mile, mountainous region located where the borders of Burma, Laos, and Thailand meet (United Nations Office on Drugs and Crime 2006). In the 1990s, it was estimated that
Burma produced more than 50 percent of the world's raw opium and refined as much as 75 percent of the world's heroin (Southeast Asian Information Network 1998). During that time, Burma was also the largest
source of heroin for the U.S. market, responsible for 80 percent of the
heroin available in New York City (U.S. Senate 1992; Gelbard 1998). In the
late 1990s, hundreds of millions of methamphetamine tablets were produced annually in northeastern Burma and smuggled into Thailand for
the booming Thai market (Phongpaichit, Piriyarangsan, and Teerat 1998;
Chouvy and Meissonnier 2004).

The major opium growing area in Burma is located in the biggest and
most populated state, the Shan State, occupied by various ethnic armed
groups (United Nations Office on Drugs and Crime 2005a). The Wa, one of
the largest of these ethnic armed groups, is in control of an area referred to
as the Wa State, or Burma Shan State No. 2 Special Region, which produced
60 percent of the opium in the Shan State in the late 1990s (Lintner 1998a).[1]

According to the United Nations' 2005 Opium survey in Burma, "94 percent of total opium poppy cultivation in Myanmar took place in the Shan State and 40 percent of national cultivation (or 42% of Shan State cultivation) in the Wa Special Region" (United Nations Office on Drugs and Crime 2005a, 3).

Shan State provided a base for the Communist Party of Burma (CPB) before the party collapsed in 1989, when leaders of the Wa area and of Kokang (another area in the Shan State that is dominated by an ethnic Chinese armed group) announced their independence from the CPB (Lintner 1990).[2] According to the Burmese government, the CPB, which had strong support from China and various non-Burmese ethnic groups, was a major threat to its authority (Smith 1999). After the disintegration of the CPB, the Burmese government quickly arranged cease-fire agreements with former CPB groups in the Shan State. The ethnic groups promised not to fight against the Burmese government and, in return, the Burmese authorities allowed these ethnic groups to keep their arms and to remain involved in the opium trade (Steinberg 2001). U.S. sources estimated that Burma's opium production rose from 1,250 metric tons in 1988 to 2,450 metric tons in 1989 and continued to increase thereafter, to 2,600 metric tons in 1997 (Lintner 1998b). Opium production in Burma began to decline significantly after 1997, and by 2003 it had been reduced to 484 metric tons, according to U.S. estimates, and 810 metric tons, according to the UN opium survey (Jelsma 2005). A subsequent UN opium survey found that opium production in Burma had continued to decline, to 370 metric tons in 2004 and 312 metric tons in 2005 (United Nations Office on Drugs and Crime 2005a).[3] Interventions (mainly suppression and crop-substitution programs) by local authorities, the Burmese government, and the United Nations; years of unfavorable weather conditions; and the loss of U.S. and European markets were all cited as reasons for the dramatic decline of opium production in Burma (Jelsma 2005). Even so, Burma is still ranked as the second-largest producer of opium in the world, after Afghanistan (Labrousse 2005; United Nations Office on Drugs and Crime 2006).

As opium and heroin production in the Golden Triangle began to take a downward turn in 1997, a year after the surrender of Khun Sa (a drug lord who symbolized the drug trade in the Golden Triangle for decades) to the Burmese government, the explosive growth of the manufacturing of methamphetamine pills in the area during the late 1990s and early 2000s raised doubts in the West over whether the Golden Triangle would ever be able to transform itself into a drug-free zone. Methamphetamine pills produced in

Burma began to saturate the Thai drug market in the late 1990s, and the use of the pills began to spread from bus drivers and laborers to students and young professionals (Chouvy and Meissonnier 2004). New towns were built along the Thai-Burma border, allegedly by drug money, to promote the drug trade. Tensions between the Burmese and Thai authorities along the border began to mount, and border clashes occurred when one side thought that the other side was intruding into its territory. The stability of the region was seriously undermined by the massive production of methamphetamine (Dupont 2001). Today, there is no sign that the methamphetamine trade is going to follow opium and heroin production and begin to fade away; this is the one business that businesspeople and political leaders in the area desperately need to offset the economic loss caused by the decline in opium and heroin production.

Burma: A Country in Turmoil

Burma is bordered on the north and northeast by China, on the east and southeast by Laos and Thailand, and on the west by Bangladesh and India. Its coastline runs along the Andaman Sea to the south and the Bay of Bengal to the southwest. Its total area is 2.6 million square miles (6.77 million square kilometers). "Burma is one of the most ethnically diverse countries in the world. Ethnic minorities make up 30 to 40 percent of its estimated 52 million population, and occupy roughly half the land area" (Kramer 2005, 33). The main ethnic groups are Burman, Kachin, Kayin (or Karen), Kayah, Chin, Mon, Rakhine, and Shan (Ministry of Information 2002). Burman, the majority ethnic group, constitutes about 70 percent of the whole population. Almost 90 percent of the population is Buddhist (Hla Min 2000). The capital of Burma was Rangoon (or Yangon) before the authorities moved the capital to Naypyidaw, an up-country site near the town of Pyinmana in Mandalay State in November 2005.

Burma was colonized by the British and became annexed to India in 1886, and it was briefly occupied by the Japanese during World War II (Thant Myint-U 2001). After the war, the British administration was reestablished in Burma. On February 1947, Aung San, a charismatic Burman leader, concluded the Panglong Agreement with Shan, Kachin, and Chin leaders that laid the foundation for the establishment of a union of equal states in Burma (Elliott 1999). Unfortunately, in July 1947 Aung San and several other prominent leaders were assassinated as they assembled for a meeting in Rangoon. After gaining independence from the British the fol-

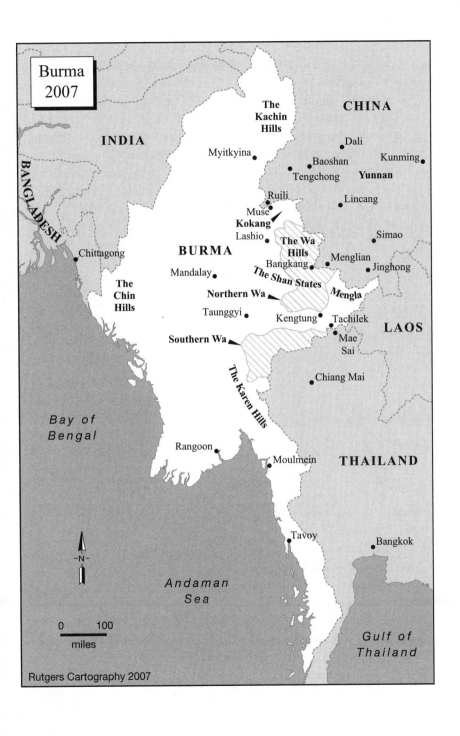

Burma
2007

CHINA

The
Kachin
Hills

INDIA

Dali

Myitkyina

Baoshan

Kunming

Tengchong

Yunnan

BANGLADESH

Ruili

Lincang

Muse

Kokang

Simao

Lashio

The Wa
Hills

Chittagong

BURMA

Bangkang

Menglian

Jinghong

Mandalay

The Shan States

The
Chin
Hills

Northern Wa

Mengla

Taunggyi

Kengtung

Tachilek

LAOS

Southern Wa

Mae
Sai

The Karen Hills

Chiang Mai

Bay of
Bengal

Rangoon

Moulmein

THAILAND

-N-

Tavoy

Bangkok

Andaman
Sea

0   100
miles

Gulf of
Thailand

lowing year, the country began to disintegrate as many ethnic groups became disillusioned with a central government that was dominated by the Burman (Callahan 2003).

Only three months after independence, the first battle between the Communist Party of Burma (CPB) and government forces broke out and fighting soon spread throughout central and upper Burma (Lintner 1990). In the meantime, many insurgencies sprang up around the country as various ethnic groups also began to fight the Rangoon government (Smith 1999). In 1949, soldiers from the armies of the defeated Kuomintang (KMT) entered Burma from China's Yunnan Province. The arrival of KMT armed groups had a crucial, long-lasting effect on the region (Cowell 2005):

> At Burma's independence in 1948, the country's opium production amounted to a mere thirty tons, or just enough to supply local addicts in the Shan states, where most of the poppies were grown. The KMT invasion changed that overnight. The territory they took over—Kokang, the Wa Hills and the mountains north of Kengtung—was traditionally the best opium growing area in Burma. Gen. Li Mi persuaded the farmers to grow more opium, and introduced a hefty opium tax, which forced the farmers to grow even more in order to make ends meet. By the mid-1950s, Burma's modest opium production had increased to a couple of hundred tons per year. (Lintner 1994b, 116–17)

On March 1, 1962, Prime Minister U Nu was ousted after a coup masterminded by a group of army officers led by General Ne Win, a career soldier who played a key role in the anti-Japanese resistance movement during World War II and in the suppression of insurgent ethnic groups after independence (Thant Myint-U 2006). "On the following day, the federal 1947 Constitution was suspended and the bicameral parliament dissolved. . . . Burma's fourteen-year-long experiment with federalism and parliamentary democracy was over" (Lintner 1994b, 170). After the coup, the Revolutionary Council was formed to implement many new policies to change Burma from a relatively liberal state into a uniquely Burmese socialist state. The Revolutionary Council formed the Burma Socialist Programme Party (BSPP) in 1962 and announced its philosophy in "The Correlation of Man and His Environment" in the following year, which provides philosophical underpinnings for the "Burmese Way to Socialism," an "inward-looking development strategy with emphasis on self-reliance, isolation and strict neutrality in foreign policy. Foreign direct investment was barred" (Collignon 2001, 87–88).

Mixing European socialist policies with Chinese Communist strategies, the Revolutionary Council began to implement dramatic policies that would eventually drive out of Burma the Indians and the Chinese, the two ethnic groups that dominated the Burmese economy. First, in February 1963 the Revolutionary Council nationalized many economic enterprises (Marshall 2002). All business firms, including many small private companies, were taken over by army personnel, and within a couple of years most of these businesses were forced to shut down because of mismanagement, embezzlement, and poor performance. Second, the regime devalued 50 and 100 kyat banknotes without compensation; the intention was to remove wealth from foreign hands. After these two policies were put in place, a large number of Indians, many of them key entrepreneurs in Burma, were expelled to India by Burmese authorities (Fink 2001). In 1967, when the Cultural Revolution was at its peak in China, clashes between Chinese Red Guards and Burmese students in Rangoon resulted in a nationwide anti-Chinese movement; by the time it ended, many Chinese had been killed or assaulted and their houses looted and burned. As a result, tens of thousands of Chinese left Burma for either China or Taiwan (Thant Myint-U 2006).

The following year, China drastically increased its support for the CPB insurgency. Several key insurgent leaders who were trained in China crossed over into Burma, took over many border towns, and set up their headquarters. A large number of young Chinese intellectuals (*zhiqing*) also voluntarily came to Burma to support the CPB. Many of them are now top leaders of the Wa, the Kokang, and the Mengla governments.

After the departure of Indian and Chinese businesspeople, Burma's economy began to falter. The establishment of Communist-style cooperatives also depressed the economy and helped to develop a vast black market where the rich still brought what they wanted by paying much more than was paid in the state-controlled stores (Fink 2001).

After the 1962 coup, in order to fight against insurgent ethnic groups in the remote areas, General Ne Win's Rangoon-based socialist government formed a number of local home-guard units called Ka Kwe Ye (KKY):

The plan was to rally as many local warlords as possible—mostly non-political brigands and private army commanders—behind the Burmese army in exchange for the right to use all government-controlled roads and towns in Shan State for opium smuggling. By trading in opium, Burma's military government hoped that the KKY militias would be self-supporting. (Lintner 2003, 256)

Many KKY leaders later became some of the most influential figures in the drug business.

From the time of coup in 1962 until 1988, Burma was wracked by armed conflict between the Rangoon government and militant ethnic groups. On several occasions, the rebel groups were poised to take over Rangoon. The Rangoon government also clashed frequently with students who participated in street protests against the government. In 1988, a brawl in a teashop in Rangoon between students and local youths turned into massive, antigovernment street demonstrations led by college students (Steinberg 2001). The Rangoon government reacted violently: many students were gunned down and thousands were arrested, and all universities, colleges, and schools were closed. However, large-scale street demonstrations continued to spread to other cities and towns, and soon the entire country was shaken by daily demonstrations. According to a friend I interviewed in Rangoon: "Nineteen eighty-eight was the best chance for the people to overthrow the military junta; once the chance was gone, people just lost any hope of getting rid of them."[4]

Ne Win resigned as BSPP chairman and in September 1988 the State Law and Order Restoration Council (SLORC) was formed to shore up the regime. The pro-democracy movement established the National League for Democracy (NLD) and Aung San Suu Kyi, the daughter of the late Aung San, was named as general secretary (Fink 2001).

In March 1989, a mutiny broke out in the CPB in the Kokang area, and a month later rebellious Wa troops captured its Bangkang headquarters, ending the forty-one-year Communist insurgency in Burma (Lintner 1990). The CPB's ageing leadership fled to China. Luo Xinghan, a Kokang Chinese who was known as the King of Opium, was asked by the Burmese authorities to initiate a cease-fire agreement. Not long after, Khin Nyunt, then head of Burma's military intelligence, visited the Kokang and the Wa areas and cease-fire agreements were signed between the regime and the two former CBP groups (Cowell 2005).

Under pressure from the international community, the SLORC conducted a multiparty general election in 1990. The NLD won a landslide victory and captured about 60 percent of the vote—and 392 of the parliamentary seats, including all fifty-nine seats in the Rangoon Division. The military-backed National Unity Party won only ten seats. However, not only did the SLORC refuse to turn over power to the NLD but it also begin to round up NLD leaders. The SLORC had put Aung San Suu Kyi under house arrest in 1989. People in Burma were again deeply disappointed with their government and their hopes for reform were completely crushed (Taylor 2001).

The regime worked to consolidate its power:

> In the years following the 1990 election, Burma's generals focused on four objectives. First, they sought to expand greatly the size of the armed forces in order to be in a stronger position against their armed and unarmed opponents. As a result, the number of soldiers was increased from 180,000 in 1988 to over 400,000 by 1999 and new bases were constructed throughout the country. Second, the ruling generals worked to break up the organizational structure of the pro-democracy movement and particularly the NLD. Third, they attempted to neutralize the ethnic nationalities by making cease-fire agreements with almost all the armed groups. And fourth, they tried to improve the economy by opening up the country to trade and foreign investment. (Fink 2001, 77)

In November 1997 the SLORC renamed itself the State Peace and Development Council (SPDC), presumably to project a softer image. However, things have remained the same in Burma since the military coup in 1962. When I visited Burma in December 1997, my first trip back to the country I had left thirty years earlier, it was as if I had never been away. Nothing had changed over the past three decades, except that some of the roads and buildings were in worse shape than before and the city now became a ghost town after dark because of a combination of curfew, repression, and shutting down of nightlife.

I visited Burma again in July 2002 to interview Burmese government and law enforcement officials. The situation then was worse than 1997 because the kyat, the Burmese currency, had taken a nosedive after border clashes between Burma and Thailand in 2001.[5] Inflation gripped the country. The unemployment rate was high and many people I talked to were extremely unhappy with the regime. A waiter in a Chinese restaurant told me he was making 8,000 kyat ($32) a month. He said waiters in small coffee shops made significantly less, about 3,000 kyat ($12) a month. He also said the only good jobs in Rangoon were for those who were well connected.

On October 20, 2004, General Khin Nyunt, sixty five, was forced to resign his dual posts as prime minister and chief of military intelligence. Burmese army chief Maung Aye was reportedly not in favor of granting too much autonomy to the United Wa State Army (UWSA), while Khin Nyunt was said to have had very close ties to it (Tasker and Lintner 2001). By coincidence, I visited Muse, a Burmese town right across from Ruili, China, several days after the removal of Khin Nyunt and when I passed by the military intelligence office there, it had already been shut down. Local people told me this was once a place no ordinary citizen wanted to go near and now it was just an abandoned building. After Khin Nyunt was ousted, State Peace and Development Council Chairman Senior General Than Shwe and Vice Chairman General Maung Aye appointed Lt.-Gen. Soe Win, SPDC secretary No. 1, as the new prime minister. A few months later, hundreds of Khin Nyunt's followers were sentenced to long prison terms, and it was reported that the followers' family members were also punished.

Three years later, in September 2007, thousands of Buddhist monks in Burma launched major protests against the military junta (Mydans 2007a). Again, as in protests past, the demonstrators were violently quashed by riot police and soldiers. The Burmese authorities shot and killed more than ten protestors (at least that is what the government has admitted to),[6] including a Japanese reporter, raided monasteries, and beat or arrested hundreds of monks who led the demonstrations (Mydans 2007b). The United Nations sent an envoy to Burma to urge the Burmese junta to take steps toward political reconciliation, but his advice fell on deaf ears as China continued to be reluctant to take a tough stand against the military regime. China's position significantly undermined UN action (Choe 2007; Fuller 2007).

Sixteen years after winning the general election, Aung San Suu Kyi, who was awarded the Nobel Peace Prize in 1991, is still under house arrest and people in Burma are still living in fear and suffering silently under an extremely oppressive regime (Skidmore 2004, 2005). The Burmese army (*tatmadaw*) is very much in control, and without many challenges internally from the various ethnic armed groups or externally from the Association of Southeast Asian Nations (ASEAN) or from China, the *tatmadaw* is most likely to continue to cling to power and do poorly in terms of economic development or the protection of human rights (Selth 2001; Callahan 2003; Steinberg 2006; Thant Myint-U 2006).[7] An international study released in 2004 listed Burma as the fourth most corrupt country in the world (U Win Naing 2004).

Chapter Two

The Wa

The Wa area is located in the Shan State of Burma (or Myanmar) and its official name is Myanmar Shan State No. 2 Special Region (Wa government). The Wa leaders refer to their region as the Wa State, to the dismay of Burmese authorities who have long resisted the idea that the Wa was a sovereign "state" or province, but was, instead, merely a special region.[1] There are other special regions in the Shan State, including the Myanmar Shan State No. 1 Special Region (Kokang government), the No. 3 Shan State Special Region (Shan State Army), and the No. 4 Special Region (Mengla government).[2] After the leaders of these zones signed cease-fire agreements with the Burmese regime that same year, these zones gradually evolved into major drug-producing areas in the Golden Triangle. In this chapter, I will discuss the history, geography, and leadership structure of the Wa State, and will describe what life is like for ordinary hill peoples in the area.

A Brief History of the Wa State

Not much has been written about the Wa society because it is located in the remote hills of eastern Burma. Only a few Westerners, mostly British officers, explorers, anthropologists, journalists, and European scholars have ever ventured into the Wa area. More recently, journalists and freelance writers from China have visited the area for brief periods of time and have written books about their adventures (Deng 2000; Li 2000; Zhao and Ke 2003; Han 2004; Zhu 2004; Xiao 2005).

A Wa official document (United Wa State Party 1999b) divided the modern history of the Wa into three stages: First Stage (before 1967), Second Stage (1968–89), and Third Stage (1990-present).

First Stage: Japanese, Tribes, and KMT (before 1967)

Bo Laikang, one of the Wa leaders, divides the first stage into three periods:

> I was born in 1940 in Northern Wa County [now Mengmao County]. For me, the years before the arrival of the Communists can be divided into three eras. The first was the war with the Japanese, when some of my relatives lost their lives. We were sometimes bombarded by the Japanese air force, and at night we did not dare light candles, and chickens and dogs were not allowed to make noise. American armed forces got local soldiers to fight by paying them with opium. After the war, a lot of arms and ammunitions were left behind; soldiers were told by their commanders to go home with their guns and rifles. Some soldiers, on their way home, would exchange their rifles for a pig or food.
>
> The second era was the time of tribal warfare, when tribes were involved in vicious fighting for land. The various tribes were involved in opium cultivation, and opium was transported to China in exchange for machine guns. We also took opium to Kengtung to convert it into cash to buy guns and ammunition. At that time there were many opium dens in Burma, China, and Southeast Asia, and so there was a huge market for opium.
>
> After the defeat of the Kuomintang in China in 1949, some of the KMT soldiers fled to Burma and occupied a vast area of land in the Wa area. They also settled at Xindifang [in Mengmao County]. The KMT army had powerful weapons, and we were no match for them. However, after Zhou Enlai [then premier of China] traveled to Rangoon and asked Prime Minister U Nu to get rid of the KMT in northeastern Burma, the Burmese drove the KMT into Thailand and Laos.[3]

Sun Chengde, the minister of the Health Bureau of the Wa government, told me: "During this stage, in the 1950s, about 99 percent of the people were illiterate. People lived simply. Women did not wear brassieres, and men wore just a piece of cloth to cover their lower bodies. At that time, if you put a gun to a man's head, he would smile at you, not knowing the danger."[4]

During this period, people from one village would go to other villages to chop off people's heads and bring the heads back to display them at the entrance to their own village. Almost everyone we talked to in the Wa area had his or her own story about the origin of head-hunting among the Wa. A man in his nineties characterized it this way:

Those who were lazy would not get involved in farming and, rather, went around robbing people, especially during the harvest season when farmers traveled to the markets to sell their opium. One day, a farmer was on his way to a market and he was cornered by a group of robbers. The farmer was carrying a long knife, and when one of the robbers approached him, he slashed the robber's neck with his knife and ran home. The robbers were from a different village, and when the farmer got home and told people from his village about the incident, the two villages started to fight one another and chop off one another's heads.

From that time on, Wa people from different villages began head-hunting in earnest. Every village had one or two households responsible for retaining the severed heads from another village. In our village, my family was the one that took care of the chopped heads. Once a family was selected to be in charge of the heads, members of that family were not allowed to get involved in head-hunting. We just had to take care of the heads other villagers brought back. Only those families that were rich were selected—that's because whenever villagers brought back a head, my family had to kill our own livestock to feed people from the entire village. Every guest was supposed to wear new clothes, and then we have a big feast that will last for five to ten days and we will all be drumming, singing, and dancing.[5]

Another villager, a woman in her seventies, offered a different reason for head-hunting in the Wa area: "Once upon a time, a group of people were trying to bring a wooden drum back home, but the drum wouldn't move. People said: 'The drum won't move because it is hungry and weak. We must feed the drum a human head.' After we placed a human head on top of the drum and sprayed blood over it, it signified the drum's stomach was filled and then it was easy to move."[6]

There is still another explanation among the Wa people as to how head-hunting originated—another group of people, the Shan, is to blame. This explanation is somehow related to the notion of bringing in a good harvest. According to a farmer:

> Many, many years ago the Wa people lived a relatively comfortable life. One day, a Shan liar approached a group of Wa and took advantage of the Wa people's innocence. The Shan man wanted to see Wa people killing one another and living a miserable life. The Shan man offered the Wa people rice seeds he had soaked in hot water. At that time, the Wa had never cultivated rice, so they were very curious about it. However, after the Wa planted the seeds, they wouldn't grow. The Wa people were perplexed; why did the same seeds grow in the Shan area but not in the Wa? The Wa people questioned the Shan man, who told the Wa to chop off a man's head and offer it to the gods. Then the Shan man gave the Wa people a new batch of seeds that had not been soaked in hot water. After the Wa did as they were told, and chopped off a man's head, they planted the rice seeds and, of course, they grew well. Since then, Wa people have followed the custom of head-hunting.[7]

Because of this custom, people in the region were afraid of traveling alone or sleeping in the poppy fields. As a seventy-year-old woman recounted:

> Do you know how horrifying it was in the past? There were people chopping off heads everywhere and if you were not careful, it could happen to you. At that time, we tried to have as many children as we could. I had ten. We women had to stay home and watch our kids, and had to rely on our husbands to support us. We were afraid to leave our homes, and we were also concerned that people would come to our village and kidnap our children and cut off their heads. The husbands of some of the women in our village went out to the fields and never returned, and that meant that their heads had been chopped off.[8]

Even though head-hunting is often mentioned as a form of violence for which the Wa people were known in the past, Fiskesjo (2000, viii) warned that "the sacrificial rituals of head-hunting should be interpreted not as the inevitable outcome of fateful processes, but as the vehicles of the making of Wa history as culturally constituted action."

In the 1950s, in reaction to the invasion of KMT troops from China, armed groups called self-defense groups were formed by various Wa leaders. These armed groups often clashed with the tribes within the Wa area. The fights were numerous and brutal and Wa people continued to suffer.

Second Stage: Burmese Communists (1967–1988)

In June 1966, Bao Youxiang and Bao Sanban formed the Kunma guerrilla group. In May 1967, Ai Ken and Ai Kelong established the Aicheng guerrilla group. A year later, Lu Xingguo set up the Hushuang guerrilla group. In February 1969, Zhao Nilai established the Shaopa guerrilla group. The guerrilla groups' names derived from the names of the towns where they were based. According to a Wa government report:

The establishment of these guerrilla groups gave hope to the widespread desire for liberation, so the Wa people supported these groups. With the active support of their people, these groups expanded rapidly. However, because these groups were formed spontaneously, they were disorganized and incapable of uniting the entire Wa Hills. Leaders of various guerrilla groups came to realize that there was an urgent need for a unified organization with a unified leadership structure. Leaders like Zhao Nilai, Bao Youxiang, Lu Xingguo, and Ai Ken started a dialogue among themselves, and after overcoming many hardships and obstacles, they contacted the Communist Party of Burma (CPB) and sincerely invited the CPB to lead the guerrilla groups in the revolution [against the KMT and the Burmese government]. (Ting 2001, 9)

In March 1969, the CPB arrived in the towns of Shaopa and Hushuang, and took over the towns of Kunma and Aicheng in July. The CPB restructured the armed groups into the 4048 Battalion (in Hushuang), the 4049 Battalion (in Shaopa), the 502 Battalion (in Kunma), and the 501 Battalion (in Aicheng). On April 30, 1970, Mengmao, and later, Yingpan, Bangyao, and Jinchang, were liberated. In 1973, the military command center of the CPB was moved to Bangkang, and in July 1978 the headquarters of the CPB was as well (Ting 2001).

Wa people welcomed the CPB at the very beginning, as recounted by Sun Chengde, the health official:

Before the CPB, no group that ever set foot on Wa soil had treated people in this area right. The British never treated the Wa area well. They never really established a good connection with the whole Wa area. Later, the KMT Third and Fifth battalions were deeply involved in the opium trade and did not have time for the Wa people. But when the CPB arrived, they accomplished three things: (1) they abolished the custom of head-hunting among the Wa; (2) they got rid of Wa blood feuds and united the Wa area; and (3) they improved the infrastructure, especially the roads, and brought some level of civilization to this area by building schools.[9]

Many people I interviewed in the Wa area thought that the Communists had changed the lives of the Wa people for the better when they first came to the Wa area. As for opium, the CPB did try to ban it in 1978, but when farmers began to protest vehemently, the CPB gave in. According to Bao Aimen, mayor of Bangkang Special District, there was another reason: "Under the CPB, opium cultivation was prohibited in 1978–79. As a result, many people in Wengao and Bangkang died of starvation [because they did not have enough money to buy the food they needed]. However, when we went to China to study, the Chinese Communists asked us why we prohibited cultivation when it was the best way to raise money. Consequently, we allowed farmers to continue growing opium."[10]

After opium cultivation was restored, the CPB asked the farmers to turn in a certain amount of their opium as tax. According to Zhou Dafu, deputy director of the Wa Central Authority (WCA):

I got married in 1976 and for the next three years I was a farmer. I also grew opium and my wife played a key role. It was hard work; there was very little water. We collected about 3 *joi* [one joi equals 3.5 pounds or 1.6 kilograms] each year and we sold them for 200 to 300 Burmese kyats. We had to give the CPB 15 percent of our opium as tax without any compensation. We sold the rest in the markets. The CPB also had its own trade team and provided advance payments to farmers for their future opium.[11]

Chen Longsheng, director of the WCA, confided: "At that time, we had a so-called Unit 51 and it was responsible for the collection of the opium tax. Then the opium was transported to the Thai-Burma border area for sale. The unit operated quite secretively, not many people knew much about it." Most of the members of Unit 51 were from Kokang. However, as

Chen commented, "With the exception of air and water, almost everything was imported from China for free, so the opium tax was not much of a big deal for the CPB at that time."[12]

Not many Wa people recall the latter period of Communist rule with fondness, because once the CPB had settled down in the Wa area, they began to focus mainly on propaganda and ideological activities and paid little attention to improving ordinary people's lives. In addition, the CPB waged a continuous war with the Rangoon government in which many young Wa lost their lives; most of the CPB troops were young Wa males.

Wa leaders were also unhappy that the CPB leadership was dominated by Burmans, and they too were more interested in promoting their own causes than in the welfare of the Wa people (Lintner 1990). Chen Longsheng summed up the reasons for the demise of the CPB:

> In 1989, the Wa decided to separate from the Burmese Communists because, one, the CPB promoted the superiority of the Burmans and they paid little respect to minorities. Two, they were still absorbed in the so-called class struggle, and paid almost no attention to what was going on in the real world. Third, of course, the changes in China were also a factor [i.e., economic changes and loosening of Communist ideology]. Moreover, Wa people are more open, they don't like class struggle. Finally, after twenty years of armed conflict under the CPB, people were still very poor and saw no future in the Communist cause.[13]

For some observers, "China's reluctance to continue its support of the CPB, combined with the party's tougher policy on the opium trade adopted at the CPB's Third Congress in 1985," were also contributing factors to the fall of the CPB (Kramer 2005, 37).

Third Stage: Liberation, Development, and Drugs (1989-Present)

On March 11, 1989, Peng Jiasheng, the deputy commander of the Northeastern Command of the CPB, announced that Kokang would secede from the CPB. Soon after this radical step, the Burmese authorities got in touch with Peng Jiasheng through Luo Xinghan, a former opium kingpin (Cowell 2005). According to Luo Xinghan:

> In 1982, two years after I was released from prison, I began to suggest to the Burmese authorities that they stop fighting with the CPB and

instead try to bring the insurgent groups into the legal fold of the Burmese government. The Burmese government was not interested. I proposed again in 1984, and it was again rejected; under General Ne Win, the Burmese were extremely reluctant to talk peace with the CPB. One of my men was jailed by the Burmese for two years just for sending messages to the CPB. I contacted Peng Jiasheng in the late 1980s, and he said he thought the time had come for peace negotiations. But only after Ne Win's resignation in July 1988 did the new government show interest in talking with the CPB. Of course, the March 1988 student demonstration against the government was also a factor in their decision. I represented Peng in the negotiations with the Burmese.[14]

Zhao Nilai and Bao Youxiang of the Wa group were dispatched by the CPB to quell Peng, but, instead, the two decided to follow Peng's step. The Wa seceded from the CPB on April 17, 1989 (Ting 2001), and signed a peace agreement with the Burmese government on May 18, 1989; six months later, the United Wa State Party (UWSP) was established.

According to various observers (Lintner 1994b; Gelbard 1998; Fink 2001; Yawnghwe 2005), after the SLORC signed cease-fire agreements with Wa and Kokang leaders, the SLORC basically granted both groups the right to produce and transport drugs with impunity in return for their support of the Rangoon government and not the National League for Democracy (NLD) headed by Aung San Suu Kyi. However, according to Luo Xinghan, the go-between between the Burmese authorities and Kokang leaders,

it is absolutely not true that the Rangoon authorities agreed to allow the insurgent groups to continue their drug production in exchange for support of the central government. There were only four conditions: (1) Kokang would support the Rangoon government, (2) Kokang would be an autonomous zone, (3) the Kokang people would keep their arms and army, and (4) when the Burmese entered the Kokang area, its leaders would be informed in advance.[15]

Promptly after the Wa announced its separation from the CPB in April 1989, Khun Sa and his army attacked the Southern Wa region because he now saw the Wa as a threat. In 1993, with the support of the Burmese government, the Wa began a major offensive against Khun Sa that lasted three years before he surrendered to the Burmese in 1996. According to Wa officials, the Wa lost two thousand men in the war with Khun Sa.

After the war, the Wa began to improve their infrastructure. With the money they presumably made from heroin and the booming methamphetamine business, and aided by professionals and laborers from China, the Wa leaders began to build roads, schools, hospitals, power plants, and factories. The Wa were confident that the best was yet to come.

However, in the late 1990s the area was hit hard by the major financial crisis that engulfed Asia, and both the Burmese kyat and the Thai baht depreciated significantly. According to Zhou Dafu of the Wa Central Authority:[16]

> The economy is really bad now [2001] because our main businesses in Burma are affected by the depreciation of Burmese kyat. We cannot refuse to accept Burmese currency because we are part of Burma; besides, most of our products, including drugs, are sold in either Thai or Burmese currencies. When the Thai baht depreciated, we had to raise prices, and that certainly had an impact on the demand side.[17]

As commercial life in the Wa area slowed down, many Chinese entrepreneurs and laborers returned home, further depressing the Wa economy. Moreover, between 2001 and 2005 there were occasional skirmishes between Burma and Thailand, prompting Burmese authorities to close the checkpoints for months at a time. These border closures also deeply affected the Wa economy. Furthermore, Thaksin Sinawatra, the prime minister of Thailand, after years of pent-up frustration with the onslaught of methamphetamine from the north, declared a war on drugs in 2003, and conducted a fierce law-enforcement campaign for several months. The crackdown inevitably hurt both legitimate businessmen and drug dealers in the Wa area who had business in the Thai-Burma border areas (Pathan 2005). Xiao Mingliang, deputy commander of the United Wa State Army, summed up the effect on the Wa economy:

> The depreciation of Burmese kyat really hurt us because the income from the gem business is mostly in kyat.[18] Besides, the financial support from the Burmese government is also in Burmese currency.[19] We also exhausted our capital over the past several years by investing money in building the infrastructure. Moreover, the Chinese economy had slowed down over the past two years and that also affected us.[20]

The fortunes of the Wa continued to slide in 2004 with the arrest and imprisonment of Khin Nyunt, who was then the prime minister of Burma. With Khin Nyunt's downfall, the Wa were not certain they would still have the support of the government in Rangoon. Moreover, starting in 2004 the Chinese authorities began to press the governments in the Wa, Kokang, and Mengla areas to curb their gambling industry because many Chinese citizens, including corrupt government officials, were losing large amounts of money in the casinos of these special regions in Burma (Zhu 2004). The Chinese also began to restrict its citizens from visiting these areas, and would not allow them to stay overnight in the border towns on the Burmese side where most casinos are located. The impact was too obvious to ignore: virtually overnight, the streets of Bangkang, Laukkai, and Mengla were much quieter than before (Yang 2005).

As if bad economic news were not enough, in January 2005 the U.S. federal court in New York charged Bao Youxiang, Wei Xuegang, and six other Wa leaders with drug trafficking; the indictment further isolated the Wa from the world community (Transnational Institute 2005; U.S. District Court 2005). The Wa announced in June 2005 that the Wa area would become a drug-free zone where opium cultivation and heroin and methamphetamine production, trading, and trafficking would be banned. A veteran Wa army officer summed up the fifteen years following liberation from the Communist Party of Burma as follows:

The first five years (1990–94) everyone here praised Bao Youxiang and Zhao Nilai for helping Wa people to leave the bitter days behind. During that time, there were not many problems; people lived and worked together well because they felt like they all belonged to one big family and that they had survived the horrors of the Communist era together. During the second five years (1995–99), people in the Wa began to pay more attention to making money. Economic development became the main concern and political ideology was put aside and forgotten. That's why some of the older officials could not stand the arrogance of those new, young officials with money. Factionalism became the norm, and quite a few zealots began to emerge in our midst. Power struggles among various government units were common, and each unit was full of itself with arrogance and ignorance. Things went downhill in the third five-year period (2000–2004), as there was quite a bit of violence in the Wa area. Some people were killed, assaulted, or arrested for no reasons.[21]

Northern and Southern Wa States

Wa State is divided into Northern Wa State and Southern Wa State. Northern Wa State is located in the northeast of Burma, and it borders Lingcang District, Simao District, and Xishuangbanna Prefecture, which are all in China's Yunnan Province. The northern area of the Wa State is also adjacent to Kokang. Northern Wa area is about seventeen thousand square kilometers, with a population of about 320,000. Southern Wa State, located north of the Thai border, is an area of about thirteen thousand square kilometers, with a population of about 280,000. Altogether, there are sixteen ethnic groups in the region; the Wa group makes up 70 percent of the population, followed by the Lahu and Shan groups. A large number of Chinese from China also live in the Wa area, and they play a key role in almost all aspects of Wa society.

The Northern and Southern Wa areas are separated by a chunk of land that is controlled by the Burmese authorities, so Wa people have to pass through Burmese checkpoints when they travel from north to the south or vice versa. A Wa official told me that if top Wa leaders from the north wanted to travel to the south, the Burmese government had to approve their itinerary.

Northern Wa State

The Northern Wa area is made up of three special districts (Bangkang, Longtan, and Nandeng), three counties (Mengmao, Wengao, and Mengbo), and two developmental districts (Mengping and Mengga).

BANGKANG SPECIAL DISTRICT

Within the district, the town of Bangkang is the "capital" of the Wa State. According to a survey conducted by the Wa authorities in 2004, Bangkang had about 12,500 permanent residents, 5,500 temporary residents, and 58,000 mobile residents or migrant workers. When I first arrived in Bangkang in August 1998, almost every building was either new or still under construction. The roads were muddy during the rainy season, but these roads were also about to be paved with cement. Electricity was provided by the power plants located across the border in China, though the Chinese often shut down the power at night without any warning. The town was populated with merchants and laborers from China. Especially on market days, it bustled with villagers and street vendors.[22] In the marketplace one would

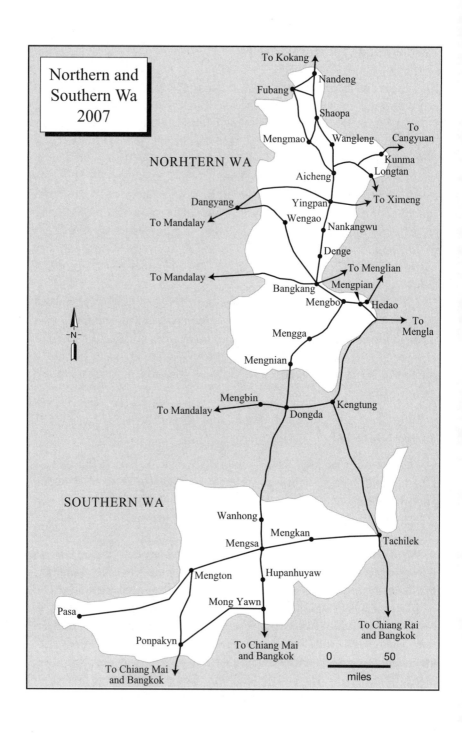

Northern and
Southern Wa
2007

To Kokang

Nandeng

Fubang

Shaopa

NORHTERN WA

Mengmao

Wangleng

To
Cangyuan

Kunma
Longtan

Aicheng

To Ximeng

Dangyang

Yingpan

Wengao

Nankangwu

To Mandalay

Denge

To Menglian

Mengpian

To Mandalay

Bangkang

Mengbo

Hedao

Mengga

To
Mengla

Mengnian

Mengbin

To Mandalay

Dongda

Kengtung

SOUTHERN WA

Wanhong

Mengkan

Mengsa

Tachilek

Mengton

Hupanhuyaw

Mong Yawn

Pasa

Ponpakyn

To Chiang Rai
and Bangkok

To Chiang Mai
and Bangkok

To Chiang Mai
and Bangkok

0   50

miles

-N-find hundred of stalls and small stores stacked with cheap goods from China. According to a Chinese businessman,

> When I arrived here in 1993 from China, it was basically a very small town. The roads were muddy and people lived in huts. Things began to change in 1996, and by 1998 the town had grown rapidly—for two reasons. First, the Wa defeated Khun Sa and became key players in the heroin trade. Second, the Wa became active in the exploding methamphetamine business.[23]

When I visited Bangkang for the second time, in 2001, the construction of the town was almost completed. The town was dotted with restaurants, convenience stores, karaoke bars, massage parlors, hotels, medical clinics, and other business establishments. The Wa now had their own power stations, and thus no need to rely on the Chinese for electricity. The new casino located at the heart of the town had the most eye-catching architecture in Bangkang. Owned and operated by a Chinese man who was one of the richest people in the Wa area, the casino was surrounded by a nightclub, a restaurant, a massage parlor, and a karaoke bar. Every evening, the vast courtyard in front of the casino was filled with people, while inside high-stake gamblers, many from China, would gamble the night away at the baccarat tables. Ordinary people, some of them farmers from the remote villages, would indulge themselves in the low-stake gambling games unique to the Wa area.

There were four other major establishments in Bangkang: the Meixin Hotel, a large bowling complex, a large supermarket, and the Kang Xiang Jewelry Company, all believed to be owned by Bao Youxiang or his family. The massage parlors (or brothels) and the medical clinics also stood out because they were everywhere. By 2001, the economy began to falter. According to a businessman from Chengdu, Sichuan, who operated a jewelry store in Bangkang: "The economy was booming when I opened this store three years ago in 1998. However, after a year, the economy slowed down. We pay 800 yuan [about $100] a month for rent, and another 400 yuan [about $50] for the small kitchen and dining room at the back. It's hard to do business because very few outsiders are coming to this town now."[24]

An intellectual from Yunnan who operated the first computer store in Bangkang told me what he thought was the basic problem with the Wa economy:

It is very hard to do legitimate business here. The only thing most people know is the drug business—that's what they are very good at. When the Thai-Burma border was closed in 2001, the impact was enormous. New drugs cannot be transported across the border, and money from former drug transactions cannot be collected. The Chinese route was also, in a sense, closed.[25]

When I visited Bangkang for the third time, in April 2005, many large businesses had closed, including the casino, the bowling complex, and the supermarket. The casino had been shut down temporarily by order of the Chinese authorities, and the other two establishments closed due to lack of business. Even so, there were also some improvements, like the opening up of a few Internet stores and a cable television system that allowed people in Bangkang to watch more than twenty channels of news and entertainment programs from Burma, Thailand, China, Hong Kong, and Taiwan. The Wa also had their own TV station, but no newspapers.

These days Bangkang looks and feels more like a town in China than like one in Burma. Because there are large numbers of Chinese in Bangkang, Mandarin is the most popular language; most of the store signs are in Chinese characters and if some are in Chinese and Burmese characters, the Burmese characters are often misspelled—and nobody seems to notice or care. Street signs are written in the Wa language, but it is rarely used otherwise. The Wa do not have their own currency and since Burmese kyats are not accepted in Bangkang, the only currency circulating is the Chinese yuan. Also, many Bangkang residents use Chinese time, which is one and a half hours ahead of Burmese time.

Denge, about thirty kilometers north of Bangkang, is the second largest town in the Bangkang Special District. It is in a major opium cultivation area, encompassing seventeen villages, including Wa, Chinese, and Lahu settlements scattered throughout the region. The people living here appear to get along very well, sometimes to the extent that there are intergroup marriages. Altogether there are about five hundred families in the district with a total population of three thousand.

NANDENG SPECIAL DISTRICT

Nandeng Special District was established in 1991 after it was carved out of Mengmao County. The district is about five hundred square kilometers with a population of fifteen thousand, and it is situated south of Kokang and on the border with China. The town of Nandeng is quite small, with a couple of streets and a few small, shabby stores and a casino. The Wa government hoped to turn the town into a major trading center for raw opium before the opium ban in 2005: it can be transported to Nandeng by truck and then sold to dealers who transform it into heroin. Nandeng is only an hour drive from Laukkai, the largest town in Kokang.

OTHER GEOGRAPHICAL LOCATIONS IN NORTHERN WA STATE

The third special district, Longtan, has had little contact with the outside world. Currently, Wa leaders are developing a tin mine in the area.

Mengmao County, established in 1974, is about thirty-five hundred square kilometers, with a population of 130,000. Xindifang is a booming town that began to grow rapidly around 1998; when we were conducting interviews there in 2001 the whole town was still under construction, with roads still to be paved, open sewers, and a few newly built small hotels. Bao Youliang (a brother of Bao Youxiang and the governor of the county) was building a large hotel that would be completed in a few months. Many Chinese from China came to settle there.

Within Mengmao County, Kunma District is notable because it is the power base of Bao Youxiang, the head of the United Wa State Army and the supreme leader of the Wa. Up to 2006, Bao spent most of his time in Kunma, traveling to the town of Bangkang only when he had to take care of business. It takes at least eight hours by car to get from Kunma to Bangkang.

Yingpan, a major opium trading town that is also located within Mengmao County, is about ninety-seven kilometers north of Bangkang. The town is populated by a large number of Chinese opium traders.

The other counties are Wengao and Mengbo. Little is known about Wengao, located west of Bangkang, and there is not much interaction between the two areas probably because the connecting road from Bangkang to Wengao is in such poor condition.

Mengbo County is located south of Bangkang and not far away from the Mengla area, another special region in northeast Burma. The United Nations Drug Control Program (UNDCP) implemented the Wa Alternative Development Project (WADP) in Mengbo in 1998. Hedao, a major town in the county, is alleged to be a center of methamphetamine production and the power base of the notorious Security Regiment (*jingweituan*), a branch of the United Wa State Army.

There are two development districts—areas designated for economic development—in the Northern Wa area, Mengping and Mengga. Mengping is also a booming town, currently ranked as the third largest Wa town.

Southern Wa State

Although the Southern Wa area is a part of the Wa State and presumably under the control of the Wa Central Authority in Bangkang, it is, at least for outsiders, a mysterious place. It began to develop rapidly after Khun Sa's surrender in 1996. "After the SUA [Khun Sa's Shan United Army] surrendered and was driven from the region in hard-fought battles, the BA [Burmese Army] ordered the Wa to vacate the region. The Wa defied the order and, with eventual government acquiescence, occupied the area, referred to as their Southern Military Region (SMR) or Southern Military Command" (U.S. Drug Enforcement Administration 2002, 7).

The Southern Wa region has been, by tradition, a region suspicious of, and generally hostile to, outsiders. Before the Wa government forced Northern Wa people to migrate there, the area had been mostly occupied by soldiers. There were two waves of forced migration, one between September 1999 and March 2000, and the other between January 2001 and March 2001. Now, with the arrival of tens of thousands of migrants, restrictions have eased up a little bit as far as physical movement is concerned. Still, according to someone who was sent to the Southern Wa region by Bao Youxiang to write and report something positive about the Southern Wa area to the world community,

Wei Xuegang [a top leader of Southern Wa State] did not see me when I visited the region. I was only met by Bao Youyi [another high-ranking official who is a brother of Bao Youxiang]. Even he was very difficult to deal with. They have a mentality that is different from that of the leaders in Northern Wa State; they don't care what other people say about them. A few years back, leaders in the north were not much different from those in the south; only recently have the Northern Wa leaders realized that there is a need for contact with the outside world. When Wei Xuegang found out that the local television station had published a magazine with his photo in it, he was extremely upset. He said the whole magazine is garbage and he ordered the military to destroy all the existing copies.[26]

Bao Youyi and Wei Xuegang are the two key leaders in Southern Wa area. Bao Youyi is believed to have been "expelled" to Southern Wa by his younger brother Bao Youxiang and the central government in Bangkang after Chinese authorities accused Bao Youyi of involvement in a major drug trafficking case. In that incident, Chinese drug enforcement agents confiscated hundreds of kilograms of heroin in Yunnan Province and they believed that the drug belonged to Bao Youyi, who was at that time living in Bangkang (Ting 2004). Bao Youxiang and Li Ziru, another top Wa leader, were summoned to Simao by the Chinese authorities for questioning, and after the two returned to the Wa, they sent Bao Youyi to the remote south.

Wei Xuegang is a Thai-Chinese who used to work for Khun Sa. After Khun Sa's surrender in 1996, Wei Xuegang began to work with the Wa. He gradually became known as Khun Sa's replacement: the most feared drug kingpin in Southeast Asia. By 1998, the United States government was offering a reward of $2 million for anyone who could provide information that would lead to Wei Xuegang's arrest. To date, he remains at large. I will discuss his role in the methamphetamine trade in chapter 5. The other key figures in the south include San Mulu, Wei Saitang (arrested and jailed in 2005 by the Wa authorities in Bangkang), and Li Laoer. The main military units are the 214 Battalion and the Independent Regiment (*dulituan*).

In 1999, the Wa authorities in the north began to move opium farmers from their region to the Southern Wa area. It was a forced migration, involving many thousands of people. The plan was to move fifty thousand people from the north to the south over five years. According to officials in Bangkang, the arranged migration was one way to stop the growing of opium. The Wa authorities believed farmers in the north who relied on opium for survival would be able to farm better in the south where the land was flat and fertile. Many observers in the West and Thailand viewed the mass movement to the south from a very different angle. These observers believe that Wa leaders were simply trying to put a tighter hold on the new territories they had received from the Burmese government after the surrender of Khun Sa (Steinberg 2001). Worse, some observers thought the Wa leaders wanted to move people to the south for a more direct connection to the methamphetamine business or to continue to grow opium nearer to the market or to the heroin refineries in the south (Takano 2002).

Whatever the true motive, the policy, drastic and haphazardly done, was bound to create all kinds of tragic consequences. A seventy-two-year-old woman in Kunma told us this story about her experience with the forced migration:

> Over the past few years, we were bothered by uncertainties and we couldn't focus on our work. That's because they [the leaders] wanted us to stop growing opium, and then they wanted us to move to the south. We did not want to leave this place; even

though this place is not a heaven, it is at least the place where our ancestors lived. When we refused to go, Wei Saitang's soldiers forced us to move under gunpoint and they burned our houses along with our grain. They wanted me to move, too, but I insisted on staying.[27]

Even though many people were forced to move and many suffered in the process, a Wa insider suggested that because "life [in the Southern Wa area] is far better than before, there is little desire to move back" (Milsom 2005, 73).

The Wa Administration

The Wa State is controlled by the United Wa State Party (UWSP), the United Wa State Army (UWSA), and the Wa government. In fact, the party, the army, and the government are virtually one organization, especially when one considers that a number of senior officials in the headquarters (called *zongbu* in Chinese) are in charge of the party, the army, and the government. This tripartite structure is copied from the Chinese setup, as are the technical terms of the units of the Wa administration (Kramer 2007). Milsom (2005) used the term Wa Central Authority (WCA) to refer to the central-level officials of the UWSP, UWSA, Wa central committee, politburo, and Wa State government. In this book, I will also refer to *zongbu* as the WCA (see table 1 for the structure of the Wa administration).

In a government document, the Wa authorities listed the principles, guidelines, and policies of the Wa State as follows (Wa State Government 2001, 3–4):

1. Hold the banner of peace and democracy, meanwhile, hold the banner of military self-defense.

2. Struggle to obtain minority autonomous power at the state level.

3. Treat economic construction as the central mission, military strength as the support mission.

4. Carry out the policies of opening to outside world, introducing techniques, persons with ability and funds.

5. All ethnic groups are equal, despite the size of the group, its wealth, or religion. All ethnic groups study and respect each other and make progress mutually, and oppose all forms of chauvinism.

Table 1. The Wa Administration

Wa Central Authority (in Bangkang) General Office			
Office/Bureau	Local administration	United Wa State Army	United Wa State Party
Finance Bureau	Bangkang Special	General staff	Chairman
Construction	District	Division 468	Vice-Chairman
Bureau	Nandeng Special	Division 421	
Political Work	District	Division 214	
Bureau	Longtan Special	Division 417	
Agricultural,	District	Division 418	
Forestry, and	Mengmao County	Independence	
Irrigation Bureau	Mengbo County	Regiment	
Public Relations	Mengping	Security	
Bureau	Develoment	Regiment	
Law Enforcement	District	Artillery	
Logistics Bureau	Mengga	Regiment	
Women's	Development	Military	
Association	District	District 171	
Health Bureau		(formed in 1996	
Investment and		after	
Tourism		combining	
Reprensentative in		Division 420	
Rangoon		and Division	
Tachilek Office		525)	
Kentung Office			
Mandalay Office			
Lashio Office			

6. Freedom for all in religion and expression.

7. The Wa State is a part of Myanmar. The Wa State never splits country, and is never independent from the country.

8. Solidarity and concord, peaceful coexistence, developing together, no intervening in other's internal affairs.

According to a Wa government report (Ting 2001, 13–14), the WCA generates its annual budget from the following sources: Burmese government (20 percent), private contributions (12 percent), business income (17 percent), taxes (20 percent), dividends (20 percent), minerals (10 percent), and tourism (1 percent).

Within the Wa administration, Wa leaders are viewed as the muscle and the Chinese as the brains. Ethnic Wa are respected for their fighting skills and, because of their ethnicity, they are the masters of the Wa area, despite the fact that some of them were born in China and came to the Wa area only recently. Ethnic Chinese are considered to be smart people with good business and organizational skills, but because they are not ethnic Wa, they can only work for the Wa people, even though some Chinese were born in the Wa area. As a result, many Wa government units are headed by ethnic Wa, but the day-to-day operations of these units are conducted by ethnic Chinese who are usually deputy chiefs. When Li Ziru (a Chinese) was alive, he was called *lideshun*, meaning he can "take care of business," and Bao Youxiang (a Wa), *baodelong*, for his ability to "unite people." Bao, though, is the undisputed leader of the Wa area. Besides the leaders in the WCA, there are leaders of the various special districts, counties, and development districts. For example, Bao Youliang, a brother of Bao Youxiang, is the mayor of Mengmao County. In addition, there are the leaders of various army divisions (468, 214, 418), military region (171), and regiments (Independent, Security, and Artillery) of the twenty-thousand-strong United Wa State Army. Bao Youhua, a younger brother of Bao Youxiang, was the chief of the Security Regiment until 2005 when he was purged from the army for drug addiction.

Among the Wa leaders, Bao Youxiang, Youyi, Youliang, and Youhua are natal brothers. The same is true with Wei Xuegang, Xuelong, and Xueyun. These seven leaders, plus Bao Huaqiang of the Finance Bureau, were indicted in 2005 by a U.S. federal court in New York for drug trafficking (U.S. District Court 2005).

As mentioned earlier, the Northern Wa area is divided into special districts, counties, or development districts. Under each special district (*tequ*) or county (*xian*), there are numerous towns or *xiang*, and under each town, there are several communes or *dajia* (big village). The Kunma Commune, where we conducted extensive fieldwork, had 158 households. Each commune consisted of several villages, and each village was further divided into two or more units or *ju*. The head of a unit was the lowest-level government official in the Wa Hills and they were the ones who actually carried out the orders from the top leaders.

In theory, the WCA in Bangkang is in charge of all local governments. In reality, local government leaders often defy orders from Bangkang. Many local leaders, including, for instance, the three natal brothers of the supreme leader Bao Youxiang, often disregarded the central government's policies. In the Wa State, the WCA collects taxes from the local authorities but provides nothing in return and, as a result, many local leaders are resentful of the authorities in the WCA. According to Bao Aimen, the mayor of Bangkang Special District,

> My district government is in charge of six towns. We have about 120 on our staff, and the annual budget is 1.5 million yuan [$183,000]. The WCA does not give us a penny; we have to rely on ourselves for all expenses. We collect taxes and are involved in all kinds of businesses. For example, we collect 20 yuan [about $2.50] per slaughtered pig. We have a real estate building where we collect 60,000 yuan [about $7,300] a month rent. We also collect 300 yuan [$36] a month per karaoke club and 200 yuan [$25] a month per massage parlor. Our district has one mayor, one secretary, and four deputy mayors. There are a number of bureaus under the district government, including public security, construction, etc. Of the six top-level administrators in the district government, only one speaks Chinese; that's why it is not easy for us to communicate with leaders from the WCA who are mostly Chinese-speaking. When our people attend meetings at the headquarters, most of the time they have no idea what is being discussed.[28]

In private, Wa leaders are highly critical of the Burmese authorities and their policies toward armed groups in the border areas. They are deeply unhappy that some of the promises made by the Burmese authority during the cease-fire agreement in 1989 (such as establishing transportation routes, communication, electricity, education, and medical services) had not materialized (Takano 2002). They think Burmese officials are incompetent, unreliable, and corrupt. According to an outspoken Wa leader: "We do not get along with the Burmese. We really don't know what their policies are. We think the Burmese authorities are like *longyi* [the Burmese dress for men]. You can wear it any way you like and it is considered appropriate. The same is true with the behavior of Burmese authorities. They say and do whatever they like and do not see anything wrong with it."[29]

Worlds of Pain: Life in the Wa Hills

In the Wa area, there are just a few rich and powerful people but many poor and powerless villagers. Even though many Wa villagers live in extreme

poverty, they are afraid to speak out. If they want to express their dissatis-
faction, there are no outlets for them to do so, as a villager in Kunma
explained:

> In Kunma, the rich have millions or tens of millions of yuan, while
> the poor may not have enough food to eat. Poor people live in dilapi-
> dated huts and their yearly income can be as low as a few hundred
> yuan [less than $50]. People like us who do not have education or
> know how to do business can only do hard labor; if we don't, we
> would starve. In this place, only government officials are rich. Some
> officials may start out poor but become rich in just a few years.[30]

A person from China who was disappointed with his lack of luck in the
Wa area after toiling there for many years said that "the only people who
are making a lot of money here are those who are close to Bao [Youxiang].
Only his relatives and the people around him will be rewarded with crucial
government positions [so that they can make money]."[31] In an area where
most people are uneducated and unskilled, loyalty and blood relationships
become critical in assigning people to different government positions.

Rich and powerful people in Bangkang live in new brick houses
equipped with chandeliers, furniture, bathtubs, and household appliances
imported from Thailand and China. These houses are designed by archi-
tects from abroad, and building materials are mostly imported. The prices
of these houses can be as high as four million yuan (half a million dollars).
The owners of these houses cruise the streets of Bangkang in their new
SUVs, and some of them can be spotted at the casino of Bangkang, gambling away tens of thousands of yuan per visit. Those who are not interested in gambling may have one or more mistresses. Some are addicted to
drugs, as it is very easy for them to be addicted to the very commodity
they are producing or trading.

Besides gambling and having mistresses, the rich and the powerful, especially their families and relatives, are also known to act recklessly and
arrogantly, as a senior police officer in Bangkang told us:

> Many family members and relatives of the Wa leaders often act as if
> they are above the law. But when they run into me, they don't get
> away with anything. Once, the wife of a Wa leader [a man who is
> believed to be a big time drug producer and dealer] ordered her fol-
> lowers to beat up a man from China. When the man came to us and
> I found out that she was the one who ordered the assault, I called her

and told her to come to the police department. She said: "Who the hell are you? Don't you know who my husband is? If you bother me again, I will order someone to take care of you!" When I heard that, I sent my men over to arrest her. I locked her up for two days. After that, she became much more humble.

If we are going to allow these sons and wives of the leaders to have their way and do whatever they want to, unchecked, then a Wa leader's family is a kind of organized crime group. What's the difference between an organized crime group and a family like this? Besides, this situation will also lead to the disarray of the Wa State. Look at what has happened in Kokang. The sons of the various leaders there were fighting among themselves. The Peng family, the Yang family, the Wei family, the Liu family, etc. fought among themselves. Kokang was eventually weakened because of all the fighting among the various families. I don't want this to happen to us.[32]

Ordinary hill peoples, on the other hand, live a very different life (Daw Tin Yee 2004). Wei Xiang, one of my interviewers, described the seasonal labor of farmers in the Wa Hills:

In May, farmers cut down the new growth in their fields, plow the earth, and plant the rice seeds. After that, the farmers go to the fields every day to keep an eye on the crop. After the plants begin to grow, the farmers have to keep weeding the fields; it is really hard work. They also have to watch the fields every day, to make sure that the cows will not eat the crop. By September, farmers collect the rice. Every year, September 20 is *xinmijie* [New Rice Festival] and by that time farmers will have collected all the rice. Farmers also plant maize, cucumber, watermelon, and other crops around the rice.

Here, the land never rests. In early October, a few days after the rice harvest, the land is burned, the ground is hoed, and the opium seeds are planted. Within a month, the opium plants will grow, and farmers have to thin out the plants that are too close, and if necessary, sow more seeds again. After the plants begin to grow, the land is hoed again to keep weeds down. Growing opium is even more challenging than growing rice. Every month, farmers have to hoe the land. After the flowers have blossomed for a month, the poppies start to grow. Farmers prepare their raw opium for the open markets by wrapping the opium sap with the poppy petals. Farmers begin to collect the opium in late January or early February, and continue the process to the end of March.

In sum, hill people are rarely idle; if a person stays home, people will say that he or she is lazy. Most people spend most of their day in the fields. If a person does not go to the fields, he or she will go into the forest to cut wood. When I was fifteen, I once refused to go to the fields with my relatives to work. My relatives told me if I do not go, they will not let me eat.[33]

Another interviewer, Wei Xiaolan, wrote the following after I asked my interviewers to write down what they observed after talking to opium farmers in the hills:

Their huts are in such bad shape that it looks like they have been dynamited. During the day, the sun just shines right through the huts and the occupants inside sweat terribly. At night, you feel like there's nothing between you and the dark sky and you can feel the wind blowing through. It seems like people there just grab something, anything, to come up with somewhere to lie down. Their food is tasteless, and that's because they cannot afford to buy things like salt or MSG. . . . Some people have nothing to eat, and they often pick things that grow in the wild to eat. People sometimes die of food poisoning. Moreover, their clothes are all worn and torn, but they can't do anything about it because they don't have needles and thread.

For people living in the highlands, life is full of hardship and disappointment, as testified to by a fifty-nine-year-old woman in Kunma:

This year, I raised a female pig for the first time in my life, and eventually she gave birth to eleven piglets. As the piglets grew, I began to dream about selling the pigs in the market and making a lot of money. My husband was ill, and I was not strong enough to build a pigpen myself. As a result, my little pigs were running all over the neighborhood. When they ran over to another family's house, the people were upset. So those people poisoned all my pigs. I was very sad when the pigs died, but I understand that it was partly my fault. Well, we ordinary people live a very hard life here.[34]

Because most young men are either required or volunteer to serve in the Wa army, households in the remote hills are predominantly made up of older men, women, and children. Without husbands around to help share the backbreaking work, most married women in the hills are living lives of grueling physical labor and isolation. Most females marry at an early age; after the marriage it is expected that the young wife will take care of her husband's parents while her husband returns to his army post. A thirty-two-year-old female talked about what it's like to be married to a soldier:

> I got married when I was fifteen. My husband is a soldier; he joined the army [as a soldier] at age seven. When we married, he was sixteen. There's no love between us and, in fact, we never really dated one another. His parents liked me, and they came to my house and proposed. My parents asked me if I wanted to get married. I was curious, but I did not know anything about getting married. After the wedding, my husband returned to his army camp, and I stayed home to take care of his parents. I was like my husband's slave—he married me so that there would be someone home. When he has free time or when he misses his parents, he will come home. Now I really regret marrying a soldier in the first place. Being a soldier's wife is really bitter, because he is not home most of the time; he will return home two or three times a year. These army people are also very poor, they get paid 15 yuan [less than $2] a month, plus a bag of rice.[35]

Another young married woman described how she was discarded by her husband and yet continued to work as a "slave" in her husband's family:

> I got married when I was eleven. My husband was a soldier. One day he came home to visit his parents, and he saw me as I was on my way to work in the fields. He liked me and chased me, and I also had a good impression of him, so I decided to marry him. We got married one month after we met each other. Everybody in my family was against the marriage because I was only eleven and he was just sixteen. After the marriage, we were not happy at all. We did not have kids for nine years, and he was away most of the time. I eventually got pregnant in the year 2000, but the child was aborted after my husband hit me in the abdomen during a fight. This year [2002], he became an officer and then got himself a mistress. I asked for a divorce, but he refused. All these years, I have been just a slave in his family.

He is now living in Bangkang with his mistress and I am the one who is working every day in his parents' house.[36]

After spending months doing fieldwork in Kunma, one of my field workers explained the predicament of the married women:

Couples here do not know what family planning is; most of them add a child every year. They also do not know how to prevent being pregnant, nor do they know how to protect their bodies. Before one baby can walk, another baby is on the way. They simply keep on having kids until they can't do it anymore. Some women know how to avoid getting pregnant, but their husbands do not cooperate. If their wives have fewer children than others, people think it's because the man is impotent. Some men insist on having boys, and if their wives do not give birth to boys, their husbands force them to keep on having children until they have boys.

Not one female villager interviewed by my field workers had a happy story to tell. I am not sure if the women we met in Kunma are representative of the entire female population in that community; it's also possible that my field workers, being young and single, may have exaggerated the plight of Wa women. One thing is clear, however: women work very hard to support their families while their husbands are away from home.

Another group that deserves our attention is the children. In the Wa area, only a small proportion of children attend school because there are only ten junior high schools and 352 elementary schools in the region (United Wa State Party 2005a). Even though the Wa authorities claim that there are more than twenty-eight thousand children attending school, it is not clear that these children are receiving any meaningful education. For one thing, most of the so-called schools are nothing more than small, shabby rooms with several rows of broken chairs and tables and occasionally a blackboard. Then, because teachers (mostly Chinese from China) are underpaid ($30 a month), they must rely on their students to boost their income and that means asking their students to spend most of the school time in moneymaking activities, including growing opium. In a Wa village, I saw students ages eight to fourteen cutting wood in a school compound after class so that the teacher could sell it in the market as firewood. The school began at eight in the morning and was over by ten. After that, the students were required to work for their teacher. All the students lived in a hut near the school compound. According to the teacher:

We do not receive much support from the local or central authorities. A student's monthly meal budget is only 5 yuan [less than a dollar], plus some rice. The money pays for salt, pepper, and vegetables. Some teachers smoke opium, have affairs with local women. Some put their personal interests above their role as teachers. I myself grow some opium, and I can make about 1,000 yuan [$120] a year from selling it. Here, people have to give the local government a certain amount of their opium as taxes, but I don't have to do that because I am a teacher.[37]

Because the opportunity to attend school is limited and because education in the Wa area is considered unimportant, most boys join the army when they are still very young while girls stay home to help their parents. When asked why young boys are being recruited into the army as child soldiers, Ailun, the commander of Division 468, explained:

We normally will recruit only young people between the ages of fifteen and twenty-five. Every year, the central government orders the local governments to come up with a certain number of new recruits. If an elder brother who is sixteen does not want to join and the younger one wants to, then we will recruit the younger one even though he may be only thirteen. The new recruits are trained for three weeks in Bangkang and then dispatched to various army divisions or regiments.[38]

In sum, ordinary people in the Wa Hills must work very hard all year round just to have enough food to eat, they live in shabby huts without electricity and water, and when they become ill, there is no place to go for treatment. Women and children suffer the most. Most Wa villagers are not happy with their dire existence, but they dare not speak out because they are afraid they might upset the Wa authorities.

Even though there is a booming drug trade in the Wa area, it obviously does not bring much benefit to the ordinary Wa people. The drug trade enriches only a small number of people, mostly Wa leaders and their families and those Chinese entrepreneurs affiliated with the Wa leadership. As a result, when we talk about the drug business in the Wa area, it is important to differentiate the Wa people as a whole from the Wa leaders and their Chinese business associates. Wa farmers only grow opium. They do not play any role in the trading of opium, the conversion of opium into heroin, and the production and trafficking of methamphetamine.

Government Officials as Businessmen

The Wa Hills have undergone major changes since the Wa leaders ended their relationship with the Communist Party of Burma in 1989 and signed a peace treaty with the Burmese authorities. In the fifteen years that followed, the Wa engaged in fierce fighting with Khun Sa and his army, established a strong base in the south after Khun Sa surrendered to the Burmese government, and began to be more active in heroin production. When Thai authorities began to crack down on methamphetamine production in Thailand, the Wa (especially the Chinese in the Wa area) gradually emerged as key players in the burgeoning methamphetamine business. At the same time, the Wa government began to invest money in the construction of roads, power plants, schools, and other public work projects. The Wa administration also began to explore a variety of legitimate businesses, including many crop-substitution projects for growing tea or rubber plants. The second five-year-plan (1995–99) of the Wa government was, at least on paper, an extremely ambitious plan indeed (Ting 2001; Wa State Government 2001).

Between 2000 and 2005, however, the area still showed the effects of the Asian financial crisis of the late 1990s. In addition, there were border skirmishes and closures between Thailand and Burma, and the war-on-drugs campaign in Thailand. Access to Thailand for the Wa was almost shut down because of these events. The development of the Wa area was also impeded by the Chinese authorities' concern over the influx of heroin from Burma and the outflow of Chinese citizens to the Burmese side to gamble. The Chinese began to restrict the free flow of people across the border (Yang 2005). In 2005, the U.S. federal indictment of several top Wa leaders for drug trafficking also hit the region hard. Many businesspeople from China left the Wa area because they were concerned that the United States might bomb the Wa. In June 2005, the Wa leaders announced their intention, effective immediately, to rid the region of drugs and the drug trade.

After visiting the Wa area on three separate occasions and spending a total of six months there, it became clear to me that every government official in the Wa was a small- or big-time businessman. Every government employee, regardless of position, was paid a standard salary of 20 yuan ($2.50) and a bag of rice a month. Everyone, therefore, had to get involved in other moneymaking activities. The same was true of the WCA and the local government administrations. The WCA received little support from the Burmese government, and the local governments received no support from the WCA. All government units and institutions, including army units, had to generate money to sustain themselves and to pay for public works projects. This was the reason why all government units functioned like business enterprises.

Moreover, it was hard to differentiate between the private moneymaking activities of a government official and the seemingly public business of his administration. Take opium, for example. A town mayor is responsible for raising money to pay for his administration's expenses. At the same time, he is also trying to improve his own standard of living (such as building a new house for his family). In the Wa Hills, it is no secret that the opium business is the one business that is the most profitable and also a commodity that people are very familiar with. When a town government is involved in the opium business, and when the town's mayor is also active in the same business, the mayor must play two roles. From the WCA's standpoint, it does not matter how a mayor raises the necessary funds to enrich his local government and himself, as long as his businesses do not hurt the incomes of other, more powerful figures. The same is true of the mayors of special districts and counties.

Of course, the highest business entity in the entire Wa region is Bao Youxiang. He is undoubtedly *the* man when it comes to business, politics, and warfare in the Wa State. Bao Youxiang needs to make large amounts of money to legitimize his power and he does this through his investments in numerous public projects. He is also personally involved in the drug business, although to what extent it is hard to judge. He can always ask his relatives or followers to operate his drug business. It appears that almost every official in the Wa Hills wants to be involved in the drug business, but his relationship with Bao determines whether he can, and to what extent.

Granted, there are also a number of businessmen who can do whatever they want as far as making money is concerned, as long as they donate money to various government projects and offer a percentage of their income to their *kaoshan* or protector. Every businessman here, most likely to be a Chinese, has a powerful figure, most likely a Wa, to fall back on; a small businessman relies on a low-level official and a big businessman on a high-level official.

To the Wa leaders' credit, Bangkang and the rest of Northern Wa State are relatively tranquil and free. Unlike other drug-infested regions in other parts of the world, drug-related violence is rare in Bangkang. Ordinary people are also highly unlikely to be unreasonably abused by those in power, even though ordinary people are afraid of criticizing their leaders. I think the leaders are genuinely concerned with the long-term benefits to their people and are at least trying to improve the livelihood of ordinary people through the upgrading of the infrastructure of the Wa State.

It is clear that ordinary villagers in the Wa area do not play any role in the accumulation and transportation of opium, the refining and trafficking of heroin, and the manufacturing of methamphetamine. It is also clear that Wa leaders could not possibly develop the drug trade in their territory and sell their drugs in the international market without outside help. All types of activities, be they political, economic, or drug related, are more likely to be initiated by ethnic Chinese in the Wa area (either long-term residents or newly arrived businessmen or immigrants) rather than ethnic Wa. Ordinary Wa farmers living in the remote villages do not play any role in the decision-making process or in the implementation of these activities.

Chapter Three

The Opium Trade

Although there are numerous estimates of the amount of opium production in the Wa territory, we do not know how reliable these estimates are. In addition to the aggregate data, we need to know how Wa farmers view the act of growing opium. What are their reasons for participating in opium production? How do opium growers manage to sell their product? How much money do they make each year? How important to them is their income from opium? What is the social organization of opium cultivation, trading, and taxation? Besides the opium growers, who else is involved in the opium trade? In sum, we need to talk to the opium farmers to learn about the social processes and social organization of growing, selling, and taxing opium.

This chapter will focus on the growing, taxing, and trading of opium in the Wa State. I will first discuss the reasons for growing opium, patterns of opium cultivation, changes in opium yields, and opium cultivation in other parts of Burma. I will also examine how farmers viewed their part in the opium culture and how they reacted to the Wa government's plan to ban opium in the year 2005. Moreover, I will examine the social organization of the opium trade in the Wa State. Finally, I will discuss the role of the Wa leaders in the opium business.

Reasons for Growing Opium

The demographic characteristics of the three hundred opium growers interviewed are shown in table 2. Most of our subjects were married Wa males in their thirties or forties. About 84 percent of the subjects were full-time farmers, growing rice, opium, and a variety of other crops. We asked the opium farmers to tell us why they grow opium. Generally, there were five reasons: to survive, to improve their living conditions, to pay the opium tax, to maintain a tradition, and to use it, either smoking it out of habit or relying on it as folk medicine. For many farmers, all five reasons were equally important.

Many subjects told us that they had to grow opium for basic survival: growing rice could only provide enough food to live on for three to four months a year. For these farmers, opium was a subsistence crop they relied on to offset the annual rice deficit. A twenty-year-old Wa male said: "The reason for cultivating opium is the same as for growing other agricultural products: to survive. Sometimes we did not have enough rice to eat, so we used the cash from selling opium to buy rice."[1]

Other subjects, especially those who had enough rice to eat for the whole year, said they used their proceeds from opium farming to improve their lives. For example, a forty-eight-year-old Wa female, laughing, said: "If we do not grow opium, we still can survive by eating rice and other stuff we grow. We grow opium to improve our living conditions."[2] Because opium could be easily converted into cash anywhere in the Wa Hills, many farmers were willing to grow the cash crop. With cash from opium, villagers could then buy a variety of items, including cooking wine, salt, soy sauce, and red pepper, so that they can add flavor to their otherwise tasteless porridge. Families that harvested several viss of opium a year could use the income to significantly enhance their living conditions by building new brick houses or buying new furniture or electronic devices.

Some farmers said they grew opium because their government asked them to. As will be discussed later, local governments in the Wa area relied heavily on an opium tax, and required farmers to turn in a certain amount of opium each year as the opium tax. The tax was mandatory; no one was exempt on the ground that he or she did not grow opium. Through years of propaganda, the Wa authorities convinced people in the region that growing opium and paying an opium tax was necessary in order to build a strong, autonomous, and modern Wa State.

Many subjects we interviewed also said that planting poppies was the only skill they had learned from their parents and that it was an ancient

Table 2. Demographic Characteristics of the Opium Growers Sample

Variable	Frequency	Percent
Sex		
Male	214	71
Female	86	29
Age $\overline{X}$ =44.68 SD=15.20		
25 and younger	25	8
26–35	77	26
36–45	65	22
46–55	59	20
56–65	43	14
66–75	25	8
76 and older	6	2
Ethnicity		
Wa	234	78
Han Chinese	34	11
Others	32	11
Number of children X=3.73 SD=2.40		
None	20	7
1–2	83	28
3–4	89	30
5–6	67	22
7 and more	40	13
Marital status		
Single	4	1
Married	263	88
Separated	2	1
Widowed	31	10
Occupation		
Has other occupation	47	16
No other occupation	253	84

Note: N=300

practice. For many Wa villagers, growing opium is as normal as breathing; it is the only thing they know how to do well. Since there are virtually no jobs in the Wa area, and they have had no education or training in business anyway, they have had to rely on the one survival skill that was taught to them by their parents.

A few subjects said they grow opium because they smoke opium. After they pay the opium tax to local authorities, they keep the rest of it for personal use. Besides smoking the opium, other subjects pointed out that they grow opium so that they can use it as medicine if someone in the family is sick. In the remote Wa villages, opium is considered the all-purpose drug for a variety of illnesses and pains. As discussed in chapter 6, many people became addicted to opium after they used opium to cure their illnesses.

In sum, the Wa grow opium because they need the income to survive, to improve living conditions, to pay the tax, to follow a tradition, and to cope with an illness or because they are addicted to it. It is grown for political and cultural reasons as well. The most powerful factor may be the opium tax, however. The Wa people must pay the opium tax, so they have no choice but to grow opium.

Opium Cultivation

From interviews with opium cultivators throughout Northern Wa State and our fieldwork in Kunma, it is clear that growing opium is a laborious task, even for the rugged Wa people. First, growers need to find an ideal site for the poppy field. According to a subject: "It is not suitable to grow opium at the top of the mountain; it is better on the mountain slopes, especially where there are plenty of dews. If you plant it on the mountain top and there's no rain when the plant begin to grow, then it won't grow well, nor will there be much opium gum in the pods."[3]

Most Wa farmers must walk about two hours to get to their poppy fields. Some respondents' opium fields were located so far away from their homes that they had to walk several hours to get there. Under such circumstances, they would stay in the poppy fields four or five days at a time. Often, farmers would erect a shelter near their poppy fields either to rest in or to spend the night.

After selecting the right place, there are basically four steps in the process: hoeing, sowing, weeding, and harvesting. My subjects asserted that each and every stage requires hard work either under the scorching sun or the pouring rain. According to twenty-four-year-old married woman,

growing poppies can very troublesome. We need to hoe the field three times before we sow the opium seeds. After planting the seeds, we must hoe the soil one more time. Once the crop begins to grow, snakes and rats will come to eat the plants. If there is rain right after the plants first emerge, the rain will wash them away. That's why we must broadcast the seeds two to three times in a given season. We also must weed the field three or four times. We also must know how to collect the opium gum from the poppy pods; if your cuts in the pods are too deep or too shallow, you are not going to get good results. Growing opium is much more troublesome than growing rice or corn, but we bought all our clothes with the money from opium.[4]

A forty-three-year-old male noted:

You need to find a good, fertile piece of land filled with small rocks and sand and an abundance of dew. The poppy field has to be hoed three or four times before the seeds are sown. When planting the seeds, one person will broadcast the seeds at the front and another person will follow behind and lightly till the field with a short-handled hoe. If you use too much strength in the process, the opium plants will not grow well. After seeding, we have to go to the field often to make sure the birds do not eat the seeds. After the opium seedlings come out, with three or four leaves, we will weed the field for the first time. This is a very delicate process because the opium plants are still very small. The removing of weeds for the first time needs to take place on a warm, sunny day. Weeds normally grow faster than opium plants, and that's why it is important to remove the weeds. If there is not enough rain, there's won't be much opium resin. If there is not enough labor for careful weeding, then the opium plants are not going to grow well. We cannot collect the entire field at once; we need to examine each and every bulb to see if it is hard, or ripe enough to be cut. If it is soft, then it's not ripe yet. Finally, the days should be dry when we are harvesting. Normally, we incise the bulbs one day and go back the next day to collect the opium resin, but if it has rained overnight, then the opium resin will turn black and it is useless. Growing opium is hard work, but if we don't grow it, we don't have money.[5]

Some basic information about opium cultivation in the eleven research sites or villages we visited is shown in table 3. Most of our subjects have been growing opium for most of their lives. The average age of the three hundred subjects was forty-four and, on average, they have been cultivating opium for twenty-four years. The average age of the participants in

Table 3. Opium Cultivation by Site

Site	Number of years in opium cultivation (mean)	Growing other crops (% yes)	Parents involved in opium cultivation (% yes)	Number of people per household (mean)
Nankangwu	24	100	88	3.4
Yingpan	17	100	79	3.3
Kunma	24	94	87	3.3
Longtan	24	100	84	3.3
Mengmao	21	100	73	3.5
Nandeng	27	59	69	3.2
Shaopa	23	97	66	3.5
Aicheng	22	100	45	3.0
Denge	35	100	67	3.5
Hedao	16	97	60	3.2
Wengao	22	92	67	2.7
Average	24	93	71	3.3

Note: N=300

Denge (forty-six) was only slightly above the average of the entire sample, but these people were involved in opium farming for an average of thirty-five years, significantly higher than the sample average of twenty-four years. The subjects in Hedao (all Hani people) and Yingpan had, on average, the least experience in opium growing.

For the majority of our subjects, growing opium is not their only agricultural activity. Almost all the subjects interviewed said that they were also involved in growing other agricultural products; they did not solely rely on money from opium to survive. As mentioned in chapter 2, Wa farmers are busy almost all year round because they grow a variety of farm products throughout the year. The only exception is the Chinese village in Nandeng. Only 59 percent of the subjects we interviewed there said they were also growing crops other than opium plants.

Not only had most of my subjects been in opium cultivation for long periods of time, but they were also familiar with it since childhood because most of their parents were also opium farmers. Seven out of ten subjects said their parents had grown opium.

Opium cultivation in the Wa area is carried out mainly by households located in remote villages. Most of these households are relatively small, with an average of three members working in the opium fields, most commonly a couple and a growing child of the family (see table 3). In other words, opium cultivation is not conducted on a state-sponsored, large-scale, collective basis but on a small-scale, family level. However, it is the state, or at least the local government, that is the force behind the opium trade because every household is required to pay the opium tax and it must be paid in opium.

Opium Yield and Income

According to the 1998 International Narcotics Control Strategy Report (INCSR), a worldwide drug report published annually by the Bureau of International Narcotics Matters of the U.S. Department of State, Burma was the world's largest source of illicit opium between 1994 and 1998, accounting for over 50 percent of the worldwide production of illicit opium (U.S. Department of State 1998). The report estimated that potential opium production in 1993 was a record 2,575 metric tons (see table 4). A Wa official from the WCA explained why there had been a marked increase in opium production: "Here in the Wa State, opium production increased dramatically after we ended our ties with the CPB in 1989. When the CPB was in control, people here could grow opium only in secret and heroin factories were not allowed. Since 1990, people began to grow opium openly, and foreign technicians were allowed to come in and participate in heroin production."[6]

However, by 1999 the INCSR report concluded that Afghanistan was then the world's top producer of opium, with Burma ranked as the second largest source of illicit opium. According to Labrousse (2005), peasants in Afghanistan increased their opium production in 1999 to 4,565 tons, in contrast to the period from 1995 to 1998 when 2,000 to 3,000 tons were produced.[7] Table 4 shows that opium production in Burma had been declining since 1997, and by 2004 production levels had hit a record low.

In 2000, the INCSR report asserted that continued eradication efforts by the Burmese government and adverse weather conditions had contributed to reduced production of opium in Burma. When I was collecting data for the first time in the Wa area in 2001, at a time when my subjects were harvesting their opium, they often mentioned that the harvest was not as good as the previous year and they blamed poor weather conditions as the key reason. A Wa official in the Longtan Special District playfully told me:

Table 4. Opium Cultivation, Opium Yield, and Other Drug-Related Statistics in Burma (1991–2007)

	Cultivation (hectare)	Potential yield (metric tons)	Seizures (opium)	Seizures (heroin)	Heroin labs destroyed (number)	Meth labs destroyed (number)
1991	161,012	2,350	1.512	0.183	6	—
1992	154,915	2,280	2.193	0.266	2	—
1993	166,404	2,575	2.265	0.3	0	—
1994	149,945	2,030	2.265	0.347	4	—
1995	154,070	2,340	1.06	0.07	3	—
1996	163,100	2,560	1.3	0.505	11	—
1997	165,651	2,365	7.884	1.401	33	—
1998	146,494	1,750	5.2	0.386	32	—
1999	99,300	1,090	1.44	0.273	23	6
2000	108,700	1,085	1.528	0.171	—	—
2001	114,317	865	1.622	0.095	14	3
2002	103,862	630	1.863	0.334	17	6
2003	47,130	484	1.481	0.568	7	—
2004	30,900	292	—	—	—	—
2005	40,000	380	—	—	—	—
2006	21,500	315	—	—	—	—
2007	27,700	460	—	—	—	—

Source: International Narcotics Control Strategy Report (U.S. Department of State 1991, 1994, 2003, 2004, 2006); United Nations Office on Drugs and Crime 2007).

This year, we did not have much rain and as a result the poppy plants did not grow well. One group of people here said that's because God knows that the Wa State is going to stop growing opium in the year 2005, and He decided to take action now.[8] Other people say that God knows that Americans are unhappy with the fact that opium is grown here, and that's why He denied rain to the Wa area.[9]

In the 2003 INCSR report, however, poor weather conditions were not assumed to be the key factor in the drop in opium production. The report stated that "eradication efforts, enforcement of poppy-free zones, alternative development, and a sharp shift toward synthetic drugs in consumer countries have combined to depress cultivation levels for the past three years. 2003 was the first year that weather was not a major factor in the declining poppy cultivation trend" (U.S. Department of State 2003, 272).

The 2006 opium survey by the United Nations stated that "in 2006, the total area under opium poppy cultivation in Myanmar was estimated at

21,500 hectares, representing a decrease of 34 percent, compared to 2005 (32,800 hectare). . . . The potential production of opium remained at 315 metric tons almost at the level of 2005 (312 metric tons)" (United Nations Office on Drugs and Crime 2006, 61–62). However, the 2007 UNODC survey found a 29 percent increase in the total area under opium poppy cultivation in Burma and a 46 percent increase in the weighted national average opium yield, mainly due to a 65 percent increase in opium cultivation in Southern Shan State (United Nations Office on Drugs and Crime 2007).

There is no doubt that opium production in the Wa area has been declining dramatically for the past several years. However, there are still two lingering questions concerning opium cultivation in Burma: First, what proportion of the opium produced in Burma actually comes from the Wa area? Second, how accurate are these estimates of opium yield in Burma, especially in the Wa region? U.S. authorities projected that, in the years 2003 and 2004, between 55 and 65 percent of the opium produced in Burma came from the Wa Hills. However, many people in the Wa area and officials in Rangoon told me that there are other areas in Burma that are producing more opium than the Northern Wa region. "The Burmese are also actively involved in growing opium," a district mayor told us. "It's just that outsiders have very little information about this. Like us, we are not hiding the fact, but it is very difficult to know exactly to what level the Burmese are involved in opium growing."[10]

Wa leaders also question the accuracy of U.S. estimates of the level of opium yield in their territory. For example, Zhou Dafu, deputy director of the Wa Central Authority (WCA), estimated that

there are about 320,000 people in Northern Wa State and I will assume that there are 200,000 people living in the opium-growing areas. If we also assume that half of them are strong enough to be involved in opium cultivation, and that each person can produce one kilogram of opium a year, then the Wa area could produce no more than 100,000 kilograms of opium a year. This means the amount of heroin exported out of the Wa area could not be more than 10,000 kilograms a year. The media always overestimates the amount of heroin we produce.[11]

According to our interviews with opium farmers in 2001, each household yielded about 7.9 *kang* (a *joi* or viss contains 10 *kang*)[12] (see table 5). The data we collected supports Mr. Zhou's assertion. For each laborer working in the opium fields, an average of 2.4 *kang* of opium was produced in 2001.

Table 5. Opium Seeds and Yield by Site

Site	Opium yield 2000 (kang)	Opium seeds 2000 (jin)	Opium yield 2001 (kang)	Opium seeds 2001 (jin)
Nankangwu	16.6	8.3	7.3	12.3
Yingpan	7.2	5.9	3.4	5.0
Kunma	4.6	5.1	3.3	5.2
Longtan	7.3	1.7	3.4	1.7
Mengmao	8.4	4.4	6.2	4.7
Nandeng	39.1	7.4	29.6	7.5
Shaopa	13.5	4.3	9.4	3.9
Aicheng	8.1	2.2	4.0	2.0
Denge	21.3	11.1	11.0	8.1
Hedao	4.3	1.6	2.0	1.9
Wengao	6.3	4.1	3.9	4.2
Average	12.5	5.0	7.9	4.9

Note: N=300

Wa farmers harvested more in 2000, but even then a household was able to collect about 12.5 *kang* of opium gum, not enough to support the assumptions that (1) 1,085 metric tons of opium was produced in Burma in 2000 and (2) the Wa area was responsible for 55 to 65 percent of the opium cultivated in Burma. Either the estimate for opium yield in Burma was grossly exaggerated or opium production in the Wa area was significantly less than other parts of Burma.

Table 5 also shows that the amount of opium seeds planted could not be used to predict opium yield. If the weather is poor (too much or too little rain), broadcasting a large quantity of opium seeds would not result in a good harvest. On average, our three hundred subjects sowed about five *jin* of opium seeds in 2000 and about the same amount the following year, even though the yields for the two seasons significantly differed. Farmers in Nandeng did not plant a large quantity of opium seeds and yet were able to collect more than three times the average yield for the entire sample of growers we interviewed.

There were significant variations in opium yields for the subjects in the eleven villages we surveyed. Subjects in Nandeng collected the most opium in 2001 (29.6 *kang* or 2.96 viss) and subjects in Hedao harvested the least (2 *kang* or 0.2 viss). Nandeng is located at the northern part of the Wa State and very close to Kokang where many heroin refineries are believed to exist (Zhao and Ke 2003). Nandeng was largely populated by Chinese; the village we surveyed in Nandeng was a so-called Chinese village. According to both Chinese and non-Chinese opium growers in the Wa State, Chinese households tend to collect significantly more opium than other ethnic peoples because the Chinese take opium cultivation seriously, even more seriously than the Wa; they work the opium fields carefully and thoroughly. The Chinese also used more workers in opium growing and often hired laborers to work in the opium fields. Hedao is located in the south, and one possible reason for the low opium yield there may be due to the existence of the United Nations' Wa Alternative Development Project in the area. The other reason could be that many people in the area were shifting to the methamphetamine business.

During the interviews in 2001, many opium growers complained that they had not had a good harvest (changes in opium yield between 2000 and 2001 are shown in table 5). For many villages in Nankangwu, Yingpan, Longtan, Aicheng, Denge, Hedao, and Wengao, the opium yield for 2001 was only half of the previous year—a dramatic drop in the harvest that meant that opium farmers in the area had had a difficult time in 2001. In sum, our data supports the suggestion by a Wa official who estimated that the Wa area could not possibly produce more than 100,000 kilograms of opium in any given year.

How much money our subjects made from opium sales is shown in table 6. Of the eleven villages, households in the Chinese village in Nandeng made the most, about $1,127 per household on average. A family in Nandeng may make almost three times as much as a family in Denge, an area where households made the second highest income from opium sales. Not only did growers in Nandeng collect more opium than growers in other communities but they were able to sell their opium for a higher price. Families in Hedao were only making an average of $59 from opium sales in 2001. The average income was $277 per household for the three hundred subjects interviewed. Table 6 also shows that opium farmers received much less from opium sales in 2001 than the year before. In 2001, villagers in Nankangwu, Yingpan, Aicheng, Denge, and Hedao made less than half of what they made in 2000. For many families who were struggling to make ends meet with an average income of $512 a year in 2000, one can understand how difficult it was for them to live on an average income of $277 the following year. The household average yearly income from opium sales continued to decline in the following years. According to a UN opium survey conducted in the Shan State of Burma, it fell to $133 in 2004 and slightly increased to $152 in 2005 and $217 in 2006 (United Nations Office on Drugs and Crime 2005a, 2006).

Table 6. Average Household Income from Opium Sale by Site

Site	Income in 2000 (in US$)	Income in 2001 (in US$)
Nankangwu	774	285
Yingpan	307	114
Kunma	210	138
Longtan	113	63
Mengmao	247	181
Nandeng	1,742	1,127
Shaopa	450	292
Aicheng	363	136
Denge	932	377
Hedao	159	59
Wengao	261	118
Average	512	277

Note: N=300

Opium Tax

Our subjects cited the need to pay an opium tax as one of the reasons for growing opium. Each year, all opium farmers are required to give a certain percentage of their opium to their local government as a kind of tax. The local governments do not place a cash tax on the opium. In certain areas, such as the Longtan Special District, farmers must also sell the rest of their opium to local authorities, rather than sell it in the marketplace or in their homes. Authorities in Longtan said this was the best way to prevent the opium from inadvertently flowing across the border into China. In other areas, such as the Bangkang Special District, farmers were allowed to sell their opium freely as long as they had paid the opium tax.

Most opium farmers were quite unhappy with the opium tax system, as one farmer we interviewed in Kunma explained:

How much opium we have to turn in to the government is decided by authorities in the district office. Right before we are about to harvest our opium, officials from the district office take a quick look at each household's opium field. The officials carry notebooks and estimate how much opium each and every household will harvest that year. When they make that quick evaluation, they do not tell the households what their estimates are. After they return to their headquarters, they send payment for the opium to the town office, and the town office will then send the money to the village section's chief. By the time the farmers receive their money, they are very upset; sometimes the women may even cry, because, very often, the official estimate of the opium yield is very different from the actual harvest. For some households, the official estimate is higher than the actual harvest and, as a result, these families have to borrow opium from relatives, neighbors, or friends; they have to pay it back the following year. We have to turn in a certain amount of opium as tax and then sell the rest of the opium to the government. We are not allowed to sell it privately. The government pays us only 40 yuan a *liang* [as opposed to the market value of 60 yuan per *liang*, or 1.7 ounce], much lower than the market price. We dare not complain, and if we do, they will yell at us.[13]

In addition to collecting opium tax, local governments can also generate income by paying opium farmers in advance for their crop. This practice is called *maiqingyan* or "buying green opium." It is the way certain local governments in the Wa area force people in their jurisdictions to grow opium. At the same time, these same local governments can generate a substantial amount of income by buying opium from their people at a price much lower than its market value. Asked about this exploitative measure, Chen Longsheng, director of the WCA, said:

The WCA does not allow local governments to buy "green opium"— that is, we prohibit local authorities from giving opium farmers payment in advance and collecting the opium later. That practice is, undoubtedly, exploitation of those poor farmers. But in some areas, local officials are still involved in it and that creates a lot of tension between the central and the local governments. We also do not allow local businessmen to buy "green opium." Of course, sometimes it was the opium farmers who asked their local leaders to buy their "green opium" because they were desperate for cash.[14]

What do the local governments do with the large amounts of opium they buy from their farmers? Do they resell the opium to high-level opium traders or heroin producers for a better price? Or do they convert the opium into heroin themselves? In the interviews with opium growers, we did not ask our subjects these questions because we thought these issues were too sensitive for ordinary people in the Wa area to talk about, nor did anyone volunteer to tell us how the local governments dispose of the opium. According to Takano (2002, 136–37), "In the Wa State, with taxes paid directly by individuals with opium, not cash, the army can systematically control the heroin business. They can acquire vast amounts of opium, process it directly into heroin and market it. They would not make as much money with opium alone, so they process it into heroin, increasing the value." In support of Takano's assertion, a businessman I interviewed in Bangkang told me that it was highly unlikely that anyone or any organization with a large amount of opium would simply sell the opium, which would yield only a small profit. The most likely scenario is for the individual or organization to convert the opium into heroin, with or without outside help, significantly increasing the profit level.

When Wa leaders are asked about the opium tax, they all insist, with a straight face, that the practice is one way for the authorities to discourage people from growing opium, even though it is not clear how this tax system could have in any way discouraged Wa people from raising poppies. Moreover, Wa leaders also know that some farmers are forced to buy opium at a higher price in the market and resell it to the local government for a smaller amount in order to meet the official estimated yield.

Even though the entire Wa area is, in theory, under the control of the WCA in Bangkang, there is no centralized opium tax policy. Officials at the county and district levels are free to implement an opium tax policy as they see fit, and, as a result, there are many localized opium policies, ranging from mildly to severely exploitative.

Farmers' Reaction to the Opium Ban in 2005

Under pressure from the world community, Wa leaders declared in 1995 that opium cultivation would be prohibited starting in 2005 (Kramer 2007). The opium ban was implemented in Mengla in 1997 and in Kokang in 2003, and the leaders of these regions erected museums in their areas to commemorate these significant events.[15] These drastic public policies may have pushed the Wa leaders to come up with a similar plan—that is, to ban opium cultivation in the Wa area in 2005.

For many Wa farmers, the ban on opium production was certainly not good news because they wanted to continue to do the one thing they knew well how to do. As one subject said, "I do not care about whether we have other alternatives. The only thing I know is growing opium, and I like doing it."[16] Many villagers also did not want to give up growing opium because it was the only way to bring them cash, and cash was needed to support them throughout the year because of the rice deficiency. One villager said: "The grains cultivated in the summer could only sustain us for four months; we need opium to live on the rest of the year."[17] For others, opium was the way to improve the infrastructure of the Wa State, as one farmer said: "We reached a cease-fire agreement with the Burmese government not long ago. Now, we need money to develop our society."[18]

There were also Wa farmers who thought it might be a good thing to stop growing opium, mainly for three reasons: opium is harmful to human beings, it gives the Wa State and its people a bad reputation, and opium is the main reason why the Wa area is extremely backward. Asked why he wanted to stop growing opium, a farmer said: "We all know that opium is a bad thing for human beings. Cultivating opium brings us food to eat, but others suffer from it."[19]

Another Wa villager thought banning opium was a good idea because the new policy would attract outsiders to the Wa area and they would develop it into a modern society: "We know that opium harms people, ruins our reputation, and brings shame to our [political] party. If we prohibit opium cultivation and open our doors to outsiders, there may be many foreign investors willing to come here and help us develop our society. Opium has ruined our reputation. No one is willing to help us."[20]

A certain number of individuals in the Wa communities will do whatever their leaders tell them to. As one respondent told us: "I heard that the central government is going to prohibit opium cultivation. I would like the central government to make a choice for me, because we rely on our government to survive. Whatever the government asks us to do, they must have good reasons."[21] Others follow orders because they are afraid they will be punished if they do not: "If the government prohibits us from growing opium and I continue to grow it, that's equivalent to getting oneself killed."[22]

My data suggests that Wa people were more likely to follow the order on the ban on opium rather than resisting it. Their respect for their supreme leader Bao Youxiang, their fear of the repercussions if they violate the order, and the fact that they had been preparing for the ban for many years may have all come into play in the process.

Western observers were concerned that abruptly ending poppy cultivation in the Wa area without any economic aid or support to the farmers was a humanitarian disaster in the making:

> Without adequate resources, the longer-term sustainability of "quick solutions" is highly questionable. Since [Wa] local authorities are eager to comply with promises made, law enforcement repression is likely to increase, with human rights' abuses and more displacement a potential outcome. The only viable and humane option lies in a simultaneous easing of drug control deadline pressures while increasing international humanitarian aid efforts. Both require stronger international engagement of a different kind from what we have seen thus far. (Jelsma, Kramer, and Vervest 2005, xiii)

Villagers' Responses to Outside Criticism

The Wa villagers' reactions to the allegation that their area was a major opium-producing area were as varied as their reactions to the plan to ban opium cultivation. Some villagers reacted angrily and defended themselves with the following explanations: (1) we do grow opium but we do not ask people to come and buy our opium; (2) we are not the only people in the world that are growing opium; (3) large numbers of Chinese are coming to the Wa area to grow opium and they should also be blamed; (4) we have no choice but to grow opium to survive; and (5) we are just following our government's order to grow opium.

My respondents were unhappy with the allegation because, even though they raise the poppies, they do not transport the opium outside of their area, nor do they sell it to outsiders. A farmer who sold his opium only to the local authorities in his area shot back when told of how the outside world saw the Wa area: "Gosh! I am, of course, mad as hell. I never travel abroad to sell my opium to them [outsiders]; I sell my opium to our own leaders."[23] Some farmers were upset because they thought people who come to buy the opium should be blamed, not the growers or sellers.

Some subjects were offended because they believed other farmers besides the Wa also grow opium and it was not fair just to blame them. One villager said: "I am angry. The Wa State is not the only place in the world that produces opium. Why do they just blame us?"[24] Some respondents were disturbed by the allegation that Wa people are predominantly opium growers because there were a large number of Chinese growing opium in their midst.

Others were angry at the criticism from abroad because they saw opium cultivation as their only means of survival in the remote, mountainous areas. They felt they were unfairly blamed by outsiders who have never paid attention to, or understood, their plight. A respondent reacted furiously: "In the Wa State, there is nothing else you can do to bring food to your table. The only way to survive is to rely on opium to improve living conditions. In other countries, people have good education and advanced technology, and they certainly do not have to grow opium."[25] An older woman replied bluntly: "As a female, I don't understand world affairs or care what other people say. I will consider myself a great woman if I can only raise my children. Other people might be able to survive without growing opium, but I know if I don't, I can't make it."[26]

Others were irritated with the accusation because they believed they were simply doing what their leaders had asked them to do. Two subjects explained why they should not be blamed: "We do not grow a lot, and we are doing it to fulfill our tax obligation. And yet, we have to hear this."[27] "I don't care what others say about is. They don't understand. We are growing opium at our government's order."[28]

Others reacted solemnly to the charge that Wa people are major opium growers. They acknowledged that, one, it is true; two, opium is harmful; and three, opium can be converted into heroin and heroin is much more destructive than opium. The fact that they are involved in opium cultivation and their awareness that both opium and heroin are harmful led some of our respondents to accept the blame readily. Some villagers were willing to take the blame because they were aware of the devastating effect of opium smoking. As one subject replied: "I am not mad, I only feel sorry for those who smoke opium because they are killing themselves slowly. It is crueler than those who kill themselves with a sword or a gun."[29] Another subject who knew the opium he grew was converted into heroin was also willing to take the blame: "I only know how to grow opium. Businessmen are so cold-blooded; they are the ones who convert opium into heroin and bring harm to others. I feel sorry about this."[30]

Buying and Selling Opium

Buying and selling buying opium was legal in the Wa State before 2005; the Wa government only required that opium buyers paid a cash tax and that opium farmers sold their opium to their local governments or local buyers, not buyers from outside of Burma. The opium trade was the major economic activity for most people in the Wa State before the ban in 2005. When people say someone is a "businessperson," it was highly likely that the person is in the drug business. Almost all the rich people in the area were thought to be involved in the opium trade, heroin production, or the methamphetamine business. As I drove around Bangkang with my interviewers in 2001, they told me that almost all the new, big houses are owned by people in the drug business. During market days, it was a common sight to see farmers arriving in Bangkang with bundles of opium leaves, and going in and out of those big houses to sell their wares. People in Bangkang all know that only high-level opium traders would buy such a large amount of opium leaves, presumably to wrap around raw opium to make it heavier, and thus more expensive.

Depending on where they lived, opium farmers sold their opium at home, in the marketplace, or to the local government. Of course, farmers who were allowed to sell freely at home or at the market to opium merchants were far better off because they received the market value for their opium. According to our survey, opium farmers in Denge, Wengao, Nankangwu, Yingpan, and Hedao were most likely to sell their opium in the marketplace (see table 7). Farmers in Nandeng, Shaopa, and Aicheng were more likely to sell their opium at home because the local authorities discouraged people from doing so in the market. Villagers in Longtan, Mengmao, and Kunma were most likely to sell all their opium below market price to local authorities. In sum, local authorities in the southern parts of the Northern Wa area were more likely to allow farmers in their areas to sell opium to private buyers either in the marketplace or at home for a better price. As one moved north, local authorities preferred to have their people selling their opium at home, even though selling in the marketplace was not forbidden. However, as one moved east toward the border with China, local authorities there were much more likely to control the flow of opium by buying all the crop produced by farmers in their jurisdiction. According to authorities in the border area, this was to prevent their people from inadvertently selling opium to buyers from China and having it end up in the hands of Chinese opium smokers or Chinese who were involved in heroin production. As the number of drug addicts in

Table 7. Methods of Selling Opium by Site

Site	Home (%)	Market (%)	Both home and market (%)	Government (%)	Others (%)
Nangkangwu	12	82	6	0	0
Yingpan	0	85	5	5	5
Kunma	52	2	0	42	4
Longtan	4	0	0	96	0
Mengmao	0	20	0	54	26
Nandeng	53	16	13	0	18
Shaopa	49	35	10	3	3
Aicheng	49	39	12	0	0
Denge	0	97	0	3	0
Hedao	3	73	0	0	24
Wengao	0	92	0	4	4

Note: N=300

China increased dramatically after the country adopted an open-door policy in the late 1970s, Chinese authorities were adamant about stopping the flow of drugs from the Golden Triangle into China, and pressured the armed groups in the border area and the Rangoon government to cooperate (Ting 2004).

Some Wa officials in government headquarters in Bangkang believe that local authorities in the border areas are simply exploiting their farmers in the name of drug prevention. According to Zhou Dafu, deputy director of the WCA:

> Every local government in the Wa area decides whether they are going to allow people in their jurisdiction to sell opium in the open market. The local officials who are sympathetic with the plight of their people will let them sell their opium openly to buyers in the market. The selfish and greedy officials will buy all the opium from the farmers at a price that is lower than the market price. When they say that this is the best way to prevent opium from flowing into China, they are lying. The same situation is true with the opium tax. Greedy local governments tax more and public-minded, responsible governments tax less.[31]

Farmers in the border areas are well aware that some local politicians are more interested in filling their coffers than in preventing opium from flowing into China. A respondent in Kunma told us: "We know the leaders will sell the opium to others for a much higher price than they pay us. We also know that they are just using an excuse when they say they buy opium from us to prevent us from selling it to the Chinese."[32]

Opium Traders

We interviewed thirty-five drug producers/traders in Bangkang, twenty-five of them opium traders. The other ten subjects were nine methamphetamine producers or dealers and one heroin producer. I will discuss people involved in the heroin and methamphetamine business in the next two chapters.

The twenty-five opium traders we interviewed were mostly ethnic Wa who were married men and women in their late thirties and considered to be low- to mid-level traders (see table 8). The majority of them had little or no education; only one subject had attended junior high school. Only one out of five had a regular job in addition to dealing in opium.

Most of them had been continually involved in the opium trade since they started trading. The average number of years in the opium trade was 6.8 years. The average annual income of our opium merchants, mostly low- or mid-level traders, was about $5,500. Compared to the average annual income of opium farmers, which was $277 in the year 2001, $5,500 was a fortune. We interviewed two subjects who each claimed to be making about $24,400 a year from the opium business. Even though the Wa government at the time required opium traders to pay taxes in cash, about 60 percent of our subjects said they did not pay taxes when they were buying and selling opium. I suspect the ones who did not pay taxes were those who were related to government officials. More than half of the opium traders we interviewed were also involved in other businesses. Buying and selling opium could be a risky business, with fluctuating prices, as more than 40 percent of our subjects had experienced business losses in the past.

Cross tabulations of the data indicate that Chinese traders, with an average of nine years in the business, in the sample were more experienced than the Wa traders, with five years. Moreover, the Chinese traders made significantly more money than the Wa traders ($8,780 vs. $4,512 a year) and were more likely to be involved in other businesses. Level of involvement/profitability was not related to the inclination to pay taxes or avoid

Table 8. Demographic Characteristics of the Opium Traders Sample

Variable	Frequency	Percentage
Sex		
Male	14	56
Female	11	44
Age $\overline{X}$ = 37 SD = 10		
30 and younger	7	28
31–40	11	44
41–60	7	28
Marital status		
Single	3	12
Married	19	76
Divorced	1	4
Widowed	2	8
Ethnicity		
Wa	16	64
Han Chinese	5	20
Lahu	1	4
Dai	2	8
Jinpo	1	4
Education		
None	11	44
Private–elementary	2	8
Elementary	9	36
Junior high	1	4
Others	2	8
Have had a regular job?		
Yes	5	20
No	20	80

Note: N=25

paying them; traders at all levels paid or did not pay the opium tax with equal frequency.

We asked opium traders under what circumstances they began their involvement in the opium business. A thirty-five-year-old Wa female who was married with three children said:

When my husband was a soldier, my family's monthly income was less than a hundred yuan [$12], plus we received some rice from his work unit. It was a hard life. I was born in a poor area, so my parents could not help me. One of my friends told me that opium could be bought for 3,000 yuan [$365] a viss in the hills, and we could sell it here [in Bangkang] for 3,500 yuan [$426] a viss. I asked my husband to borrow 10,000 yuan [$1,219] from others and we started buying and selling opium, even though we only made a profit of 500 yuan [$61] a viss. That's how we got started.[33]

Most of my subjects who were opium traders gave the following reasons for their involvement in the opium business: (1) it was perfectly legal to buy and sell opium in the Wa area; (2) I needed money; (3) there was no other business opportunity here; (4) many people were involved in it; and (5) unlike other businesses, I could get into the opium business with a small amount of start-up money.

Low-Level Opium Trade

The social organization of the opium trade could be divided into at least three levels: low level, mid level, and high level. Of course, there could be more than three levels. Obviously, there were no standard criteria to separate a low-level opium trader from a mid-level trader. According to a Chinese businessman in Bangkang, "There are small, medium, and big opium dealers. You can see the small dealers buying raw opium from farmers in the open market. Medium dealers would buy the opium from small dealers and then sell it to big dealers. Big dealers would either sell their opium to heroin producers or they, themselves, were heroin producers."[34] A local government that buys from farmers and sells to heroin producers is most likely to be a high-level trader because of the large amount of opium involved. Opium buyers who were operating at the low level could buy their opium either in the villages or in the marketplaces.

Buying Opium in the Hills

In the Wa State, some opium buyers would venture up into the mountains and buy opium directly from farmers in their villages. These opium buyers sometimes would barter with the farmers, offering household items or clothes to villagers in exchange for raw opium. Many villagers in the remote areas preferred to receive household goods instead of cash because they lived so far from a market town and it was inconvenient for them to travel to town on market days.

A twenty-one-year-old Wa woman was an opium buyer when she was still a teenager. Her mother was once an opium buyer and is now involved in the retailing of both opium and methamphetamine tablets in Bangkang. Her father was a Wa army officer and a heroin producer/trader who was arrested by the Thai authorities near the Thai-Burma border in the early 1990s for heroin trafficking and sentenced to a long prison term. Not long after his release, he died because he was an opium addict and an alcoholic:

Three months before I was to graduate from middle school, I quit school because I wanted to get involved in some kind of business. When I told my parents I wanted to get involved in the opium business, they said no because I was only fifteen. So I went to a relative in Kunma without telling my parents. The relative told me if I wanted to be an opium buyer, I first had to learn the whole process of opium growing. I observed firsthand how farmers planted the seeds and collected the opium. When I went with them to the poppy fields, they allowed me to keep the opium I collected. The first day I went into the opium field, I was able to collect only a small amount of opium because I was not good at it. However, the farmers taught me how to do it, and told me to spit on the opium resin if it is too dry. They also taught me how to wrap a small amount of opium resin in opium leaves and bundle it, in the hope that the opium would "bite" [suck] the leaves so that the leaves could not be separated from the opium. That is how you make a small amount of opium become heavier. After working in the fields for a few weeks, I came home with a viss of opium. When my father saw it, he was delighted and said that I was good enough to go into business.

My family was poor, and my parents told me that they could only gave me 2,000 yuan [$243] to start my business. With that money, I bought a whole bunch of clothes, especially children's clothes. I also bought some army blankets. I traveled across the Wa State for months, going from village to village, selling clothes. If the farmers gave me money, that was fine. And if they didn't have money and were willing to pay me opium, that was better. I brought a pair of scales with me. After a season, I came back to Bangkang with a bag of opium and sold it to the opium bosses in the town.

I stopped doing that for a year. Later, I went to the villages again with 10,000 yuan [$1,219]. This time, I did not bring any clothes, just cash. It was hard; I had to travel on foot, and many times, I almost starved to death. Besides, at that time, I did not know it was a good idea to wear a hat. My skin was very dark because of the sun, and my lips were dry and cracked. Once, I had to walk for days.

When I met with the farmers, they liked it when they saw that I used bullets to weigh their opium. They didn't like old coins or batteries because those things could be tampered with by the buyers. I normally was very aggressive. If I saw someone with a basket, I would grab the basket and take out the opium brick wrapped in leaves or paper and cut it with a scissors. After I cut it, the farmer was more or less forced to sell it to me, because the carefully packed opium brick had been cut. If he did not sell it to me, he might have a hard time selling it to another buyer because the cut brick was an indication that it might have been examined by a buyer and rejected.[35]

A twenty-three-year-old Wa male who is also a mid-level army officer told us how he normally went about buying opium in the villages: "I would go to the hills to buy opium. I normally would go straight to the farmers' homes. We could buy it cheaper right after the farmers began to collect their opium. That's because at that time businesspeople from other places had yet to come to the hills. Farmers were desperate for money at that time, and they were willing to accept a low price for their opium."[36]

As will be discussed later, mid- and high-level opium traders also traveled to the remote villages to buy opium at the farmers' doorstep.

Buying Opium in the Marketplaces

In the Wa State, there is a market day every five days. During my stay in Bangkang, on market day I would usually see several groups of buyers buying opium from farmers in front of a small hotel owned by a Wa leader. Typically, two buyers would work as a team: one person would examine and weigh the opium paste wrapped in opium leaves and formed into bricks and the other person would work as the cashier. Farmers wandered around, checking every buyer's price, attitude, and practice before they handed over their opium to a particular buyer.

Once a farmer turns in his or her opium to a buyer, the buyer first tries to remove the outer leaves wrapped around the cake of opium. Then the buyer weighs the opium with a hand-held scale, using either old English silver coins or bullets as counterweights. Then, the buyer cuts the opium with a scissors to check the quality. Opium paste that appears to be fresh, not watery, and does not contain opium flowers or leaves is considered good quality. Typically, the buyer examines the opium cake by its texture and smell. The marketplace was filled with the musty opium smell. Very often, this type of conversation went on between buyer and seller:

Buyer: Why should I take all these leaves? I can't eat them.
Seller: Please do not remove the leaves.
Buyer: Then don't pack your opium with layers and layers of leaves.

If a buyer removed a lot of leaves from the bundle, some farmers would complain and move on to another buyer. Or they would ask a buyer to weigh their opium and then go to another buyer and have the opium weighed again, just to make sure that both buyers had the same result.

A thirty-five-year-old Wa female trader explained to us the advantages of buying opium in the villages instead of in the marketplaces:

Sometimes, I buy opium from the peasants in the countryside, while occasionally I buy it at the market. Of course it is better to buy at the farmers' houses because, as long as you have the money, you can buy it any time. If you have to buy it at the market, it's frustrating because you have to wait until it is a market day. Besides, there are too many buyers at the market who compete with you.[37]

A fifty-year-old ethnic Chinese who was born in Kunming, China, told us why it is an advantage to buy opium in the hills but also about the importance of flexibility: "If there is enough opium in the hills, I would prefer to buy as much as I can in one trip. Of course, we can also buy it at the market, but if there are too many buyers, you may miss your chance. That's why we do not have a fixed buying strategy. We buy whenever and wherever it is convenient and available."[38]

After these small dealers bought their small quantities of opium, they would go home and repack it into viss. They may be able to sell a viss to a mid-level opium trader for about 3,200 yuan ($390), making one to two hundred yuan (about $18) as profit. Of course, they could also keep the opium for a while and sell it to a mid-level dealer when the price is higher.

These small dealers usually made about 20,000 yuan ($2,430) a season, and when conditions were right, they could make 30,000 yuan ($3,650) a season. For them, it was good money.

In the Bangkang marketplace, the majority of the low-level opium buyers were women. An opium buyer explained why: "Most opium buyers are women in their thirties and up. You don't see many young women doing this, or men. Men are not as industrious as women, nor are they as patient. We have to wait for the farmers to come to us [buyers], and often we have to wait for hours. Men would not have that kind of patience."[39] Besides, most street-level opium buyers were ethnic Wa, not Chinese. The main reason was because most opium farmers were Wa or other hill peoples who did not speak Chinese. To be an effective street-level buyer, one had to speak the languages of the Wa, Lahu, or Shan. Otherwise, the buyer would not be able to communicate with the farmers.

These low-level buyers could be working for themselves or working for a boss. At the Bangkang market, we interviewed a twenty-year-old, married Wa woman who was her own boss. She said that she had two children and had been buying for the past four years. She considered herself to be a small-time trader; she made about 3,000 yuan ($365) a year. She was not involved in any other business. Sometimes she would go to the marketplaces to buy opium and sometimes she would buy it at her home. Because she examined all the opium before buying it, she did not have to worry much about buying poor quality opium. However, she did occasionally lose money from the business, from 3,000 to 6,000 yuan (from $365 to $730), because of falling prices after she bought the opium. She said that it was a tough business, but it had helped her family enormously. It was important for her to keep on working because her family had food only when she was trading.

We also interviewed two opium buyers who were working for a boss. Both of them were Wa women in their fifties who not only spoke Wa and Chinese but also Burmese, Shan, and Jingpo. After buying opium in the market all day, they had the following to say about their work when I talked to them in their home:

We just got back from a place where we packed the opium. Today, we bought altogether ten viss, four viss in the morning and six viss in the afternoon, at about 3,000 yuan [$365] a viss. We sold them to an army officer right after we packed them. We made a profit by cheating with the weight. We are working for a *laopan* [boss]. The boss invested money in the business and we help the boss buying and selling. For our service, the boss paid us 200 yuan [$24] each for a day's work. It is hard work because the opium is dirty and the smell is awful. Besides, farmers are very cautious and think over and over before they sell. They also shop around, and that's why it is not that easy to be buyers. But we have to do it because we could not rely on the 20 yuan [$2.50] standard monthly salary from the government.[40]

These opium buyers also make money on the side by referring buyers to sellers in Bangkang. According to one of the subjects, she made 600 yuan ($73) last year when she helped a person with fifty viss of opium find a buyer. She complained that the seller did not give her a good commission. She thought she should have been paid at least 1,000 yuan ($120).

In sum, trading opium is a unique fixture in the marketplaces of the Wa area. Besides the normal scenes of what one would expect to see in an open market in Southeast Asia—a huge crowd of hill peoples in colorful dress, women with their smoking pipes dangling from their mouths, stacks and stacks of cheap goods from China, vendors selling all kinds of home-grown vegetables and live animals—there are also teams of opium buyers working diligently to buy as much opium as possible on a market day. During harvest season, farmers arrive in the marketplace of a town with their precious, small amounts of opium. They pack their opium carefully, and are very cautious about who they sell the opium to and at what price. They talk to various buyers before they make the decision to sell. Some sell only a small quantity if the price is not good, just to have some money to sustain themselves until the next market day.

After farmers have made their sale, usually amounting to 200 to 300 yuan (about $30), they then go shopping for food, clothes, and other necessities such as red pepper, salt, and soy sauce. If their young children are with them, they will go to a food stall and buy a bowl of noodle soup for their kids, who are always excited to be with their parents in the marketplace, where they will have a chance to buy some good food.

Mid-Level Opium Trade

Most low-level traders buy and sell only a few viss per transaction, or in an entire market day. Mid-level traders are those who buy a few viss of opium from low-level traders, then accumulate a number of purchases (normally about twenty to thirty viss) before selling them to high-level traders. Transactions between low-level and mid-level traders are carried out in one another's home. Either side can take the initiative because most of them know one another. According to a street-level opium trader in Bangkang,

> after I bought the opium from the farmers in the mountains, I would come back to Bangkang and sell it to the bosses. From an early age we knew who the opium traders were. We just walked in and told the bosses we had opium and they would take a look at it and buy it. They always bought, regardless of the quality of the opium; it was just a matter of how much they would pay. The same was true with quantity. No matter how much you had, they would take it.[41]

Like low-level opium collectors, mid-level traders could also go to villages to buy opium directly from villagers. The only difference was that mid-level dealers were more likely to have much more cash with them, to travel in a group, and to arrive by car. According to the two female opium traders quoted above:

> We could go to the hills to buy opium instead of the market. In the market, we could not buy in large quantities because the Wa government was trying to stop the opium trade. However, if we went up to the hills to buy, we could buy as much as we wanted and nobody would bother us. All we had to do was to make sure we bought the opium tax ticket, which was 100 yuan [$12]. A person with the tax coupon could buy and sell as much opium as he or she wanted, and the tax was always 100 yuan.[42]

Other mid-level traders from Bangkang would travel to other towns and buy opium in the marketplace, pack it, and then sell it in that same area. The boyfriend of one of my interviewers worked for a mid-level trader who was a Chinese male and a relative. According to the interviewer:

> My boyfriend came back last night after spending about five days in Yingpan. He went there with his *laopan* and his wife. They stayed in a house in Yingpan they own. The boss stayed home while his wife and my boyfriend went to the markets to buy opium, which they repacked and sold to local businessmen. He said they made about 1,000 yuan [$120] a day. They did not bring any opium back to Bangkang. This is the time of year [late March through early April] when large numbers of people like my boyfriend's boss go around buying and selling opium. After a few weeks there won't be any

more opium coming from the farmers. My boyfriend's boss could make a profit and compete with local traders because he is good at cheating when weighing the opium. He also knows how to repack the opium with leaves to make it heavier, and knows how to mix good opium with poor opium so that the buyer will not reject the poor opium.[43]

As we moved from low-level to mid-level opium trade, we also noticed that the ethnicity of the traders begin to shift from Wa, Kachin, or other hill people to ethnic Chinese. In the many Wa villages we visited, a few Chinese families dominated the opium trade within their respective villages and they were the mid-level traders who buy opium from their villagers and sell it to high-level traders from the outside. The mid-level trade was much more discreet than the street-level trade. Once opium was packed in viss, it became a sensitive commodity, even in a place like the Wa area where buying and selling opium was legal.

High-Level Opium Trade

High-level traders are those who buy and sell opium in hundreds of viss per transaction. They either sell opium to heroin producers or they themselves are heroin producers. According to my interviews and fieldwork, most big-time opium traders are believed to be (1) high-ranking government officials and army commanders; (2) family members or close relatives of top-level officials; or (3) rich and influential people with close ties to powerful authorities.

An opium trader in Bangkang described how large opium transactions were usually carried out:

Bosses may not conduct opium transactions in their own houses. Here, if we learn that someone from the outside is here to buy opium, we will check out their background first. After meeting them, we show them the opium. If they want to buy it, they will come back with cash and take the opium away. If the order is small, we may not allow a buyer to come to us. Instead, we will simply ask someone to take the opium to his or her place, as long as both sides agree on a price.[44]

A businessman in Bangkang further explained why buyers of large amounts of opium typically would go to the seller, and not vice versa:

"Heroin producers are willing to go pick up the opium because it is not easy for an opium merchant to travel around the Wa State with a large amount of opium; plus heroin factory owners might not want opium sellers to know where their heroin factories are located."[45] Heroin producers are normally much more powerful and well-connected than opium traders at any level, and as a result heroin producers are in a better position to move around large amounts of opium in the Wa Hills and need not be concerned about being robbed by armed rivals or having their goods confiscated by the authorities.

Problems Associated with the Opium Trade

We asked opium traders what kinds of problems they normally encounter in the opium business. The following are the most likely "problems" or "headaches" buyers have to deal with.

First, there is not enough opium to buy. Some traders who are determined to get involved on a large scale because they have the capital and the people to do so are frustrated when they cannot find enough opium to buy, either in the marketplaces or the remote hills. Most of the demand for a large amount of opium must be met within a short period of time; if not, the demand may simply disappear and never return.

Second, opium traders are always leery of buying poor quality opium. To be a successful opium merchant, one must have the ability to tell instantly the difference between good and poor quality, real and fake opium. Otherwise, a trader may end up buying heavily diluted or poor quality opium and will have a hard time finding a buyer or will lose money after selling the opium for a lower price.

Third, most opium traders who travel to the hills to collect opium say that it is grueling, difficult work. Many have to walk long hours, or even days, along dusty or muddy roads, with little food and in unbearable heat. Finally, some subjects said they were most frustrated by their lack of capital. Without a considerable amount of capital, a trader can only buy and sell a relatively small amount of opium at a given time and, as a result, can make only a small profit. These are the people who are forced to remain small-time traders simply because they do not have the money to expand their business. According to a businessman in Bangkang, a person needs to have at least 400,000 yuan (about $50,000) in start-up money if he or she wants to be a key trader.

These opium traders were also asked about the problems associated with selling opium. The two problems most often described were:

1. Fluctuating prices. All traders are extremely leery about a possible drop in opium prices whenever they buy a large amount of opium for a relatively high price. Opium prices in the Golden Triangle fluctuate unpredictably, and traders can lose a large amount of money when the price drops.

2. Buyers failing to pay. Some traders may extend credit to their buyers, but there is always the chance that they will not be paid on time, or the buyers will say they are out of cash and offer to pay for the opium with cars or other commodities.

Opium Trade between Wa and Kokang

Before 2002, Kokang, located north of the Wa territory, was also a key opium cultivation area for many decades. As the first armed group to break away from the CPB and sign a cease-fire agreement with the Burmese authorities in 1989, the Kokangnese were allowed by the Rangoon government to remain armed and autonomous. However, when there were conflicts between the Yang clan and the Peng clan in the mid-1990s, it gave the Burmese an opportunity to move into the Kokang area. Hkam Awng, a drug enforcement official in Rangoon, said: "We took advantage of the infighting to move our troops into the Kokang area; they actually invited us to move in. Of course, Kokang is a part of Myanmar anyway."[46] As a result, there are now about six thousand Burmese soldiers in the Kokang area and many checkpoints there are manned by Burmese soldiers (Zhu 2004).

In 2002, Kokang's leaders declared that their farmers were not allowed to grow opium anymore; the region was transformed into an opium-free area in 2003 (Milsom 2005; United Nations Office on Drugs and Crime 2005a). However, many people I interviewed, including the Wa leaders, believed that as late as 2005 opium cultivation was still going on in certain parts of Kokang. Moreover, many active heroin refineries are located in the Kokang area. Opium production there is not as massive as in the Wa State; heroin producers in Kokang often buy large amounts of opium from high-level traders in the Wa State. According to a low-level opium trader, "The major opium traders here in Bangkang buy the opium and then someone from the Kokang area will come down to buy it from them. These people are the agents of the heroin factory owners in Kokang. The owners are not going to come here to buy the opium themselves, they just send one of their agents to Bangkang." [47]

When I asked an official in the WCA about the transportation of opium from Wa to Kokang, he admitted that the Wa government is aware of this and in fact "when opium from the Wa area is transported to Kokang, the Wa government collects 10 to 15 percent opium tax." [48] Besides buying opium from high-level traders in Bangkang, Kokang's opium traders also travel to certain Wa villages to buy opium directly from the farmers. For example, a significant portion of the opium farmers we interviewed in the Chinese village of Nandeng stated that they sold most of their opium to Chinese buyers from Kokang. Kokang traders may only be active in the Chinese villages within the Wa area that are not far from Kokang. Nandeng is located in the northernmost region of the Wa area, just south of Kokang.

Wa Leaders' Involvement in the Opium Trade

After Khun Sa surrendered to Burmese authorities in 1996, journalists and law enforcement officials in the West shifted their attention to the Wa State and its leaders and claimed that the United Wa State Army (UWSA) had emerged as the most powerful organization in the drug trade in the Golden Triangle (Lintner 1998a). Western government officials, law enforcement authorities, and journalists began to characterize the UWSA as essentially a heavily armed drug trafficking organization (Gelbard 1998; Hawke 1998), and Wa leaders as "drug kingpins" or "drug warlords" who were in charge of the best-organized and the largest drug-trafficking organization in the world (Eads 2002; Jelsma, Kramer, and Vervest 2005). Even so, no Wa leader was arrested, let alone convicted, for drug trafficking after the downfall of Khun Sa in 1996. The question became—and remains—to what extent are the Wa leaders involved in the opium trade and in what role?

When asked whether Wa leaders are involved in the drug trade, the mayor of a special district frankly stated that

> I myself am involved in the opium trade. I will buy and resell it. My wife is the key person in the business because she does most of the work: examining the quality of the opium, negotiating the price with sellers, completing the transactions, repacking the opium, and selling the opium to buyers. My local government is also involved in the opium trade; we collect tax in opium from farmers and later sell it to

buyers. A few days ago, the leaders from a county called and said they could not meet a big order for opium and asked us to help. So we sold them fifty viss of opium. My rule with the opium trade is that as long as we do not transport the opium out of the Wa State ourselves, that's fine. [49]

Another influential Wa leader told me how common it was for people in the Wa area, including government officials, to be involved in the opium business:

It is completely legitimate to buy and sell opium here. I, myself, will buy opium and resell it for a higher price. I mean, the trade is just a very normal thing for us to do. Nobody here questions the ethical and legal aspects of the trade. Potential buyers come to my house and I just sell them the commodity if the price is right. When I collect the money and they leave with the opium, whatever they do with the opium later has nothing to do with me. The trade is completely a domestic trade, not an international trade. In the past, I was also involved in transporting opium from the Wa area to the Kokang area. For me, this is just a business: moving a commodity from one market to another to make money. This mode of operation is not for everybody; it is only for those who are in power and those who are well connected. [50]

Like the official quoted above, this Wa leader also relied heavily on his wife to run the family business. A businessman in Bangkang explained why family or relatives of top Wa leaders are in a better position to buy and sell opium:

Here, buying and selling opium starts with buying the opium tax tickets. These tax tickets are not publicly available; you need to know where to go to buy them. With these tickets, you can go anywhere to buy and sell opium. You need not show these tickets when buying or selling opium but you need to show these tickets to Wa soldiers at the various checkpoints. If they discover you have opium but not the tax tickets, you will be in trouble. Those who are in power can use their government vehicles to transport opium without having to worry about tax tickets. Sometimes, opium traders may use army trucks to transport opium without tax tickets if they are close to the army commanders. [51]

Even those few Wa officials who are thought by people in Bangkang to be "clean" and "incorruptible" cannot completely dissociate themselves from the drug business. For example, a high-level Wa official who lives modestly is believed to have never been involved in the drug business, though his daughter is heavily involved in both the opium and the methamphetamine businesses. Even the one WCA official who, along with his family, is not involved in the drug business admitted he accepted bribes from people in the drug trade.

Not all Wa leaders I talked to admitted that they were involved in the opium trade. For example, Ailun, the commander of Division 468, denied that the Wa army was involved in the drug trade as an organization:

> Our troops do not rely on opium to survive. Our soldiers absolutely are not involved in the opium business. Our troops are not good at doing business and they are not allowed to do so. Our priority is to keep the army united and involved in agricultural activities as much as possible. Unlike the local governments, the troops are mostly supported by the central government. The central government provides us with ten months of food and we have to rely on ourselves for the other two months. In fact, we often produce three months of food a year on our own. Our troops even help law enforcement authorities fight against drugs. Some soldiers may, however, help their families grow opium or buy and sell opium when they go home.[52]

Notwithstanding what this army officer had to say, my research in the Wa area convinced me that the majority of the Wa leaders are involved in the opium trade, both privately and publicly. Privately, they or their spouses or other family members or relatives are involved in buying and selling opium on a relatively large scale, and they use the public resources they have at their command to promote their business or to avoid paying the tax. Most Wa leaders, however, are not directly involved in the opium trade; they let their family members conduct the business. Yet, it is clear that the Wa leader do not stay idle if there is a problem with the business. Publicly, they are in charge of the taxing of opium farmers or the buying of green opium from growers. As local or central authorities, these Wa leaders are responsible for the "handling" of the large amounts of opium that are considered to be government property. Handling could mean, in the Wa area, trading or transporting the opium, or even converting it into heroin. As a result, both as a government official and as an individual entrepreneur, it is inconceivable that most Wa leaders are not somehow implicated in the opium trade.

Even though it is no secret that most Wa leaders are involved in the opium trade, few people know how the large amounts of opium collected annually by local authorities are disposed of. Western observers are convinced that the Wa army or the Wa government plays a key role in the opium or heroin business, but they are not sure how. According to a mid-level Wa army officer, the social organization of the opium business in the Wa State is structured this way:

After local governments collect opium from growers, the local authorities turn over a certain percentage of the opium or the equivalent amount of money to the central Wa government. The very top leaders in the central government then ask a businessman who is not a Wa official nor a member of the inner circle of the central government to handle the opium. He will take full charge and dispose of the opium as he sees fit, and if something goes wrong he will take full responsibility and will make sure that it has nothing to do with the top leaders or the central government.[53]

A government official in Longtan (the special district where farmers were not only required to pay the opium tax but also to sell all their opium to local authorities) stated that his office, after collecting all the opium from the farmers, would sell it to the central government in Bangkang. It is clear that the central government in Bangkang regularly received not only a certain portion of the opium tax collected by local authorities but also opium that local authorities were willing to sell to them. A little-known "businessman," most likely an ethnic Chinese, is then assigned to convert the opium into cash, either selling the opium outright or converting it into heroin and then selling the heroin.

It is not clear how much the central and local governments rely on opium (including the opium tax and the opium trade) to survive. Observers in the West suggest that revenues from the opium business might be one of the main sources of wealth for both the central and local authorities. A Wa official in the central government disagreed:

We do not receive much opium tax. The central government collects about several million yuan [less than a million U.S. dollars] a year from all kinds of taxes, and the opium tax represents about 20 percent of the overall tax. This means we take in about $140,000 a year as opium tax. Of course, this is the money that we in the central government receive and I do not know how much the local authorities collect in tax from opium farmers.[54]

The Political Economy of Opium in a Global Context

The Wa opium economy is not unique. Poor farmers in many parts of the world often rely on the cultivation of opium to sustain themselves while living under difficult conditions (Westermeyer 1982; Booth 1997). These farmers do not get rich by growing poppies, nor do they play a role in the opium trade or in the transformation of opium into heroin.

The taxing of opium farmers by the Wa authorities is also nothing new. Local authorities in the opium-growing areas all over the world almost always play a key role in the social organization of the opium economy by encouraging, taxing, buying, and trading opium. A state-sponsored opium economy is the norm rather than the exception (Meyer and Parssinen 1998; Haq 2000). Insurgent and other clandestine groups also often rely on the opium economy to support their activities (McCoy 1972, 1991; Lintner 1994b; Smith 1999).

Different levels of opium merchants play key roles in the collecting, packing, and trading of opium, and they all help to consolidate the opium crop that is scattered throughout the Northern Wa region and eventually funneled to a handful of heroin refineries located in the Wa area or in the neighboring Kokang or Mengla areas. Although the low-level buying and selling of opium in the Wa area can be observed in the open in the marketplaces or the villages in the remote hills, mid-level and high-level transactions are conducted out of sight by a tight network of opium merchants. Even though street-level opium merchants are most active during the harvest season, mid- and high-level opium traders conduct their transactions all year long. These merchants will hold on to their opium when the price is not good and sell it when the price is good.

Local and centralized Wa authorities also facilitate the free flow of opium from farmers to heroin producers by taxing, purchasing, and trading opium both as individual entrepreneurs to enrich themselves and as representatives of their respective official units to fill their government coffers. Wa leaders began to encourage their people to grow more opium after the 1989 cease-fire agreement with the Burmese authorities. The increase in the opium tax, the stringent requirement to turn in opium rather than cash, and the buying of "green opium" all worked in concert to put pressure on farmers to be aggressively involved in opium cultivation. Indeed, the opium economy is orchestrated by the state, though individuals were willing to go along with the state plan because opium growing also enabled them to have some cash. For farmers, it is their only way to survive, whereas for Wa leaders it is a business opportunity that enables them to get rich and simultaneously generate money for state building.

All these activities were made possible by the arrival of Chinese nationals in the Wa area after China began to embark on economic reform in the late 1970s and encouraged cross-border trade with Burma and other neighboring countries. The Chinese not only brought the technical know-how, the management, and the precursor chemicals but also the connections to the heroin markets in China and other parts of the world. Without the heroin industry to absorb the opium produced in the Wa area, opium growing, taxing, and trading in the Wa area could not have been as active as they were when this study was conducted. The impact of China and Chinese people on the drug trade in the Golden Triangle, especially in the Wa area, will become clear when I discuss the heroin and methamphetamine trade in the next two chapters.

When Leach (1954) examined the political systems of highland Burma, he found that Kachin societies there continuously oscillate between *gumsa* (chieftain) and *gumlao* (egalitarian) in a state of unstable equilibrium due to internal contradictions embedded in these two types of systems. After exploring the relationship between social reproduction and the opium trade in the Kachin area, Nugent (1982) concluded that opium production was the most important factor in the *gumsa* economy, and as the opium business was disrupted by events in China, it undermined the basis of chiefly authority and led to revolts and the establishment of a hitherto unknown *gumlao*-egalitarian polity. Friedman (1987, 27), on the other hand, argued that the opium trade was more likely to be associated with a *gumlao* polity because "there is a tendency for everyone to be able to cultivate this cash crop, to accumulate cash that is convertible into prestige, and thus to undermine the conditions for the existence of hierarchy, which is dependent on the increasing monopolization of the distributable wealth in a society" (Friedman 1987, 27). In Friedman's view, social structure, social reproduction, and the modes of production in highland Burma were deeply influenced by global economic and power structures because these highland communities were "surrounded by larger state economies and strategic trade routes between China, Burma and India" (Friedman 1998 [1979], 33).

No doubt opium cultivation in the Wa area has always been deeply influenced by political and economic events in the greater Golden Triangle. The intrusion of the KMT in the mid-1940s, the expansion of the CPB in the late 1960s, the U.S. involvement in the Vietnam War in the 1970s, the reform and open door policy adopted by China in the late 1980s, and the development of a methamphetamine industry in the 1990s all played a key role in not only determining social structure and social reproduction in the Wa area but also the scope and patterns of the cultivation, production, and trafficking of opium, heroin, and methamphetamine in the area.

The opium trade in the Wa area cannot be eliminated simply by removing one or two opium kingpins because the trade is not under the control of one or two powerful figures. How much to grow and the actual amount of opium harvested annually depend on (1) the relationship between the Wa Central Authority and the various local administrations; (2) the dynamic between the Wa and other regions in the Shan State; (3) the relationship between the Wa and local governments in neighboring countries such as Yunnan in southwest China and Chiang Mai and Chiang Rai in northern Thailand; (4) the relationship between the Wa Central Authority and the central governments in Rangoon, Beijing, and Bangkok; (5) the demand for heroin in the international market; (6) the availability of other moneymaking opportunities such as the production and trafficking of methamphetamine; and finally (7) weather conditions. All these factors affect the cultivation, transportation, and price of opium in the region.

It is also clear that the opium trade is not the result of a simple political-criminal nexus in the Wa area. As in many other parts of the world, the flourishing of corrupt exchanges between criminals and politicians is made possible by the participation of otherwise legitimate businesspeople in the process. In the Wa area, many legitimate Chinese businesspeople play a key role, as they always have, in the buying and selling of opium on a higher level and in the transportation of large amounts of opium to the heroin producers. For them, opium is just a commercial commodity to be bought at a lower price and sold at a higher price to make a profit.

Finally, in the Wa area many people are simultaneously politicians, criminals, and businesspeople. Many Wa leaders are conscientious political leaders who are trying hard to bring peace and prosperity to their people. However, they become criminals, at least in the eyes of outsiders, when they get involved in the production and trafficking of heroin and methamphetamine. They are also legitimate businesspeople because they are also involved in the buying and selling of opium (that is legal in the Wa area) and many other business ventures. Their ability to move freely among these three roles enables them to make legal and illegal deals with people from both the regular economy and the irregular economy and blurs the distinctions between politicians, criminals, and businessmen and between politics, crime, and business. That is why I argued at the beginning that Wa leaders are essentially entrepreneurial state builders and we must deal with them as such to be able to understand the nuances of the political economy of the drug trade in the Wa area, and probably in other drug-producing areas of the world as well.

CHAPTER FOUR

HEROIN PRODUCTION AND TRAFFICKING

Because of the international subculture of heroin use, the opium business in the Wa Hills attracts the rapt attention of the world law enforcement community. According to the 1994 International Narcotics Control Strategy Report of the U.S. Department of State, approximately 60 percent of the heroin consumed in the United States in 1994 came from Southeast Asia (SEA), and almost all of that was from Burma. Between 1986 and 1992, U.S. authorities solved more than twenty major heroin trafficking cases involving Chinese participants (Chin 1996). All the heroin had come from the Golden Triangle; the Chinese in Asia and the United States were alleged to be key players in the emerging heroin trafficking route between Asia and the United States (U.S. House of Representative 1987; Posner 1988; U.S. Senate 1992). In the late 1990s and early 2000s, however, heroin from Colombia began to show up in the United States and gradually replaced SEA heroin (Jelsma 2005). Even so, the heroin markets in China (Ting 2004), Thailand (Phongpaichit, Piriyarangsan, and Teerat 1998; Chouvy and Meissonnier 2004), Hong Kong (Chu 2002), Taiwan (Ministry of Justice Investigation Bureau 2003), Australia (Australian Crime Commission 2007), and other countries (Haq 2000) were reported to be mainly supported by heroin from Burma. As a result, heroin production in the Wa Hills is still a major concern for drug enforcers around the world.

Over the years, the heroin trade has been the subject of many movies, novels, documentary films, and scholarly reports. And there has been much speculation about the roles played in the heroin trade by Kuomintang troops (Bo 1987), the U.S. Central Intelligence Agency (McCoy 1972), the South Vietnamese government (McCoy 1991), Khun Sa (Boucaud and Boucaud 1992; Belanger 1989; McCoy 1999a), high-level Thai officials (Phongpaichit, Piriyarangsan, and Teerat 1998), Hong Kong triad groups (Posner 1988; Black 1992; Booth 1999; Chu 2002), and U.S.-based Chinese street gangs and tongs (Chin 1990, 1996; Sack 2001). In 1996, the surrender of Khun Sa to the Burmese authorities turned the world's focus to the Wa leaders and their involvement in the heroin trade (Marshall and Davis 2002; Takano 2002; Zhao and Ke 2003; Zhu 2004).

The production, sale, and trafficking of heroin in the Wa area are illegal under the Wa Basic Law.[1] A Wa government document acknowledged that "between 1990 and 1994, the Wa government allowed businesspeople to set up heroin refineries in the Wa region. The government collected a small amount of tax [in cash]. But starting in 1995, nobody was allowed to refine drugs in this area" (United Wa State Party 2001c, 9). The same document also claimed that "between 1990 and 1994, the government collected around 6 million yuan [$730,000] each year as a heroin refinery tax; a total of 30 million yuan [$3.65 million] was collected over the five-year period" (United Wa State Party 2001c, 11). The Wa leaders said they began to prohibit heroin production in 1995 because of pressure from Burmese authorities and the world community. Regardless of the Wa officials' assertion that heroin manufacturing has not been allowed in their territory since 1995, many observers continued to view the Wa as a key player in heroin production and trafficking (Gelbard 1998; Lintner 1998a; Takano 2002).

According to our key informants, opium prices in the Wa area increased dramatically in the late 1990s after the surrender of Khun Sa. A *joi* or viss of opium worth 1,000 yuan ($120) in 1993 increased in value to 4,000 yuan ($485) in 1998, presumably as a result of the establishment of many heroin refineries in the Wa area.

When I asked the Wa leaders about this, they stated emphatically that the region to the north—the Kokang area—was the center of heroin production, not the Wa area. In fact, many opium farmers we interviewed in Nandeng (in the Wa area just south of Kokang) did tell us that they sold most of their opium to buyers from the Kokang area, which suggested the presence of heroin refineries in Kokang. However, opium farmers in other Wa villages seldom referred to buyers from Kokang. My key informants also claimed that the opium that Wa farmers provided to local governments (either as payment of the tax or as a commodity sold below the market price) was used to produce heroin. These informants believed that Wa authorities were too astute to sell their opium to heroin manufacturers in Kokang; the Wa knew full well that the heroin business was much more lucrative than the opium trade.

The Politics of Heroin in the Golden Triangle

The Disintegration of the CPB

As mentioned earlier, the Communist Party of Burma (CPB) began to collapse after Peng Jiasheng announced in March 1989 that Kokang, under his control, was breaking away from the CPB. The following month, officials of the Wa area also stated that they were following Kokang's lead. The Burmese authorities quickly signed cease-fire agreements with leaders of the two areas (Lintner 1990). It is widely believed that, in return for their promise to be loyal to the Rangoon government, former CPB groups were allowed to have a free hand in the drug business (Dupont 2001). According to Lintner (1993a, 25):

> Since the mutiny and the subsequent cease-fire with Rangoon, many former CPB members have enjoyed excellent relations with Burma's military government. Prior to 1989, most of the opium grown in the northeast was convoyed down to the Thai border, where it was converted into heroin in a string of laboratories located in an area controlled by drug warlord Chang Chifu, alias Khun Sa. But the former CPB forces soon established their own refineries along the Sino-Burmese frontier. US sources estimate that Burma's heroin production rose from 53 tonnes in 1987 to 128 in 1989 and 185 in 1991.

Davis and Hawke (1998, 28), on the other hand, theorized that the arrival of the Wei brothers in the Wa Hills in 1992, almost three years after the cease-fire, was the turning point in the development of the Wa area into a major heroin producing region:

> UWSA [United Wa State Army] entry into the heroin trade was expedited by three ethnic Chinese brothers, Wei Xuelong, Xuegang and Xueyun, who had earlier been involved with Taiwanese intelligence and the WNA [Wa National Army] on the Thai border. In late 1992 Wei Xuelong moved north to UWSA HQ at Panghsang [Bang-

kang] and before long had established a string of refineries in the Wa hills. The Weis were to provide the commercial know-how and international connections to complement the military muscle of Pao Yu-chang [Bao Youxiang] and Li Ziru, transforming the UWSA into what has been described as the world's largest armed narcotics trafficking organization.

A key informant, a twenty-one-year-old Wa woman, told me that heroin refineries were first established in the Wa area in 1994: "My father was involved in the drug business. Before he died, he was moving opium from here to the Thai border. Before 1994, there was no heroin factory here, so the opium had to be transported to Thailand for refining into heroin."[2]

According to the above-mentioned three sources, it appears that Wa leaders began to allow the establishment of heroin refineries in their territory right after the cease-fire agreement with the Burmese authorities in 1989, the heroin business began to take off with the arrival of the Wei brothers in the Wa area in 1992, and, despite what the Wa leaders have said, and what their laws stipulate, the production of heroin in the Wa area did not end in 1994.

The Surrender of Khun Sa to the Burmese Government

From 1962 to 1996, before his surrender to the Burmese authorities, Khun Sa was, along with Luo Xinghan, one of the two most powerful drug lords in Southeast Asia (Lintner 1994b; Renard 1996; McCoy 1999a). As the leader of the Mong Tai Army (MTA), earlier known as the Shan State Army (SSA), Khun Sa commanded one of the strongest drug armies in the world in the early 1990s (Maung Pho Shoke 1999). Even though Khun Sa did not occupy the best opium-producing area, he was in control of heroin processing and marketing along the Thai-Burma border (McCoy 1999b). Before the collapse of the CPB and the opening of the Sino-Burma border, opium cultivated in the northern Shan State was mostly transported to Khun Sa's territory and then processed into heroin for the overseas market.

According to Bao Youxiang, Khun Sa's MTA began to attack the Wa a few weeks after they had reached a cease-fire agreement with the Burmese regime in April 1989. The Wa retaliated. With the help of the Burmese army, the Wa began to put the MTA on the defensive. According to an MTA leader, during the six years that the MTA fought with the Wa, over thirteen hundred MTA soldiers were killed and fifteen hundred were wounded (Maung Pho Shoke 1999). In June 1995, several MTA leaders and their followers in the thousands defected from the MTA to the Burmese authority. At the same time, U.S. authorities were able to arrest and extradite more than a dozen key figures in Khun Sa's heroin business, a result of an enormously successful international joint effort called Operation Tiger Trap (U.S. Department of State 1995). On January 7, 1996, Khun Sa abruptly announced his surrender to the Burmese authorities, and an official ceremony of surrender was held in Ho Mong, the MTA's headquarters near the Thai-Burma border. By April of that year, fourteen thousand men, over eighty-three hundred assorted arms, over two million rounds of ammunition, and more than forty-seven hundred assorted mines were surrendered to the Burmese government (Maung Pho Shoke 1999).

According to many observers, the drug trade in the Golden Triangle continued to flourish even after Khun Sa's capitulation and the disintegration of his Mong Tai Army (Gelbard 1998; Lintner 1998a). Soon, new drug lords such as Wei Xuegang, Bao Youxiang, Li Ziru, Peng Jiasheng, and Lin Mingxian, among others, began to emerge. In 1998, U.S. authorities announced a $2 million reward for the arrest of Wei Xuegang, a move that promptly elevated him to a new status as the major drug kingpin of the Golden Triangle. Consequently, the group that was alleged to be providing muscle to Wei—the United Wa State Army (UWSA)—was also dubbed "the leading trafficking organization" in Burma (Gelbard 1998, 189).

A brief review of the politics of heroin in the Golden Triangle makes it very clear that heroin production in the region had undergone a dramatic change with the disintegration of the CPB and the subsequent cease-fire agreements between the Burmese regime and insurgent groups in the Kokang, the Wa, and the Mengla areas. Heroin laboratories began to emerge in the newly established special regions located on the Burmese side of the border with China to compete with the heroin refineries along the Thai-Burma border area formerly controlled by Khun Sa. After Khun Sa quit the drug trade under pressure and retired to Rangoon, the drug business was simply picked up by other powerful figures in the area.

People in the Heroin Business

Even though there is an extensive literature on the few well-known drug kingpins in the Golden Triangle, little is known about the majority of the people who are involved in the heroin business. In the Wa area, there are many successful "businessmen" and many of them are, in one way or the other, involved in the drug trade.

According to our interviews, one of the key figures in the heroin business was a relative of a top leader. Uneducated and destitute, the woman had worked as an ice cream vendor fifteen years ago. Around 1991, the woman's sister, who was the wife of a top leader, gave her some money to start a small opium business. At the very beginning, she went to villages to buy opium; after her business began to grow, she stayed home and waited for sellers to come to her home. She is now a key figure in both heroin and methamphetamine production. The forty-two-year-old woman teamed up with her husband in the drug business as well as in many other businesses. They transported their heroin to Tachilek, a Burmese town just across from Mae Sai, Thailand, to sell. The woman eventually owned one of the grandest mansions in Bangkang and could be seen gambling tens of thousands of yuan away almost every day in the town's casino.

One former heroin merchant whom we interviewed was a fifty-year-old, high-ranking Wa army officer who was involved in heroin production between 1990 and 1995, when it was permitted by the Wa authorities. He told us how he got involved in it and his experience as a heroin producer:

> Coming home after the war [with the Burmese during the CPB era], I felt like I was a hero because I survived the war. However, a starving hero could soon become a coward. I heard about the existence of this heroin factory and I was excited because I needed money and I was confident that I could make money from this business. Even if I had wanted to do something else, I had no idea how to do it, anyway. That's why I decided to get involved in this business.
>
> In the beginning, it was a small business. However, as time went by, it got bigger and bigger. You can say I was greedy and I did not care how this drug might affect people. All I knew was that this was a very lucrative business, and people would come and buy it [heroin], right after I produced it.
>
> I was making a profit of about 12,000 yuan [$1,500] per *jian* [unit] of heroin.[3] To produce one *jian* of heroin, I needed to buy 4 *joi* [viss] of opium for 20,000 yuan [$2,500]. The expenses and taxes for producing a unit of heroin amounted to about 8,000 yuan [$1,000]. I could sell a unit of heroin for 40,000 yuan [$5,000] and that meant I made 12,000 yuan [$1,500] per unit. When it was good, I was making about 2 million yuan [$250,000] a year.[4]

After 1994, the Wa authorities occasionally arrested people who were involved in the drug business and would make a major announcement whenever they did so. For example, after a China-born heroin trafficker committed suicide in August 14, 1994, the Wa government made the following announcement:

> Liu Ming, whose real name is Liu Zhiang, was born in Chengdu, Sichuan, in 1953 and he was forty-two years old when he died. He arrived in the Wa area in 1987 through his connections with a Wa army officer and later became a member of the Wa army. When in May of 1994 the Chinese authorities arrested Xiao Pa in Menglian and Xiao Ke in Kunming, Liu Ming had already smuggled 122 *jian* [units] of heroin into China. Liu Ming committed suicide in Mengpo on August 14, 1994. A person by the name of Peng Jinliang was believed to be the man behind Liu Ming's drug business. Peng escaped.

The 1996 incident involving Zhao Sanmuli, the brother of Zhao Nilai, is probably one of the most significant heroin cases ever to be solved in the Wa area, mainly because Zhao Nilai is considered to be the founding father of the Wa State (he was the former chairman of the UWSP and the former commander-in-chief of the UWSA) and Zhao Sanmuli was a substitute member of the party central committee before his downfall. The following announcement was widely circulated in the Wa State after Zhao Sanmuli was punished for his involvement in the heroin business (United Wa State Party 1996, 1):

A Decision on the Punishment of Zhao Sanmuli for Privately Allowing the Establishment of a Heroin Refinery in Yongbang of Northern Wa County

In early June 1996, Zhao Sanmuli, former substitute member of the United Wa State Party Central Committee and general party secretary of Northern Wa County, privately allowed ten businesspeople from abroad to set up a drug manufacturing factory in Yongbang, Northern Wa County, and dispatched armed troops to provide what was illegal protection of the factory. These kinds of behaviors are openly against the policy of our party and army, which is to ban opium growing and drug production, and they not only cast a shadow over our party and the general society but also damage our plan to eradicate drugs. As a result, the Central Committee made the following decisions:

1. All weapons, machines, precursor chemicals, cars, and drugs found on the premises of the heroin factory will be confiscated and destroyed.
2. Zhao Sanmuli will be discharged from the Central Committee. He will also be seriously chastised for his mistakes.
3. Zhao Aiben [unknown] will be discharged from his job for six months and will be asked to engage in self-examination. This punishment will be carried out by the County Committee of Mengmao County.
4. The ten foreign businessmen will be fined 100,000 yuan [$12,000] each for a total of a million yuan. The Political Legal Bureau will be responsible for collecting the fines.

United Wa State Party Central Committee
August 2, 1996

From this announcement, it is clear that certain high-ranking Wa officials were involved in the heroin trade, heroin refineries were guarded by Wa soldiers, and "businessmen" from abroad played a key role in the development of a heroin manufacturing venture. It is also apparent that not all Wa leaders can do whatever they want to do when it comes to heroin production. There are norms and rules to be followed, and if one completely disregards these norms and rules, his drug business, or the drug business he is protecting, could be in jeopardy. Of course, in an attempt to understand why such a high-ranking Wa official was heavily penalized for something other Wa leaders might have also been involved in, we also need to take into consideration the fact that Zhao Nilai was in poor health and his political power was declining. Moreover, the incident took place in 1996, one year after the Wa leaders' new policy of forbidding outsiders from setting up heroin refineries in the Wa area. The arrest of Zhao Sanmuli was also may have been related to the confiscation of 598 kilograms of heroin in the cities of Guangzhou and Shenzhen by the Chinese authorities in April 1996 (Ting 2004). The drug seizure was not only the largest in China up to that point but the heroin was believed to have originated in the Wa area. The case will be discussed later in this chapter.

The Social Organization of the Heroin Trade

Although it is widely believed that there are many "businessmen" in the Wa area who are involved in the *baifen* ("white powder") or *sihao* (number four) trade and that there are *jiagongchang* or "factories" in the area, the use, production, and trafficking of heroin are all extremely sensitive issues there. In the Wa Hills, it is not unusual to see people buying and selling opium openly in the markets, but nobody there would dare sell heroin in plain sight. In any given town, most local people know who the big-time opium traders are, but few people know who is involved in heroin production. One of my key informants told me that her boyfriend kept her in the dark for years about his working in a heroin factory. Unlike those in the opium trade, people in the heroin business are highly unlikely to identify themselves as heroin producers or traffickers or to talk about their social organization. Nonetheless, we learned a lot about the heroin trade through our discussions with a former heroin producer, various Wa leaders, and key informants (many of them former drug entrepreneurs) in Bangkang and northern Thailand. In this section, I will explore the structure of the heroin trafficking organization, the relationship between the Wa government and the heroin trade, and the role of the Kokang and the Mengla areas in the heroin business.

Structure and Group Characteristics

Most people I talked to in the Wa area stated that both Wa and Chinese are involved in the heroin trade. Very often, a Wa official (or his close relative) will work with a Chinese "businessman"; the Wa official provides the muscle (his army) and the political power (his government position), while the Chinese businessman offers his money, brains (business acumen), and connections (to the outside world, especially buyers in China, Thailand, Hong Kong, and Taiwan).

The Wa official or his close relative will be primarily responsible for locating a suitable place to set up the refinery, hiring the right people to guard the refinery (primarily UWSA soldiers), making sure that relevant Wa government units or officials are informed and bribed, and that the so-called manufacturing fee is paid accordingly. From the fifty-plus Wa government documents and announcements I have reviewed, it is clear that occasionally the Wa authorities would go after people who were producing or trafficking heroin in their territory. These crackdowns could be the result of one or more of the following reasons: no Wa official was involved; the involved Wa official was not powerful enough; the involved Wa official did not pay tribute to the correct, higher-up official or government unit; the involved Wa official did not pay the "manufacturing fee" to the Wa authorities; or, when the heroin was smuggled into China, it was confiscated by the Chinese authorities who then pressured the Wa authorities to do something about it.

The Chinese partner, on the other hand, is mainly responsible for coming up with the start-up money, finding the right chemist, importing the necessary precursor chemicals such as acetic anhydride, and marketing the heroin. Many of these Chinese "businessmen" were born and grew up in China, Thailand, or other parts of Burma and are better connected to the outside world than their Wa counterparts. A top drug enforcer in Muse, Burma, characterized those who are active in the drug business this way: "Most drug dealers in this part of the world are ethnic Chinese, be they Burmese or Chinese citizens; they are smart and they have good connections. You've got to be smart to be a drug entrepreneur; and if you do not know any people, you don't know how to get into this business. The right connections are everything."[5]

Profiles of two Chinese drug lords are provided here to illustrate the characteristics of drug "businessmen" in the Golden Triangle.

TAN XIAOLIN

Tan Xiaolin was born in Lezhi County, Sichuan Province, in 1962. In 1992, he left home to work in the China-Burma border area. There, he met Yang Guodong, a major drug producer from Burma. Later, Tan married Yang's daughter and moved to the Burmese side, probably to Kokang:

With the help of Yang Guodong, Tan Xiaolin quickly followed the drug trafficking road, which was very common in the locality. At first, he traded drugs mainly in the border area between Thailand and Myanmar. He changed his status constantly, going from a hired hand for making drugs to a drug lord. Just when his business was growing, something went wrong with the route on which he depended for transporting his drugs. After 1994, because of the incessant wars on the border between Thailand and Myanmar, his drug transportation route was often cut off, and the drug lords also bullied each other in the process. Tan Xiaolin decided to find another route to get his drugs through. In 1995, he left the place where he had lived for three years and moved his family to Muse town in Myanmar. (Ting 2004, 80)

After Tan moved to Muse, opposite the town of Ruili, China, he began to transport heroin into China via the Muse-Ruili route. He also established a well-organized drug trafficking organization with a clear division of labor. His organization "set up a number of bases inside and outside of Myanmar, established a warehouse, rebuilt camouflaged vehicles, used code words for communication, supervised each other, transported drugs in sections, had a single line of contact and used other devious means to avoid police and customs inspections" (Ting 2004, 79). According to Chinese authorities, Tan's organization was responsible for the trafficking of three tons of heroin into China between 1995 and 2001, including the 490 kilograms of heroin confiscated by the authorities in Guangzhou City in November 1999 (Chen 2006).

Tan Xiaolin came under the radar of the Chinese drug enforcement authorities as soon as he arrived in Muse in 1995, and he knew it. However, he decided to carry on with his drug activities, often conducting trial runs to evade the Chinese authorities. He also stopped going to China after the November 1999 drug bust, believing that if he stayed on the Burmese side, the Chinese could not touch him.

On November 4, 1999, authorities in Guangzhou City confiscated more than one hundred kilograms of heroin transported from Muse to China overland by truck. It belonged to Tan Xiaolin. In the process, Chinese authorities accidentally discovered more than twelve tons of amphetamine inside the warehouse where Tan's heroin was found. The 554 boxes of amphetamine belonged to Tan's partner in China who was producing amphetamine with a group of offenders while simultaneously working with Tan to import hundreds of kilograms of heroin into China from Burma (Hu and Li 2005). On April 12, 2001, the Chinese authorities finally made a formal request to the Burmese authorities to arrest Tan Xiaolin for drug trafficking. Eight days later, the Burmese authorities arrested Tan, and the Chinese authorities followed by apprehending eighteen associates of Tan in the cities of Kunming, Diqing, Baoshan, and Chongqing. On April 23, 2001, Chinese officials arrived in Muse to bring Tan back to China to stand trial for his drug crimes. Tan was found guilty of drug trafficking and executed in Kunming on June 25, 2004 (Ting 2005).

LIU MING

Liu Ming (not related to the above-mentioned Liu Ming who committed suicide) was born in 1959 in Yunnan Province and went to Kokang in 1992 after serving time in prison in China for human trafficking. In Kokang, Liu married a local woman who was a major drug dealer. After the marriage, Liu got involved in the drug business, and within ten years had emerged as one of the major drug lords in the Kokang area. According to Chinese authorities, over a period of seven years Liu had trafficked a total of 510 kilograms of heroin from Burma to the Chinese provinces of Yunnan, Hunan, Guangdong, and Shantong (Ting 2004).

Zhao Shilung and Ke Shuya (2003), two Chinese journalists, reported that in 2000, when Kokang leaders established a drug eradication museum to commemorate the ban on opium cultivation in their area, Liu Ming personally donated 20 million yuan ($2.4 million) to the museum, 60 percent of its total budget of 38 million yuan ($4.6 million). When the Burmese leader Khin Nyunt came to Kokang on December 27, 2000, to participate in the opening ceremony, he and other dignitaries were greeted by Liu Ming, museum benefactor and financial kingpin. Liu was then the deputy director of the finance department of the Kokang government and deputy director of the development department of Dongcheng (a newly developed area adjacent to Laukkai), where the museum is located (Zhu 2004).

Despite Liu Ming's contributions to the area's culture and prosperity, on December 27, 2001, the Chinese government asked the Burmese government for assistance in his arrest:

> On the morning of January 15, 2002, the Myanmar military and police authorities organized forces to surround and arrest him in Kokang but did not succeed. . . . Opportunities came again on January 28. According to accurate information, Liu Ming was driving a Mitsubishi cross-country vehicle alone to a school not far from his home that day. After receiving this news, the Kokang government immediately sent forces to surround the school. At 6:50 a.m., Liu Ming drove his car out of the school when a Kokang soldier signaled him to stop. Liu Ming refused and opened fire first to resist arrest. The two sides exchanged fire, and Liu Ming was shot dead. (Ting 2004, 88)

At the time of Liu Ming's death, Laukkai (the "capital" of Kokang), was divided into five turfs, with each turf under the control of a Kokang leader and his personal army. Liu Ming and a partner were in charge of Dongcheng. Liu Ming, unlike other Kokang leaders who had been living in Kokang for several decades, was viewed as "arrogant." Liu's abrasive personality irritated other Kokang leaders, and it was believed that many Kokang leaders were simply happy to take advantage of the opportunity to have him killed (Zhu 2004).

In the years between 1996 and 2004, besides Tan Xiaolin and Liu Ming, several major heroin producers in Burma, all of them Chinese citizens, have been arrested by the Burmese authorities and handed over to the Chinese. Once they were back in China, the Chinese authorities executed them promptly.

From Production to Distribution

According to a heroin manufacturer, he had little problem selling his heroin once it was produced: "After processing opium into heroin, I kept it at home and waited for buyers to come to me. Sometimes, people working in the heroin factory would come to buy. Most of these workers are from outside of the Wa area [they are mostly Chinese], or they are from other groups [other groups within Burma, mainly the Shan people]."[6] Asked what kinds of problems he encountered in the selling process and who the buyers were, he said:

> Nothing troubled me in the selling process. I never had to worry about not getting my money. It was quite usual for buyers (mostly Chinese from Thailand and Burma) to look at heroin samples first, then, if they liked what they saw, they would come back with money to buy my heroin. I would not let them just walk away with my heroin. It's as simple as that.
>
> I did not really hang out with these buyers, so I don't know much about them. But they all seemed to be smart businessmen and I sort of idolized them. They were not local people, so they were also somewhat leery of us and that's why they would not try to cheat us, and they would be very honest in dealing with us. The heroin business in this area was not like Hong Kong, where heroin dealers often kill one another over business-related disputes. Here, things go rather smoothly.[7]

A Chinese intellectual from China, who came to the Wa area to open a computer store but later became a Wa official, told me the following when I asked him about the connection between local heroin producers and overseas heroin traffickers:

> Those who are involved in the heroin trade here do not have much connection with outside heroin traffickers. Wa people are not very wise businessmen and they do not have overseas connections. Once the drug leaves Burma, they are not in charge anymore. They may have some connections with heroin traders in Thailand but they have little or no connections with traders from China. The Thai part is controlled by Thai and Burmese Chinese and they have to work with traders from the United States and the West to move the drug from Thailand to the West.[8]

A United States General Accounting Office report (1996, 11–12) on the social organization of the Southeast Asian heroin trade also indicated that the business is not controlled by one organization from start to finish:

> Heroin-trafficking organizations are not vertically integrated, and heroin shipments rarely remain under the control of a single individual or organization as they move from overseas refinery to the streets of the United States. These organizations consist of separate producers and a number of independent intermediaries as financiers, brokers, exporters, importers, and distributors. Since responsibility and ownership of a particular drug shipment shifts each time the product changes hands, direct evidence of the relationship between producer, transporter, and wholesale distributor is extremely difficult to obtain.

The Wa Government and the Heroin Trade

A discussion of the social organization of the heroin trade in the Wa area is incomplete without exploring the role of the Wa government. In the West, the United Wa State Army (UWSA) is now considered to be one of the most powerful drug trafficking organizations in the world (Gelbard 1998; Marshall and Davis 2002). Leaders of the UWSA—Bao Youxiang, Wei Xuegang, and Li Ziru (before his death in 2005)—are all viewed as "drug lords" or "drug kingpins," and the entire UWSA organization is primarily seen as a heavily armed drug trafficking organization.

Two Asian researchers who spent some time in the Wa area in the late 1990s have agreed with the Western observers' viewpoint. Shi Anda (1996), a researcher from Yunnan Province, has concluded that leaders of the Wa army are armed drug kingpins; the basic economic structure of Wa society has not changed, and as a result, the army still has to rely on opium and the drug trade to survive. In Shi Anda's opinion, the Wa's current leaders are essentially third-generation drug warlords, after Luo Xinghan and Khun Sa.

According to Takano (2002, 137), the UWSA is the key organization in the heroin business because it needs the money from the heroin trade to survive: "Some military leaders undoubtedly are involved in the heroin business at a private level, but the largest producer and source of sales is the Wa army. With that money, they purchase arms and military equipment."

When Bao Youxiang in 2001 was interviewed by Bill Curtis, an American television journalist with A&E, Bao told Curtis that "between 1990 and 1994, we did allow businesspeople to refine heroin in the Wa State. But by 1994, there was too much pressure [from the outside] and we dared not to continue. At that time period, we only collected about 6 million yuan [$730,000] a year from the heroin business, and that income was less than 10 percent of our total income" (United Wa State Party 2001d, 14).

Even though the Wa leaders did approve a certain number of people to operate heroin refineries, they were reluctant to allow people to retail heroin in their territory, presumably to prevent local people from using heroin. For example, according to an official announcement dated November 26, 1991, "Anyone who is involved in heroin *chaimai* [retailing], regardless of which organization, government unit or army unit he or she belongs to, the drug will be confiscated and the offender will be fined twice the value of the drug confiscated" (United Wa State Party 1991, 1).

Moreover, the Wa government appeared to be very concerned with the trafficking of heroin via China. For example, in an announcement dated July 24, 1994, the Wa authorities stated that anyone smuggling five units of heroin into China would receive the death penalty; four units—twenty years; three units—fifteen years; two units—ten years; and one unit—five years. There were other announcements related to the prohibition of smuggling heroin via China. Peculiarly, in all the government documents I collected, there is no mention of prohibiting people from transporting heroin out of the Wa area through Thailand or other neighboring countries.

From my fieldwork in the Wa area, it is a definite possibility that heroin refineries still exist there, even though Wa leaders I interviewed would not admit to it, nor would I be able to say how many such refineries are in operation. According to one of my key informants, a businessman who himself was twice arrested for transporting precursor chemicals from China into the Wa area, "all heroin factories are connected to the central authorities and that's the only way you can be involved in this business. If you are not backed by a high-level government official, there is no way you can operate a heroin factory here."[9]

A Wa official familiar with the inner workings of the Wa Central Authority said, "No doubt there are refineries in the Wa area, but they are located in remote areas and outsiders could not possibly know where they are. Some of the heroin factories in the Wa area are probably located within the army compounds of the USWA, which means the commanders of these military units are actively involved in the heroin business."[10]

At one point in 2001, I asked a group of well-connected Bangkang residents to rank their leaders' involvement in the opium and heroin business. The group considered almost all Wa leaders to be involved in the opium and heroin trade. Some leaders were thought to be exclusively involved in the opium and heroin trade, some involved only with methamphetamines, and some involved in both trades. It is no surprise that some of the Wa government documents openly declared that "according to the current situation [2001], some officials do not know how to contribute to society during a peaceful period; some officials are feudalistic; some are old and their minds are rigid; some are heavy drug users; some greedy, corrupt, and involved in embezzlement . . . a variety of undesirable characteristics are manifested among a substantial number of officials" (United Wa State Party 2001b, 4). Bao Youxiang once chastised his people by declaring that "a substantial number of officials are officials in name only and focus primarily on their own businesses, or they treat their losses as the government's and profits as their own. Some are consistently violating our regulations in order to benefit themselves" (United Wa State Party 2001a, 3).

The problem is, if a leader at the very top is himself or members of his family are involved in the drug business and it is an open secret among his followers and the general public (excluding the farmers in the remote hills), it is almost impossible to ask his colleagues and followers to not do what he or his family members are doing. When a top leader and his family members are all living in newly built, expensive houses, it is also almost impossible for his colleagues and followers not to dream of living in a new house. However, in the Wa Hills, there is simply no other means to get rich besides the drug business. Conservative Wa leaders will get involved only in opium buying and selling, and the aggressive ones will produce heroin and/or methamphetamine. The trick is to get rich without getting into trouble.

The Role of Kokang and Mengla in the Heroin Trade

An evaluation of the Wa government's involvement in the heroin trade is complicated by the existence of other drug-producing special regions near the Wa State. To the north, there is the Kokang area. With a population of 180,000 mostly ethnic Chinese, the Kokang area was—and is considered by many observers to be still—a major heroin production center. Even though Kokang is significantly smaller than the Wa area and its army is less powerful than the Wa army, it has long been considered to be active in both the production of heroin as well as trafficking it through China. Whereas Chinese authorities believe the Wa to be fairly cooperative and candid about their promise not to transport heroin through China, they are suspicious and distrustful of Kokang's leaders. For example, according to a number of popular books on the case involving a Kokang leader who was arrested in China during a major heroin bust, the Kokang authorities showed no remorse and even vowed to retaliate if the Chinese government dared punish the arrested Kokang leader harshly. In response, the Chinese government promptly executed the Kokang drug trafficker (Jin 2003; Zhao and Ke 2003; Zhu 2004). On the other hand, in 1996, when Bao Youyi, the elder brother of Bao Youxiang, was implicated in a major heroin trafficking case in China, not only did the Wa leaders promise to stop heroin trafficking through China, they banished the elder Bao to the remote Southern Wa area as a form of punishment. To this day, the elder Bao remains in the Southern Wa region and his desire to return to Bangkang is repeatedly denied by his younger brother, Bao Youxiang.

Many Wa leaders I interviewed argued they are blamed for the heroin trade when it is, in fact, dominated by the Kokang people, as Wang Keqiang, minister of Investment and Tourism Bureau, explained:

I will say 70 percent of the opium cultivated in the Wa State is refined into heroin in the Kokang area. Many Kokang businessmen come here to buy opium. We know for sure that a large amount of Wa opium is transported to the Kokang area. However, there is not much we can do about this. We know opium, heroin, and methamphetamine are transported back and forth between the Wa State and Kokang but we cannot crack down on the Kokang businessmen because if we do, we would end up arresting our own people, people who are in our government and army officials or their close relatives. We know our people are working together with the Kokangnese in the drug business.[11]

An official in Bangkang told me that heroin from Kokang did go through the Wa territory: "Heroin from the Kokang area can be transported to Thailand via two routes: the Wa route and the Burmese route. Of course both the Wa and the Burmese tax the heroin transporters but the Burmese are much greedier than the Wa. Besides, there is still a kind of friendship and brotherhood that exists between Kokang and Wa leaders."[12]

Police officers in the Wa area also asserted that heroin dealers from Kokang are active in the Wa state. The chief of police of Bangkang claimed that many heroin traffickers or distributors arrested in the Wa area are Kokangnese and he allowed me to interview some of the Kokangnese drug entrepreneurs locked up in a detention center not far from Bangkang. A heroin trafficker told me this story:

I am twenty six years old and I was born in Gunnong [a Burmese territory]. I am a Kokangnese. I am married and have a kid. Before I was arrested, I was operating a car garage. In fact, the day before I got involved in this drug deal, I had just come back from Mandalay [the second largest Burmese city] with some car parts for my garage.

I was arrested in Fusan [a Wa territory] with thirty-two units of heroin. The drugs belonged to my uncle. He asked me to deliver them to Xingdifan [an area in Mengmao County of Northern Wa State]. I didn't know where the drugs would be going after Xingdifan; my responsibility was to call someone after I arrived there in my car. However, I was arrested at the checkpoint in Fusan and I believe someone must have tipped off the Wa authorities. I was driving a jeep all by myself.

I was promised 10,000 yuan [$1,200] for this service. Before I left Kokang, I knew I was transporting heroin to a certain point. Of course, I needed the money, but it was also because the man who ordered me to do this was my uncle—I can't say no to an elderly relative. I did make one successful drug delivery before this. I transported five units of heroin to a certain point and I was paid 5,000 yuan [$600].[13]

As mentioned earlier, many opium growers in Nandeng told us that they sell most of their opium to buyers from Kokang. Several opium traders we interviewed in Bangkang also revealed that they often sell a hundred viss of opium at a time to buyers from Kokang. It is safe to conclude that there were, at the time of my fieldwork in 2001, heroin refineries operating in the Kokang area. However, the question is, where were the majority of the heroin refineries located? The Wa Hills or the Kokang area? According to one individual in Bangkang:

All the opium the Wa farmers sell to the local governments is used to make heroin. Heroin is much more profitable than opium. Kokang refiners need only go to Nandeng and other northern parts of Wa to get some opium for themselves, but the majority of the opium grown in the Wa area ends up in the hands of the rich and powerful Wa officials and they do the refinement themselves.[14]

Another special region in the Burmese part of the Golden Triangle, Special Region No. 4, or the Mengla area, was declared opium free in 1997, and was the site of Burma's first drug eradication museum. Since the early 1990s, leaders of the area have been aggressively promoting the area as the Las Vegas of Southeast Asia. The streets of Mengla are dotted with extravagant casinos, hotels, nightclubs, and massage parlors (or brothels). Every day, hundreds of Chinese visitors pour into Mengla from the Dalou border checkpoint near Jinghong of Xishuangbanna, the Dai prefecture in Yunnan Province. Even though the area's economy is very much sustained by the booming entertainment industry, people in the Wa area I interviewed suggested that there are heroin refineries and methamphetamine laboratories located in the Mengla area but not opium cultivation. A Chinese businessman in Bangkang who is familiar with the drug trade in the Mengla area told me that "even though the No. 4 region [Mengla] is reported to be a drug-free area, many people there, especially the leaders, are still involved in the drug business. The leaders are also involved in the trafficking of methamphetamine into the Xishuangbanna area."[15]

Dong Sheng, the deputy director of the Yunnan Provincial Anti-Narcotics Bureau, also confirmed that the Mengla area is not drug free: "In 2004, the amount of drugs coming out of Special Region No. 4 was significantly higher than in the past several years. That does not mean, however, that all the drugs coming out of the area were produced there."[16]

In fact, it is very hard to draw a line between the various special regions in the Shan State. The leaders of the various zones know one another very well, and some of their assistants or partners in the drug business often change bosses or partners. In Bangkang, it was not unusual to meet a former "business" assistant or a partner of a Kokang leader who was now working for or with a Wa leader and still often visited his former boss or partner in the Kokang area. The same is true with individual drug entrepreneurs. Some Kokang people move to the Wa area to get involved in the drug business, and there are also Wa drug businesspeople active in the Kokang and Mengla areas.

Heroin Routes

Even though there are heroin users in the Wa and Kokang areas, the population of addicts is relatively small because both governments do not allow people in their jurisdictions to use heroin. As will be discussed in chapter 6, the authorities in these two areas are much more willing to tolerate opium use than heroin use. There is no question but that the bulk of the heroin produced in these areas is not for local consumption, but is designated for overseas markets.

Although a small amount of the heroin produced in the Wa and the Kokang areas is smuggled through Bangladesh, India (Haq 2000), Laos, and Burma, heroin from the Wa and Kokang areas was mostly transported to the world market via two routes: the Thai route and the Chinese route.

The Thai Route

Before the Chinese route became significant in the mid-1990s, Thailand was the main way that heroin from the Golden Triangle reached the world market. In the late 1980s, Belanger (1989, 11) observed that:

> Thailand is positioned geographically so that it contains ideal routes for the transport of heroin from its mountains origins to jump-off points for the international markets. Some elements of the Thai government work hard to intercept and destroy any drugs being transported through the country, but the flood is overwhelming. Over the past several years, narcotics produced in the Golden Triangle have been transported from northern Thailand to Bangkok where they are expedited on their way around the world. In Thailand the major drug kingpins behind the trafficking are mainly Chinese Haws [Muslims] and Taechews [Chiu Chau] who have been naturalized while living in Bangkok. About one hundred of these affluent immigrants are believed to be financial backers for the illicit trade.

Bertil Lintner (1994b, 253), an expert on the drug trade in the Golden Triangle, suggested that "Thailand was a transit country for narcotics from Burma as well as the nerve-center of the trade, where deals were organized, couriers were hired and money was laundered." Klong Toey, a huge slum in Bangkok, was known as the country's biggest wholesale heroin marketplace, while Don Maung Airport of Bangkok was commonly used for smuggling heroin out of Thailand (Phongpaichit, Piriyarangsan, and Teerat 1998).

Before Khun Sa's surrender in 1996, most heroin refineries were located near the Thai-Burma border area under his control (Worobec 1984; Lintner 1994b). After his downfall, many heroin factories were set up in northeastern Burma and, consequently, the first step in the international movement of heroin involved the transportation of the drug from refineries in the Kokang and the Wa areas to the Thai-Burma border. Because Kokang is located in the northern part of the Shan State, heroin from Kokang must go through either the Burmese or the Wa-controlled territories to arrive at the Thai-Burma border. Regardless of where it passed through, the authorities along the route had to be bribed to allow the drug to go through.

If a Wa official was involved in heroin transportation, he most likely used his cars or trucks and members of his government or army unit to facilitate the movement. Because motor vehicles belonging to high-ranking officials could be easily identified by their license plates, officers and soldiers manning checkpoints were reluctant to closely check motor vehicles that belonged to their leaders. Whether the Wa official paid the heroin tax depended on how he saw it and on his influence. A Wa official who believed it was unfair to be taxed and was confident that he was powerful enough to get away with it was likely to ignore the tax. My fieldwork in the Wa area suggests that it was highly unlikely for a buyer from overseas to have the ability to transport a large amount of heroin from refineries in the Northern Wa area or from Kokang to the Thai-Burma border on their own. The buyer certainly needed the help of high-ranking Wa or Kokang officials and their army units.

When heroin arrived in the border area, it was transported across the border by people living on the Thai side of the border. According to a subject in Mae Sai: "Many hill peoples living on the Thai side of the border with Burma, especially the Lahu, Ahka, and Lishu, were involved in the drug trade, plus the Chinese from Yunnan. Most of them were drug couriers, capable of moving only a relatively small amount of drugs. Whenever Thai people were arrested, however, the arrest typically involved a large amount of drugs."[17] High-ranking Thai officials in Bangkok and local politicians in the border area were believed to be active in the heroin trade as well (Phongpaichit, Piriyarangsan, and Teerat 1998).

There are many customs posts along the Thai-Burma border for legitimate cross-border trade and visits. However, there are also many remote areas where drug couriers can simply walk across. Only a tiny river, the Mae Sai River, exists between Mae Sai (Thailand) and Tachilek (Burma), the two border towns that account for the bulk of the cross-border trade between the two countries. Certain parts of the river are so narrow and shallow that people from both sides can swim over to the other side with relative ease. A *jao pho* (influential figures who are also called *kamnan*) in charge of the area can smuggle almost anything across the border at will with impunity.[18] According to the subject in Mae Sai cited above:

Village residents elect village heads. However, once elected, these village heads only care about making money. Local thugs support them. One way for them to make money is the selling of Thai IDs to migrants from the north. When a villager dies, his or her family is unlikely to notify the Thai authorities; instead, the village head would collude with the family in order to sell the ID for 120,000 baht [$2,800]. Village heads are also involved in bid rigging and collecting kickbacks from local construction projects. Even though the border is closely watched, you can still smuggle a huge amount of Chinese goods and products into Thailand.[19]

The same subject, a Muslim Chinese woman in her forties, told me how she got involved in the heroin trade when she was a teenager:

My father was a Kuomintang soldier. After we arrived in Thailand from Burma, we lived in Mae Sa Long before we moved to Mae Sai. My father had been involved in opium smoking and opium and heroin distribution for a long time. In Thailand, he was arrested for drug dealing and jailed for a few years. After he came out of prison, he went right back to his drug business. Later, he was arrested in China for spying for Taiwan and locked up for several years. He quit smoking opium while he was imprisoned. After he returned to Thailand from China, there was no way for him to resume his drug business.

When I was seventeen, I smuggled heroin from Tachilek into Mae Sai for my father. My younger sister went along with me, and we smuggled half a kilo every trip. We divided half a kilo of heroin into four packages and my sister and I would each hide two packages on our bodies. We did that right before we went to school and during lunchtime we would go again to bring in the other half kilo. My father would threaten to withhold our allowances if we did not help him. My mother would yell at my father for asking us to do these things. At that time, it was no big deal, even though it was illegal. The worst that could happen to us if arrested was to pay a fine.

During that time, there was no phone. So when a buyer came to my father, he paid my father first and returned in two days to pick up the heroin. My father was involved in selling a few kilos or retail sales. He also operated a gambling place and an opium den.[20]

I interviewed another former heroin trader, a Thai whose brother was a major figure in the underworld of Mae Sai. Thakoo (not his real name) was a heroin transporter who worked for one of his elder brothers. Thakoo's brother was almost killed one day and after that incident, he went to Mong Yawn (Southern Wa State) and never returned to Mae Sai. Thakoo began by telling me his background: "We were poor when we were young. When I was still in elementary school, I used to deliver flowers for my cousin who owned a flower shop. I dropped out of school after attending only one year in the middle school because my family could not afford it. My third brother joined a street gang."[21]

Thakoo explained how he and his third brother became involved in the heroin trade:

Later on, third brother and I began to operate a small transportation business. He drove a van and I collected the fare from the passengers. Not long after, we were asked by an Ahka village head to provide our service exclusively to Ahka people in his village and we did. We later changed our business; instead of transporting people we began to transport goods for the Ahka. We delivered the goods midway to their hill and they would transport them by mules to the hilltop.

Even though we were transporting goods for the Ahka, we had no idea what the goods were. We were somewhat skeptical about the goods but we dared not ask about them. One day, while I was sleeping, the Ahka came in and started weighing heroin. When I walked out of the room, I saw what was going on. They asked me to smoke a cigarette stuffed with heroin and I did and I vomited right after I finished smoking. I used to smoke opium, but I was not addicted to it. Since that incident, the Ahka were more open with us about what they were doing.

My brother and I began to deliver heroin to various places. My third brother was responsible for transporting a large amount of heroin to Bangkok and I was mainly involved in delivering the drug to the Mae Sai area. When I was first asked to deliver two kilos of heroin, I did not dare use my car, afraid that the authorities would confiscate my car if they discovered what I was doing. I put the heroin into a bag, walked down the hill, and took a bus. After the first successful delivery, I began to use my car. Later on, I began to act as a middleman; that is, in addition to delivering the drugs for the Ahka, I also sold heroin on the side. This way, I can make more

money. The Ahka were mainly involved in supplying the local market in Mae Sai and drug dealers in Ban Hin Taek. They were not involved in exporting the drug overseas.

At that time [late 1970s], the police were not concerned with heroin
trafficking. We need not bribe them; only after we were arrested did
we have to pay a fine. I was making a lot of money, so much so that I
did not have time to count it. I always packed my car with heroin.
The heroin was transported into Thailand from Khun Sa's base.

When I was at my peak, I was making an average of 20,000 baht
[$460] a day. All I needed to do was to sell two kilos of heroin to
make that amount of money. I can sell a kilo of heroin for 25,000
baht [$583] and I can get it from the suppliers [the Ahka] for 15,000
baht [$350] a kilo. If I transport the drug for a seller to a buyer, I earn
5,000 baht [$115] a kilo. But if the buyer is my contact, than I make
10,000 baht [$230] a kilo. I don't know at what price the Ahka ob-
tained a kilo from the producers in Burma.[22]

Thakoo explained how he left the drug trade:

After my third brother fled to Burma to avoid being killed by his rivals in Mae Sai, he asked me not to be involved in the drug business
anymore. Besides, the Thai police had noticed my involvement in
the drug trade and they were following me all the time. I was convinced that if I kept on, I would be arrested sooner or later. On top of
this, the Thai royal family, upset with the Ahka's involvement in the
heroin trade, ordered the police to shut down the village and, as a
result, the supply routes were cut.[23]

There are a large number of Chinese villages located near the
Thai-Burma border, and the Thai media has reported that residents of
these villages are heavily involved in the drug trade (Suksamram 2005). I
visited a Chinese village in Ban Yang that is considered to be a transshipment point for drugs from Burma and interviewed a sixty-seven-year-old
Chinese woman whose son was arrested for dealing heroin:

My eldest son was arrested seventeen years ago for selling three kilograms of heroin to an undercover agent not far from our home. But
when he was charged, he was charged for only one and a half
kilos—half the heroin simply disappeared. We were not in a position
to say anything. When he was arrested, he had been in the heroin

trade for only a year and had made six or seven successful transactions. My son was a nice boy; he's the eldest son and after my husband died when my son was about seventeen years old, he felt he was the head of the household and was under enormous pressure to support the family. I was selling food on the street, but it was not enough. Although we were not starving, we needed money and when he saw neighbors getting rich from the heroin trade, he decided to join them.

After he was convicted, he was sentenced to life. He is in a prison in Bangkok and I visit him once a year. When I visit him, he says he is extremely sorry for what he did. I had told him not to get involved in the heroin business but he said, "If I don't do it, what are we going to eat?" Now he says he regrets saying that. After my son was arrested, we did not dare give the authorities the name of the person who supplied the drugs to him. Otherwise, our whole family would be killed. If you get arrested with the drugs, you have to take the heat.

Some of my neighbors encouraged and supported me, but others looked down upon me for having a son jailed for a drug sale. There are many households in this village with a family member involved in the drug business. Some of them are not caught because they are lucky. People in this village are poor and there's not much to do here.[24]

It was easy for heroin producers in Burma's Shan State to smuggle their drugs across the border into northern Thailand. Many hill people and ethnic Chinese living in the border areas who were not well integrated into mainstream Thai society were recruited by heroin producers and big-time heroin dealers in Bangkok to work in the illicit drug industry. After the heroin arrived in Bangkok, dealers there would sell it to buyers from abroad.

But time brings change. According to a subject I interviewed in Mae Sai, the Thai route for heroin trafficking shifted dramatically between 1992 and 2002:

Nowadays, it is highly unlikely for a drug dealer in Thailand to order heroin from a Burmese producer without knowing in advance that there is a buyer in Thailand. Even so, the dealer would not handle it as a stand-alone order; he would ask the dealer in Burma to send the heroin along with his order for methamphetamine pills. That is, you may find one or two kilograms of heroin along with millions of methamphetamine pills.[25]

Even though the Thai route is believed to be on the decline for moving heroin to the international market, it is by no means obsolete, as attested by a report in the *Bangkok Post* (March 21, 2005, 1):

Marine police intercepted a fishing boat carrying 546kg of heroin on Saturday, their largest drug seizure in 10 years. Police said they found the drugs, worth at least 1.6 billion baht [$37 million], during a search of a Hong Kong-registered fishing boat, the Yueng Shing, near Koh Kut off Trat. The search was made after the drugs were delivered to the fishing boat by a speedboat from the mainland, they said. Police said they believe the heroin, which was later moved to the marine police office in Songkhla, was destined for Hong Kong. . . . A source said heroin seized from the boat was believed destined for Australia or the United States, where the drugs could fetch up to 5 million baht [$116,000] per 700 grammes.

The Thai route is also utilized by drug traffickers from Malaysia, Indonesia, Singapore, and Taiwan. Heroin in Thailand can be transported overland into Malaysia and continue to move to Singapore and Indonesia. There are a substantial number of Taiwanese tourists and businessmen in Thailand and some of them are involved in the transportation of heroin from Thailand to Taiwan by air or sea.

The Chinese Route

Before the mid-1980s, heroin produced in the Golden Triangle was mostly smuggled into Thailand overland, and then to Hong Kong on Thai fishing trawlers before being transported to the United States, Europe, and Australia (Belanger 1989; Dobinson 1993; McCoy 1999b; Chalk 2000). Bangkok and Hong Kong were the organizational and financial centers for the region's heroin trade (Lintner 1993b; Gaylord 1997). However, this pattern changed with China's economic development and population migration in the late 1970s (see below), which opened up the drug trade along the China-Burma border in the early 1980s (Lintner 1990, 1994a; Thayer 1993; Kuah 2000).

Before
Burma → Thailand → Hong Kong → International Market

Present
Burma → Yunnan → Guizhou → Guangxi → Guangdong → Hong
Kong → International Market

In the late 1970s, not long after the end of the Cultural Revolution and its ten years of turmoil, China decided to adopt an open door policy in order to improve its stagnant economy. As China stopped supporting Communist insurgent groups in neighboring countries, its relationships with these countries also improved (Spence 1990). When China switched from a centrally controlled planned economy to a market economy and encouraged people to become private entrepreneurs, people living in the border areas took advantage of their strategic location and began to get involved in cross-border trade (Evans, Hutton, and Eng 2000). All of a sudden, cross-border activities exploded in China, and border controls were significantly loosened (Kudo 2006).

As cross-border trade between China and Burma began to take off in the 1980s and continued to expand rapidly in the 1990s, drug trafficking along the border areas also began to flourish. On April 12, 1986, twenty-two kilograms of heroin was seized by the authorities in Yunnan, the province in southwest China that borders Burma, Laos, and Vietnam. That botched delivery of heroin—which was traced to drug traffickers in Thailand and Hong Kong—became China's first major case since Communist control began in 1949 (Ma 1999). Between 1987 and 1990 there was a dramatic increase in the number of detected cross-border drug trafficking cases and the amount of drugs seized along the China-Burma border (Ma 1994). In May 1994, the police in Yunnan caught Yang Maoxian, a major drug trafficker from Kokang, and sentenced him to death (National Narcotics Control Commission 1999). The drug lord was a brother of Yang Maoliang, a Kokang leader. Also in 1994, the U.S. State Department's International Narcotics Control Strategy Report indicated for the first time that China had became a major transit route for heroin and other opiates from the Golden Triangle. A year later, Li Guoting, a Kokang leader and a well-known heroin dealer, was arrested and executed by the Chinese authorities. Nevertheless, the Chinese route remained popular for drug traffickers in 1996. For example, in March 1996, 221 kilograms of heroin from the Golden Triangle were confiscated in Guangzhou, the capital of Guangdong Province, which borders Hong Kong. A month later, authorities in Guangzhou again confiscated more than 598 kilograms of heroin, a record at that time, after they arrested a group of thirty-nine drug traffickers, including seven from Hong Kong.

The multikilo trafficking of heroin from Burma to China began to slow down after 1996, however. According to various sources, the involvement of a Wa leader in the record-breaking heroin trafficking case forced the Wa and other armed groups along the China-Burma border to scale down the movement of heroin into China. A Wa official told me:

> Before 1996, large amounts of heroin had been smuggled into China from the Wa area. In 1996, Chinese authorities in Guangdong confiscated a huge amount—about 590 kilograms of heroin. They arrested smugglers in Guangdong and Hong Kong and traced the heroin trail back to Yunnan and arrested several accomplices there. After a thorough investigation, Chinese authorities discovered that the man behind the whole scheme was Bao Youyi, Bao Youxiang's elder brother. Liu Shuanyueh, then head of public security of Yunnan Province, summoned Bao Youxiang and Li Ziru [another Wa leader] to Simao City [about a five hours' drive from Bangkang]. At the meeting, Liu said he had evidence to suggest that Bao Youyi was responsible for the huge amount of heroin; both Bao and Li sat there for ten minutes without saying a word. Liu told the two that, if necessary, he could ask the arrested accomplices to come forward and testify that they all worked for Bao Youyi. Li Ziru told Liu that Bao Youxiang had been one of the most ardent supporters of the CPB years earlier when the Wa leaders were talking about separation from the CPB. Li also spoke of the many good deeds of Bao Youxiang. As a result, the two sides signed a memorandum stipulating that the Wa leaders would not use the Chinese route to smuggle heroin. After Bao Youxiang returned to the Wa State, he ordered his elder brother to leave Bangkang and move to Southern Wa State. Since then, the Wa leaders rarely use the Chinese route, even though a few individuals may try it on their own.[26]

Not long after Bao and Li returned to Bangkang, a meeting was held among Wa leaders, who issued a statement on June 20, 1997, that ordered exact and very harsh sentences for anyone caught selling heroin to buyers from China. The statement also included remarks from Bao Youxiang: "To have a good relationship with China is the utmost assurance to the Wa people's survival and development."[27]

As a result, Wa leaders became reluctant to take full advantage of the China route, fearing that if China shut down its border, the Wa area would be completely isolated. Ironically, in 2000 a major confrontation about drugs erupted between the Burmese and Thai border forces, and the Burmese authorities shut down all the border posts in retaliation. The Thai-Burma border trade all but came to a complete halt and the flow of drugs from Burma to Thailand was severely disrupted. This incident prompted drug traffickers to once again search for a safe route through China (National Narcotics Control Commission 2003). On April 20, 2001, two drug traffickers were arrested by Yunnan railway police for importing more than five hundred kilograms of heroin into China (Yunnan Province Narcotics Control Committee 2003). Seven months later, police in Luoping County, Yunnan, discovered 672 kilograms of heroin inside timber. At that time, it was the largest-ever drug bust in China (Yunnan Province Narcotics Control Committee 2003). In 2002, the Chinese authorities seized thousands of kilograms of heroin in Yunnan or Guangdong and arrested drug traffickers from Burma, Thailand, Hong Kong, and China. The 2002 DEA Drug Intelligence Brief reported that "China's Yunnan Province has become the primary transit point for Burmese heroin. It is estimated that over 50 percent of Burma's opiate production enters China. Over the past decade, increasingly large amounts of opiates have been smuggled from the Shan State to China's Yunnan Province toward the southeastern coast and onward to Guangzhou and Hong Kong" (U.S. Drug Enforcement Administration 2001, 5). In 2003, the UNDCP estimated that 60 percent of Burma's opiate production was shipped through China (Emery 2003). In 2004, Chinese authorities cracked another heroin trafficking ring and confiscated 463 kilograms of heroin originating from the Wa area and destined for the international market (Jinakul 2005).

The booming drug trafficking business in China can be attributed to two main factors. First, a sizeable domestic drug-consumption market has emerged and China has become a kind of black hole for heroin from the Golden Triangle (Fabre 2005). By the mid-1980s, drug addiction was no longer confined to the border areas. The Chinese government now openly acknowledges that every province and all major urban areas have drug problems; China is no longer just a transit country favored by transnational criminal organizations, it has a sizeable addict population of its own (Ting 2004). According to official statistics, there were 148,000 officially registered drug addicts in China in 1991; a decade later (in 2001), the number had jumped to more than 900,000. By 2004, there were 1.14 million known drug addicts in China (Chen 2006). Heroin was the predominant drug used by addicts.

Second, for drug traffickers in the Golden Triangle, who are mostly ethnic Chinese, the Chinese route is far better than the Thai route because of geographical proximity (the major towns of the Wa, the Kokang, and the Mengla areas are all located just along the Burma-China border), better road conditions, and familiarity with the language and customs.

As drug traffickers in the Golden Triangle were busy expanding the Chinese route, Chinese authorities also increased their countermeasures against drug kingpins. In 2001 and 2002, several Burma-based but China-born heroin kingpins were arrested by the Burmese authorities and handed over to the Chinese government. One drug lord was shot and killed in Kokang. The Chinese authorities also execute scores of drug traffickers and dealers each year after they are put on trial. Even so, the Chinese authorities admit that they are not gaining the upper hand in the war against drugs in the border areas because more and more traffickers, many of them peasants from interior provinces of China hired as couriers (or "mules"), continue to cross the long and porous border regions. According to the Chinese authorities,

in order not to be caught, drug smuggling groups, inland and overseas, use such methods as breaking the whole into parts like "ants moving their food," smuggling drugs piecemeal, a few at a time. They frequently use body concealment to smuggle drugs in small quantities, thus making their smuggling activities even more difficult to detect. Yunnan has become a transit spot for the "Golden Triangle" drug traffickers and faces a very serious situation. (Yunnan Province Narcotics Control Committee 2003, 27)

These low- and mid-level heroin dealers are a different breed from those dealers involved in the trafficking of very large amounts of heroin for the international market. A street-level dealer in Kunming, a twenty-eight-year-old Muslim male, explained the social organization of the heroin trafficking "ants":

My uncle is a major drug dealer. In the early 1990s, he was involved in opium buying and selling. One day, he was arrested with more than forty viss of opium and was sent to prison. In prison he became acquainted with someone from Laukkai, Kokang. After my uncle got out of prison, he traveled to Laukkai and got involved in the heroin business. Typically, my uncle traveled to Laukkai, ordered a few kilograms (from two to six kilograms) of heroin and paid a certain amount of money as down payment, about 10,000 to 20,000 yuan [$1,200 to $2,400]. Then he came back to Kunming and waited for the heroin to be delivered; once it got here, he sold it immediately to drug dealers. For example, if he ordered two kilograms, there would be four or five buyers who took four to five hundred grams each. My uncle paid the balance due his contact in Laukkai once he received the drug. At that time, in 1998 and 1999, my uncle paid the seller in Kokang between 50 to 80 yuan [$6 to $10] per gram, depending on the quality of the drug. He in turn sold the drug to others for 110 to 130 yuan [$13 to $16] per gram, making about 40 to 50 yuan [$5 to $6] per gram. People who bought the drug from my uncle retailed the drug for 140 to 150 yuan [$17 to $18] per gram, and made 10 to 20 yuan [about $1 to $2] per gram only.[28]

Unlike mid-level heroin dealers in China who import a few kilograms of heroin from Burma directly to China, low-level drug retailers in China are mostly drug addicts who must rely on mid-level drug dealers for supply. According to the above-mentioned subject in Kunming:

I was a drug retailer for about two years, between 1998 and 2000, and had been using heroin for a while before I started selling it. At one point, I was using heroin heavily and was running out of money and did not know what to do. My uncle came to my home and when he saw me, he said: "Look at you! You are eating so much 'seafood' [*haichan* or heroin]!"[29] I told my uncle I might have to sell heroin to support my habit. My uncle said: "Look, if you are going to do it, I know a friend from whom I can get ten grams for you. You can sell it and use the money as your seed money to start your own drug retail business. Or you can use up the heroin yourself and forget about the drug business." So he gave me ten grams for free. At that time, I did not know he was involved in the heroin business. People normally won't tell anybody that they are doing it, including their wives. Why should they? After I got the ten grams, I used one gram and sold the other nine grams to my *duyou* [drug-using friends]. After that, I was in.

This was how it worked. My uncle would sell me 100 to 200 grams per transaction. Often, I had to pay him for the entire drug right away; sometimes, he would let me leave with the drug after paying for half of it. After I left my uncle's place with 200 grams of heroin, I went home right away and immediately took 150 grams of it and hid it. I then packed the other 50 grams into one gram or half a gram bags. I did not add anything to the drug. Normally, I would sell the 200 grams in seven to ten days. When I was down to 30 grams, I would call my uncle and ask him to get another 200 grams, and he would tell me when to stop by to pick it up at his place. At that time, people had money and it wasn't that hard to distribute 200 grams in a week or so. Now, people are selling one quarter gram or even one-fifth gram bags. Users nowadays do not have money like the users in the late 1990s.[30]

Drug enforcement authorities in Yunnan Province are overwhelmed by the large number of drug mules arrested each year. The majority of these heroin traffickers, usually carrying a few hundred grams, are arrested near the border area and sentenced to long prison terms. Those arrested with several kilograms of heroin generally receive a death sentence.[31] In sum, the business of drug trafficking in China is most rampant in Yunnan Province, as attested by a government report: "In the last five years [1998–2003], 66,978 drug cases have been dealt with [in Yunnan] that included the seizure of 42.1 tons of drugs, including 33 tons of heroin. The average seizure of heroin [in Yunnan] accounts for 70% of the total seizures in China per year. 32,926 suspects have been captured, and 23,467 of them have been tried" (Yunnan Province Narcotics Control Committee 2003, 75).

After heroin from Burma enters China via Yunnan Province, a large proportion of the drug will travel to Guangdong Province through the provinces of Guizhou and Guangxi (Cui 1999). Guangzhou City, the capital of Guangdong Province, is considered to be both the heroin distribution center for the domestic market and the transshipment point for heroin headed for Hong Kong or the international market (Ma and Ren 1999).

From the Golden Triangle to Southeast Asia and the West

Before its fall to the Communists in 1975, South Vietnam was a major destination for opium from the Golden Triangle. Opium from the hills in Burma and Laos was transported to Saigon by corrupt Laotian and Vietnamese officials; it was then converted into heroin before being shipped to Hong Kong, the United States, and Europe. The massive production of heroin in South Vietnam had also led to the heroin epidemic among American GIs in Vietnam (McCoy 1991).

Hong Kong and Taiwan

As a British colony before it was returned to China in 1997, Hong Kong, a well-established transportation and financial hub, had always been the center of the Southeast Asian heroin trade (Bresler 1981; Posner 1988; Gaylord

1997; Booth 1999). McCoy (1992, 255) characterized the role of Hong Kong in the heroin trade as follows:

> After the collapse of the Nationalist [KMT] regime in 1949, Shanghai's narcotics syndicate [called the Green Gang] fled to Hong Kong where they opened heroin refineries in the early 1950s.[32] Suffering reverses in a struggle for control of the colony's heroin trade against local syndicates, the Green Gang faded by the mid 1950s and was replaced by small syndicates of ethnic Chiu Chau criminals who traced their origins to nearby Swatow on China's south coast. Using the Green Gang's chemists, these new narcotic networks expanded the colony's heroin consumption during the 1950s and then extended their operations into Southeast Asia in the 1960s. Significantly, Hong Kong syndicate chemists opened the first No. 4 heroin laboratories along the Thai-Burma border in the late 1960s, introducing the technology that made the Golden Triangle the world's largest heroin producer.

Over the past several decades, rarely has there been a major SEA heroin trafficking case that did not involve people from Hong Kong as either organizers or financiers. Before the establishment of the Independence Commission Against Corruption (ICAC) in 1974 to fight against corruption, a large number of police officers were corrupted by high-profile heroin kingpins in Hong Kong (Lo 1993). Even after the British returned Hong Kong to China in 1997 and it became a special administrative region of China with its own political and judicial systems, its role in the SEA heroin trade remains vital, as more and more heroin is being smuggled into Hong Kong overland through China (Finckenauer and Chin 2006). However, most drug experts in Hong Kong do not think that the triads such as the Sun Yee On and the 14K, powerful organized crime groups in Hong Kong, are involved in heroin trafficking as organizations, nor do individual triad members dominate the heroin business (Chu 2002).

Like Hong Kong, Taiwan not only had a relatively well-established local market for heroin but it also is strategically located and commercially developed enough to occasionally serve as a transshipment point for SEA heroin to the West. In June 1991, U.S. drug enforcers found more than twelve hundred pounds (486 kilograms) of heroin in a warehouse in Hayward, California. The drugs were imported into the United States from Bangkok via Kaohsiung, Taiwan, in a container. So far, it is the largest heroin seizure in the United States (Chin 1996). Beginning in 1987, when people in Taiwan were for the first time allowed to visit China since the Communist takeover in 1949, many Taiwanese are now visiting, living, or doing business there. In the mid-1990s, concerned that too many of its businesspeople were flocking to China (which views Taiwan as a renegade province), the Taiwanese government began to encourage its entrepreneurs to look for commercial and investment opportunities in other countries in Southeast Asia. As a result, the number of Taiwanese firms in Thailand, Cambodia, Laos, Burma, and Vietnam began to grow. According to a drug expert in Taiwan, "In the late 1990s, as people in Taiwan became active in both China and many Southeast Asian countries, their role in the heroin trade also began to change. After 1998, Taiwanese businessmen who went to mainland China and Thailand to conduct business were able to contact foreign drug producers. These businessmen established a direct channel of heroin trading and trafficking from producers to Taiwan. Since then, the supply channel of Hong Kong gangs has been gradually replaced" (Finckenauer and Chin 2006, 65). After gaining access to heroin resources in Southeast Asia, Taiwanese drug organizations have partly replaced the Hong Kong gangs' role in Taiwan. These groups traffic heroin to Australia, Japan, and the United States. Their criminal activities have extended worldwide. The same expert characterized heroin traffickers and their organizations in Taiwan:

Drug groups in Taiwan recruit members based on whether a person has the connections and the ability to contribute in the drug trade. Having a fishing boat or a crew license, owning a company with a legal permit for exporting and a customs declaration, maintaining good relations with local drug dealers, or engaging in the business of chemical materials or medical equipments—all these characteristics may decide whether a person has the potential to join. There is no strict discipline or set of rules. Among all the actions or interactions of members, the most important thing is to keep the drug trade moving smoothly. Making money is their priority. Meanwhile, as ordinary businessmen, they also emphasize prompt delivery, quality of drugs, and on-time payment. In a relatively large, professional drug trafficking or manufacturing group, most members do not use drugs. Their behavior patterns are similar to ordinary businessmen. They rarely use violence against other drug group members or law enforcement authorities. (Finckenauer and Chin 2006, 66)

The United States

Ever since their first arrival in the United States in the 1850s, the Chinese have been viewed as being heavily involved in opium use and trafficking (Mark 1992). In U.S. Senate hearings on Chinese immigration in 1877, government officials and police officers testified that San Francisco's Chinatown was overrun with then-legal opium dens (U.S. Senate 1978 [1877]). It was reported that there were two hundred opium dens within the core area (about nine blocks) of the community (McLeod 1947). According to Mark (1992), during the late nineteenth century, a significant number of Chinese businessmen in the San Francisco area were actively involved in the importation and distribution of opium on the West Coast.

Little is known about the role Chinese dealers played in the American drug trade between 1914 and 1965. It is alleged that, after the liberalization of the immigration laws in 1965, Chinese criminals, many of them sailors, brought heroin into the United States (Chou 1993). The seamen turned the heroin over to drug dealers in Chinatown, who sold it in its entirety to mid-level drug dealers of other ethnic groups. The Chinese were not themselves involved in street-level sales.

After 1983, the amount of heroin imported into the United States from Southeast Asia increased dramatically (Bryant 1990). In 1984, law enforcement officials claimed that Chinese drug traffickers were responsible for about 20 percent of the heroin imported into this country. They also alleged that 40 percent of the heroin in New York City was of Southeast Asian origin (President's Commission on Organized Crime 1984).

In 1986, the number of heroin cases involving Chinese offenders began to rise dramatically. Drug enforcement and customs officers took notice of the increase in the number of Chinese heroin couriers arriving in American airports from Hong Kong and Bangkok. Each courier concealed ten to fifteen pounds of high-quality Southeast Asian heroin in luggage, picture frames, and other items, in an attempt to bypass customs checkpoints. A number of Chinese drug couriers, most of them otherwise legitimate community leaders, business owners, or restaurant and garment factory workers, were arrested at airports in Hong Kong, New York City, Los Angeles, and San Francisco.

In 1987, there was a dramatic change in the importation methods employed by the Chinese (DeStefano 1988). Instead of using drug couriers, Chinese heroin traffickers began to make use of their expertise in international trade. Large quantities of heroin (from fifty to one hundred pounds or more) began to arrive in the seaports of Newark and Elizabeth, New

Jersey, and in Chicago, hidden in cargo containers shipped from Asia. The drugs were carefully stuffed in furniture, frozen seafood, and nylon sport bags, in order to evade customs officials (U.S. Senate 1992).

In addition, Chinese drug traffickers began to stack ten to fifteen pounds of heroin in parcel boxes containing commodities that could conceal the odor of the drug (Lay and Dobson 1993). The boxes were sent from either Thailand or Hong Kong, and arrived in New York City via Oakland, California. Chinese drug traffickers also began to utilize air cargo to smuggle large amounts of heroin into the United States.

In 1987, law enforcement authorities solved more than twenty heroin-trafficking cases involving Chinese importers and seized a record 200 kilograms of 95 percent pure Southeast Asian heroin and millions in drug money (Huang 1988). Drug enforcement authorities suggested that of all the heroin seized in New York City in 1987, 70 percent was of Southeast Asian origin, compared to 40 percent in 1984 (Koziol 1988). The purity of the heroin on the streets of New York City rose from 5 percent in the early 1980s to 40 percent in 1987. The American drug enforcement community was overwhelmed by the sudden surge in heroin importation implemented by the Chinese (Stutman 1987).

Despite law enforcement efforts, Chinese involvement in heroin trafficking continued to increase in 1988 (Erlanger 1990). In Chicago, drug enforcement authorities seized 160 pounds of heroin hidden in religious statues arriving from Bangkok. Top-level Chinese smugglers were arrested in New York City for importing several hundred pounds of heroin into the United States. In Boston, 180 pounds of heroin were found inside a bean-sprout washing machine shipped from Hong Kong. In the meantime, law enforcement authorities in Asia, especially in Thailand and Hong Kong, were stunned by the amount of heroin the Chinese were trying to send to the United States. Thai authorities confiscated 2,800 pounds of heroin destined for New York City (Esposito and McCarthy 1988), and Hong Kong authorities seized a record 861 kilograms of heroin bound for the United States.

The arrests of major Chinese heroin traffickers continued unabated in 1989. In February, as the result of a worldwide drug enforcement operation known as Operation White Mare, the Organized Crime Drug Enforcement Task Force seized approximately eight hundred pounds of heroin and $3 million cash in Queens and arrested thirty-eight defendants in the United States, Hong Kong, Canada, and Singapore. The drugs were imported into the United States via Hong Kong, hidden in hundreds of rubber tires for lawn mowers. A Chinatown community leader was indicted for his role as middleman for the foreign-based sellers and the American buyers (Marriott 1989). Throughout 1989, other Chinese heroin trafficking groups were apprehended by drug enforcement agencies in the United States, Canada, Hong Kong, and Australia (Kinkead 1992).

By 1990, it was estimated that 45 percent of the heroin smuggled into the United States, and 80 percent of the heroin smuggled into New York City, was Southeast Asian (McCoy 1992; U.S. Senate 1992). By that time, law enforcement authorities in the United States (Bryant 1990), Canada (Dubro 1992), Australia (Dobinson 1993), the Netherlands (Schalks 1991), and Britain (Black 1992) claimed that the Chinese dominated the heroin trade in their respective jurisdictions.

In June 1991, drug enforcement authorities found twelve hundred pounds of heroin in a warehouse in Hayward, California (Morain and Hager 1991). The drugs were imported into the United States from Bangkok via Kaohsiung, Taiwan, in a container. Four Taiwanese merchants residing in California and a Hong Kong citizen were arrested for the crime. So far, it is the largest heroin seizure in the United States, surpassing the one thousand pounds imported by a Hong Kong businessman in 1988 and the eight hundred pounds hidden in the rubber tires for lawn movers in 1989 (Treaster 1991).

In 1992 and 1993, many high-level heroin traffickers in New York City's Chinatown were convicted and incarcerated by the U.S. government, thus putting many Chinese heroin trafficking groups out of business. Even so, according to various sources, almost 70 to 80 percent of the heroin seized by U.S. law enforcement officers in 1993 originated in the Golden Triangle (Witkin 1994; Greenhouse 1995). In 1994, U.S. authorities conducted Operation Tiger Trap to stop the flow of heroin from the Golden Triangle to the United States, and its enormous success was believed to have caused the dramatic decrease in the amount of SEA heroin being smuggled into the United States.

The social organization of the heroin trade between Burma and the United States, unlike the cocaine trade between Colombia and the United States, is horizontal rather than vertical:

The Colombian cocaine cartels are vertically integrated: A single organization may control everything from production to street sales. But in the heroin trade, independent entrepreneurs are involved on several levels. The Shan, for instance, have brokers with seemingly legitimate businesses in various Thai cities. One such broker, Lin Chien-pang, now imprisoned in New York, ran a Bangkok karaoke nightclub. A broker such as Lin might be approached by another broker representing Hong Kong businessmen who want to invest in a shipment of heroin. Typically, DEA officials say, the investors strike a deal with a group of ethnic Chinese in the United States—for example, New York businessmen who own legitimate restaurant or retail stores. The heroin may change hands several more times between these U.S. importers and street retailers, who for the most part are not Chinese but Italian-American, African-American or Dominican. (Witkin 1994, 44)

In the aftermath of Operation Tiger Trap, the trafficking of SEA heroin into the United States began to decline. In the early 1990s, the Cali cocaine cartel also began to enter the more lucrative heroin business. Within a few years, heroin from Colombia quickly replaced SEA heroin in the U.S. heroin market. In a January 1, 1998, *New York Times* article, U.S. authorities claimed that Colombian heroin accounted for more than 60 percent of the heroin smuggled into the United States. In a major assessment of international crime threats, U.S. officials concluded that heroin produced in Colombia and Mexico accounted for about 75 percent of the U.S. heroin market, with heroin from Southeast Asia making up most of the remainder (National Security Council 2000). By 2003, it was estimated that Colombian drug cartels were providing 80 percent of the heroin market in the United States (Forero and Weiner 2003). Jelsma (2005, 153) summarizes how Colombian heroin pushed SEA heroin out of the U.S. market:

By 1999, heroin from the Golden Triangle accounted for only 10 percent of the analyzed heroin sample. Data for 2001 showed that 56 percent originated from Colombia, followed by Mexico (30 percent), Southwest Asia (7 percent), and Southeast Asia (7 percent). Most recent data available from the DEA heroin signature program mention a source figure for Southeast Asia as low as 1 percent, with Colombia now dominating 80 percent of the U.S. market. It seems that today no more than a few hundred kilos of Burmese heroin makes it to the U.S. market, probably less than 1 percent of Burmese production.

Even so, in May 16, 2003, American and Chinese authorities arrested Wang Jianzhang, a major drug trafficker who was a Fujianese from Tingjiang, a county near Fuzhou City that is a major sending community of illegal Chinese immigrants to the United States. Wang, aka Tingjiang125 (reportedly because he weighed 125 kilograms), was arrested in 1989 in

New York for drug sales and served four years in jail. After his release, Wang was deported to Hong Kong because he was a Hong Kong resident. Wang later returned to Fuzhou and resumed his drug business. This time, Wang was arrested inside his sauna establishment in Fuzhou City while conducting a drug transaction. Between 1997 and 2000, Wang was alleged to have imported 680 kilograms of heroin from the Golden Triangle into the United States via China. American DEA officers in Bangkok and Beijing were directly involved in the joint operation (Chu 2004; Ting 2005).

Heroin as a Commodity

Wa farmers rely on opium cultivation to offset their rice deficiency and to have a little extra cash to buy basic necessities such as spices, clothing, and utensils. Local authorities in the Wa area depend on the opium tax and the opium trade to finance their offices and to enrich themselves. Top leaders in the local and the central levels, along with Chinese "businessmen," play a crucial role in the accumulation and distribution of all the opium produced in the Wa area. Some of them may sell their opium to heroin producers, some of them may convert their opium into heroin themselves, and some of them may work with groups of people who are capable of refining the opium into heroin. Small and big buyers from overseas, mostly from Thailand, China, Hong Kong, and Taiwan, will get in touch with heroin producers in the Wa area, and they will transport the heroin to another set of buyers in the international drug markets. Opium growers make an average of a few hundred dollars a year from opium cultivation, and local authorities in the Wa area also do not make much from the opium tax and the opium trade. A few powerful Wa leaders in Bangkang and other special districts and counties are getting relatively rich through the heroin business, but it is that handful of "businessmen," predominantly ethnic Chinese born in Burma, Thailand, or China, who benefit the most from the heroin trade in the Golden Triangle. Of course, compared to heroin dealers in the international markets, the heroin "businessmen" in the Golden Triangle are not making that much; the price of heroin doubled, tripled, or quadrupled as the drug moved from refineries in the jungles of the Wa area to the border area, to China or Thailand, to distribution centers in Bangkok, Guangzhou, and Hong Kong, and to markets in Australia, the United States, and many other international destinations.

Like opium, heroin is a commodity that needs no marketing. In other words, both the opium and the heroin trades are a sellers' market, in which buyers will always try to find the sellers and not the other way around. In fact, if there were no demand for the drug, and buyers did not take the initiative as they do now, there would not be much that opium and heroin producers could do to move their "products" to the middlemen's or the consumers' hands.

The economic reforms in China beginning in the late 1970s certainly played a critical role in the transformation of the drug trade in the Golden Triangle. The arrival of a large number of Chinese from China in the Golden Triangle starting in the early 1980s not only increased the production of heroin but also helped develop a new route for heroin via China. In the early 1990s, when the heroin trade via Thailand was deeply affected by law enforcement efforts in the United States and the subsequent surrender of Khun Sa, the heroin trade via China emerged to fill the void.

Initially, heroin from the Golden Triangle only passed through China before it was transported to the various international markets after the drug arrived in Hong Kong or Guangzhou. However, as China began to embark on economic reform, a heroin market in China also began to develop as the so-called *getihu* or individual entrepreneurs began to experiment with heroin. The trafficking of heroin into China was made possible not only by a dramatic increase in border trade between Burma and China but also by the network established between people on both sides of the border after years of going back and forth between the two sides, either for business, work, or sightseeing. Few Chinese from China go to Burma with the intention of entering the drug trade, but when they are presented with the opportunity at a time when things are not going very well with their business or legitimate work, many of them take it. These are the PRC Chinese who are confident that they might be able to pull off a drug deal mainly because they are familiar with both the supply side (Burma) and the demand side (China). They become the bridge between the producers and the buyers.

Like the opium trade, the scope and patterns of the heroin business are also very much influenced by global and regional politics, the availability of precursor chemicals, the opening and closing of trade routes, the demand for heroin, the constraints of operating in an illegal market, and traffickers' responses to law enforcement measures. As a result, it is not possible to have much impact on the trade by simply arresting or prosecuting a few heroin kingpins. The Chinese authorities have executed quite a few major heroin traffickers in the past fifteen years, and yet new drug entrepreneurs quickly emerge to replace those that were removed. When so many people from some of the poorest areas of China are willing to face the death penalty for transporting just a few kilograms to make just a few thousand dollars, it is not hard to imagine how unlikely death could be a deterrent for a major heroin dealer who could be making millions of dollars by moving hundreds of kilograms across the border.

The political-criminal nexus certainly moves up a notch and becomes much more intensified when the switch is from the opium trade to the heroin trade. The ability to accumulate and transport hundreds of viss of opium and locate a suitable place to produce heroin, the power to order soldiers to guard the refinery, and the need to prevent intervention by outsiders, including the authorities, are all critical factors in operating a thriving heroin business. These arrangements or needs could not be secured without the complicity or involvement of high-level Wa authorities.

After production, heroin must be transported to the markets in Burma, Thailand, China, Hong Kong, and other destinations. The heroin trade is made possible not only by corrupt exchanges between politicians and criminals but also by the participation of large numbers of otherwise legitimate businesspeople who simply take advantage of their connections, opportunities, and business acumen to move the heroin from one place to another and, in the process, reap a huge profit. Most of them are not professional criminals, nor members of a criminal organization, but owners of legitimate businesses in Rangoon, Bangkok, Kunming, Hong Kong, and New York.

Those who are key players in the heroin trade are mostly people who simultaneously occupy a major role in politics, the military, the underworld, and the legitimate business sector. Most Wa leaders, the *jao pho* of Thailand, the gangster politicians of Taiwan, and community leaders of the Chinatowns in Bangkok, New York, and other major Chinese communities around the globe fit the profile of a person with enormous power both in the mainstream society and the underworld.

The heroin trade has also been affected by the development of an alternative way for drug entrepreneurs in the region to make money. For example, after the mid-1990s, when China and the rest of the world began to exert pressure on the Wa to eliminate opium cultivation, Chinese "businessmen" from Thailand and China began to develop an alternative commodity that is actually more lucrative than heroin. The opportunity to make money through the methamphetamine trade either moved some of the heroin producers and traffickers into the methamphetamine business or created a whole new generation of drug entrepreneurs.

Chapter Five

The Methamphetamine Business

While the Golden Triangle in Southeast Asia has long been known as a major opium cultivation and heroin production center, in the past decade the area has also developed into an important base for methamphetamine production.

According to Chartchai Suthiklom, deputy secretary-general of the Office of Narcotics Control Board (ONCB) of Thailand, methamphetamine (or meth) tablets or speed pills (called *yaba* or mad drug in Thailand) were originally produced in Bangkok in the 1970s. At that time it was legal to possess ephedrine, the main ingredient in the production of methamphetamine. When the Thai government banned the production of meth tablets in the early 1990s, meth factories were first moved from urban centers to the country's remote hills in the north, and then to the Wa area not long after.[1] Wang Keqiang, minister of the Wa Investment and Tourism Bureau, acknowledged that his government was implicated in the establishment of meth factories in the Wa area in the mid-1990s and explained why that happened:

In 1996, Thai and Burmese businessmen—mostly Chinese in Thailand or Burmese who had been living in Thailand for a long time—came to Bangkang to establish meth factories. They had already contacted businessmen in China and all parties came here to meet. They sat down with us and struck a deal about setting up speed pill factories here; all they needed from us were places to set up the factories and our protection. At that time, there were no difficulties whatsoever about bringing in [from China] the necessary precursor chemicals for meth production here. We allowed them to set up meth factories here because the Wa State was in a dire financial situation at that time. We had fought with Khun Sa for many years and that had depleted our treasury. Plus, we were having problems moving heroin through China because there had been several major arrests involving our people and the Chinese authorities had ordered us not to transport heroin via China.[2]

A Wa government document also indicated that "in the three years between 1996 and 1998, the government permitted businesspeople to operate 'ice'-producing factories in the area, for which the authorities collected a small amount of tax. Starting in 1999, the production of 'ice' [methamphetamine] was prohibited. But between 1996 and 1998, approximately 8 million yuan [$960,000] was collected [per year] as ice production tax. About 24 million yuan [$2,880,000] was collected over the three-year period" (United Wa State Party 2001c, 11).[3]

Even though the Wa government has claimed that the production of speed pills was prohibited starting in May 1999, Thai authorities estimated that one million speed pills per day were flowing into Thailand from Burma in 1999 (Khuenkaew 1999a), and the Thai ONCB estimated that the United Wa State Army produced more than three hundred million meth tablets for the Thai market that year (Khuenkaew 1999b). The 2000 U.S. International Narcotics Control Strategy Report concluded that production of methamphetamine had skyrocketed over the preceding few years; by 2001, Burma was producing an estimated eight hundred million meth pills a year (U.S. Department of State 2001).

Wa leaders I interviewed in 2001 all denied that there were speed pill factories in the Wa area and blamed Kokang for the meth epidemic. Zhou Dafu, deputy director of the Wa Central Authority, said:

We do not have any speed pill factories here anymore. The pills that are being smuggled into Thailand are all produced in Kokang, but the pills are marketed as Wa products because we are bigger and more likely to be noticed by outsiders than the Kokang.[4] Plus the pills that were once produced in the Wa State are known to be of better quality, unlike the pills from Kokang that are often diluted with other chemicals. Kokang is exploiting us. So, why are we accused of being the major meth producers? That's because people say once a thief, always a thief![5]

Regardless of the Wa leader's denial, all my key informants told me that the methamphetamine business in the Wa area was the engine of economic growth there and had surpassed the heroin business in terms of scope and profitability. Several subjects estimated that, by the early 2000s, the meth business in the Wa area has been five times bigger than its heroin business.

From Heroin to Methamphetamine

The Golden Triangle's methamphetamine business had been first noted in the 1996 U.S. International Narcotics Control Strategy Report, which stated that an increasing amount of methamphetamine was said to be produced in labs located side by side with heroin refineries along the China and Thailand borders (U.S. Department of State 1996). Several years later, a DEA report also suggested that many drug laboratories in the Wa area were involved in the production of both heroin and methamphetamine (U.S. Drug Enforcement Administration 2002).

Opium has been the lifeblood of the remote Wa Hills for many decades. Farmers grew opium to offset the annual rice deficit, local authorities relied on the opium tax as their main source of revenue, and businesspeople bought and sold opium just like any other commodity. The arrival of the Kuomintang in the Wa area in 1949 transformed the production, taxation, trading, and transportation of opium into a much larger and better organized system. The cease-fire agreement between the Burmese government and the Wa in 1989, coupled with the surrender of Khun Sa to the Burmese authorities in 1996, shifted heroin production from the Thai-Burma border in the south to the Burma-China border in the north.

Under pressure from the world community, two other special regions adjacent to the Wa area—the Mengla and the Kokang—announced in the late 1990s and early 2000s that opium cultivation in their territories had been banned. To sustain the local economies, authorities in Mengla and Kokang made a concerted effort to develop their areas into a gambling resort for Chinese (Yang 2005). When Wa leaders were forced to follow the example of Mengla and Kokang, they agreed to ban opium cultivation but they came up with a better idea to generate money. Instead of developing a gambling industry, the Wa decided to establish a methamphetamine industry.

The Wa government's plan was to allow Chinese and foreigners to mass produce methamphetamine in the Wa area, collect large fees from the drug producers, and then ship the drugs out of the area to be consumed elsewhere. Under this plan, everything would be discreet and controlled, and the drugs produced in the Wa area would not affect Wa society. The idea was not much different from establishing a *jiagongchukouqu* (a manufacturing zone for export only). To prevent the drugs produced in the Wa area from being locally consumed, the Wa authorities penalized only those who were retailing (*chaimai*) meth or using it. The regulated production and trafficking of drugs on a large scale were never targeted by the Wa authorities.

The shift from heroin to methamphetamine also served another important goal for the Wa leaders (and the Burmese authorities), and that was to avoid upsetting the Chinese. There is a saying in Burma: "When China spits, Burma swims" (Marshall 2002, 47). A high-ranking drug enforcer in Rangoon also stated that "the Wa are more concerned with how the Chinese react to what they do rather than with how we in Burma would react."[6] From the Wa leaders' standpoint, it was better to saturate Thailand with methamphetamine then to send heroin to China.

However, the Wa leaders' well-laid plan backfired. First, it was not possible to prevent their people from gaining access to the methamphetamine tablets that were produced in their territory and soon large numbers of Wa students and soldiers were addicted to the drug. Second, it became clear that the Wa could not hide their role in the methamphetamine trade as hundreds of millions of the tablets were smuggled into Thailand from Burma. As a result, the Wa regime was later labeled by the world community as one of the most powerful drug trafficking organizations on earth. In the meantime, heroin production and trafficking continued, and it still found its way into China and thus angered the Chinese.

According to people I interviewed in Bangkang, some drug producers are indeed simultaneously involved in the manufacturing of both meth and heroin. A Wa official made the following comments about the relationship between the production of the two drugs: "The meth and heroin businesses are inseparable. They are all businesses. Someone in the drug business is like a vegetable seller who will sell whatever vegetable will bring him the highest profit. It does not make a difference whether you sell potatoes or tomatoes; you just sell whatever has the highest profit margin."[7]

However, other subjects suggested that many heroin producers left the heroin business completely after they became speed pill manufacturers. A businessman in Bangkang pointed out that many former opium and heroin traders shifted to the methamphetamine business because meth tablets are much easier to produce and transport. Another respondent in Bangkang indicated that powerful people were getting into the methamphetamine business and transferring their heroin operations into the hands of their associates and followers. A businessperson in Mae Sai, Thailand, explained why many heroin entrepreneurs are switching to yaba:

> The yaba business is more lucrative than the heroin trade and yaba is much easier to produce and transport. To refine heroin, you need about ten types of precursor chemicals, but not with yaba. With heroin, you also need a really good chemist to produce it. If you don't have a good chemist, the heroin that is produced could be brown and the market value for brownish heroin is not good. As far as yaba is concerned, you can produce yaba with a machine twenty-four hours a day. That's why many of those who were in the heroin trade switched to the yaba business.[8]

In addition, the speed pill business, like the crack cocaine business in the United States, appears to have attracted a large number of people who would have not participated in the making and selling of heroin (Williams 1989; Bourgois 1996; Jacobs 1999). The above subject made a key point:

> There is no doubt that the emergence of the meth business has increased the number of people who are involved in the drug trade. In the past, only a small number of people were dealing heroin. Heroin is bulky and not very lucrative. For example, my father was in the heroin business for more than twenty years, but he never became rich. With yaba, it is a different story. You can make tens of thousands of baht, or even millions, within a relatively short period of time. You also need not invest any money in the yaba trade. The producers will provide the distributors the drug on credit. I saw many people both in Tachilek and Mae Sai become rich within a year or so. I have some friends who are now in the yaba trade who would not have gotten into any drug business if not for yaba.[9]

In sum, a large number of opium or heroin traders have given up those drugs and picked up methamphetamine in order to generate much more income while working with a less cumbersome drug. Some drug entrepreneurs have passed on their opium or heroin business to their subordinates and now devote themselves exclusively to the meth trade. Still, there are others who engage in the opium, heroin, and meth business at the same time. Many others, including the offspring of opium or heroin traders, have also been recruited into the booming meth business.

Methamphetamine Dealers and Producers in the Wa Area

Of the thirty-five drug dealers or producers we interviewed, nine identified themselves as meth dealers or producers. We also interviewed many well-placed informants with intimate knowledge of the meth business. Individuals involved in the meth trade in Bangkang can be categorized as retailers, wholesalers, and producers.

Retailer

Unlike the legalized status of opium, the buying or selling of meth tablets was and is illegal in the Wa area. Even so, some people, especially women, sell meth tablets from their homes. We interviewed a forty-four-year-old female retailer, married with three children. She said she had never attended school, had sold heroin in the past, and was now a full-time methamphetamine retailer:

> I began to sell speed pills in 1998. I saw other people selling, and they were making a lot of money. My whole family relied on me for support and I did not have enough money to conduct other businesses, so I decided to sell speed pills. I went to the bosses and asked them to give me one or two bags of speed pills to sell and said I would pay them the money after I sold the pills. Because selling speed pills is illegal here, I am selling them clandestinely. I keep the drug home and people will come to me to buy. If the government finds out, I have to go to jail. Before I sold speed pills, I used to sell heroin. I can make as much as 5,000 yuan [$600] a month from selling speed pills.[10]

Another methamphetamine retailer we interviewed told us that she normally would buy a *bao* (bag) of speed pills (two hundred tablets) from a wholesaler and repack them in 10 yuan ($1.20) bags with about five to seven tablets each. In the Wa area, one unit (*jian*) of meth contains ten bags. Normally, a retailer buys a unit of speed pills from a wholesaler for 1,000 to 1,200 yuan ($120 to $150), though it could be as high as 1,350 yuan ($164). If a retailer repacked the pills into 10 yuan bags, he or she can take in around 3,000 yuan ($360) per unit. A retailer can make a profit of 2,000 yuan ($240) per unit. This is lucrative if one considers that many people in Bangkang make about 300 yuan ($36) a month. She also said she reluctantly lets buyers smoke speed pills in her house. There are so many people going in and out of her house, she is concerned that the authorities are going to get her one day.

Wholesaler

A methamphetamine wholesaler we interviewed was a thirty-five-year-old Chinese from Kokang, married with two children. She said she dropped out of elementary school and that she had been distributing speed pills for five years. Once, she stopped selling the pills for six months because she was arrested by the Wa authorities. She was released after paying a fine because it was her first arrest. After she returned home, she noticed that she was being watched by the Wa authorities, so she stopped selling drugs. Six months later, after she was certain that she was out of the radar of the authorities, she resumed her drug distribution:

It is a family business. If I am busy, my husband will help me. That is, when people come to buy bags of drugs, my husband will count the drugs. My business is medium size; many retailers buy speed pills from me. I do not do retail, just wholesale. I go to the bosses' homes to buy the speed pills; that's because I don't know where the factories are. When business is good, I make up to 100,000 yuan [$12,000] a year.

My major concern is that I will make a mistake and buy poor quality speed pills. Or I will bring in good quality speed pills for a very high price and will not able to sell them promptly. You can't keep these things in your home for a long time; the authorities are going to come to search your house anytime they want.

I have no problem dealing with those bosses from whom I buy the speed pills; they are honest people and I am an honest person, too. Besides, this is an illegal business; nobody is willing to create unnecessary problems just to have a little advantage.

After I buy the speed pills, I do not need to do much, just keep them at home and wait for retailers to come. My only headache is that I could be arrested anytime. I only sell the drugs to old customers. If the person is a stranger, I don't care how sweet he or she is, or if the buyer comes with cash; I will not deal with the person. I was burned once, and I will not trust a stranger again.

I don't have a good impression of the retailers. They are not a nice bunch of people to work with. They are sometimes very pushy and tell you they need the drugs in a hurry, and that they need this or that amount of drugs, and they demand the best quality drugs. And we also have to decide what the price is going to be. I wait for them and then they don't show up. They will call and say they are busy today and will come tomorrow. But you can't show your anger to these people, otherwise they can hurt you by letting the authorities know what you are doing. My goodness, it is really a pain in the neck dealing with these people.

In fact, this business is very lucrative. The pills are very light and easy to hide. It's just that it is very risky; every minute you worry that you might get arrested. Before I was arrested, I was making a lot of money. I built a new house and bought a new car. After I was caught, they confiscated my house and my car, and they fined me a lot of money.[11]

While I was doing fieldwork in the Wa area, I came to know a Chinese woman from Kokang. She was twenty-one years old at that time, a pretty woman had who arrived in Bangkang in the mid-1990s and, according to one source, was responsible for the recruitment and training of half of the speed pill retailers in Bangkang. She was working with her boyfriend, an ethnic Chinese who was a methamphetamine wholesaler and well-connected in the Wa area. She was also a heavy user, and I often saw her smoking the drug with her friends in the hotel where I was staying. After my return to the United States, one of my interviewers told me she had been arrested by the Wa authorities for dealing speed pills and was confined to a so-called hole (a hole in the ground that functions as a prison cell) for more than three months. After she was released, she disappeared.

In Bangkang, I was also acquainted with several young women who were the children of wealthy Chinese businesspeople or powerful Wa officials. Most of their parents were either involved in the opium trade or the heroin business, or both. These young women, who are considered to be the luckiest ones in the poor Wa hills because they are young, rich, and protected by their well-connected parents, are also involved in the methamphetamine business. In Bangkang, I was often told that it is not unusual to see parents involved in the opium or heroin business while their children play key roles in the methamphetamine business. In the Wa area, the drug trade is a family business that can be passed from one generation to the next and, if necessary, diverted to other types of drugs.

Producer

A methamphetamine producer we interviewed in 2001, a forty-five-year-old Wa man, married, with five children, said he had never attended school and had been involved in the production of meth tablets since 1996. This is his account of how he entered the drug business:

One day I was on my way to the market on my motorbike and a car hit me. The driver was a businessman from Kengtung. Because I was injured, he drove me home. He saw how poor I was, and he asked me to work in his "company" [a meth factory] after I recovered from the injury. After working for him for a year, I saved enough money to start my own business.

My drug business is considered medium sized, because I am making only a few million yuan a year. In a good year, I make about 6 million yuan [$730,000] and in a bad year I earn about 1 million yuan [$120,000]. I need to pay tax to the government, about 1 to 2 million yuan [$120,000 to $240,000] a year. Besides this meth business, I also buy and sell opium. I also own gas stations and poultry farms. I had a garment factory in Lashio and a hotel in Rangoon.[12]

Asked what kinds of business-related problems he normally encountered, he said:

My headache is when I cannot buy good precursor chemicals. If there is too much salt in the precursor chemicals, not only are we unable to produce many speed pills but the salt might also damage our machines. Those people who are selling me precursor chemicals are not honest people. Well, what can you say, they are Chinese and they are going to cheat you, regardless.

After I convert the chemicals into speed pills, I transport the pills to Thailand for sale. As far as the sale is concerned, my only worry is that I won't be paid in cash. This business has been in decline over the past two years. Buyers will take away speed pills and they don't come back with cash. These past two years, they have traded cars for the drug. You see how many cars I have here.[13] [There were twenty to thirty cars parked in front of the subject's big house.][14]

Another methamphetamine producer said he entered the drug business inadvertently: "At one point, a group of people from Thailand and Kengtung came and they said they wanted to rent a house I owned; the house was big, and they said they could use it to produce methamphetamine there. Later on, I joined them as a partner. That's how I got involved in this business."[15]

A businessman in Bangkang talked about the transportation of pills from Bangkang to Tachilek, near the Thai border:

I was arrested by Chinese authorities for transporting ephedrine [the main ingredient for the production of meth] from China to Burma. After being locked up for more than twenty days, I was released. [The subject told me later that he was able to buy his way out at that time, which was around 1997.] Not long after my release, a group of friends were arrested for the same crime, and because my friends had my beeper, the Chinese authorities thought that I was the main figure behind that deal. After that, I decided to get out of the drug business. When a group of friends asked me to be a partner in the transportation of methamphetamine tablets from Bangkang to Tachilek, I turned down the offer, even though it was tempting. You can sell the pills in Tachilek for twice the amount of money you pay in Bangkang. Plus, you can move a large quantity of the pills in one trip because they are small. We can't bribe the Burmese authorities, but we don't have to because we can hide the pills in the trucks.[16]

When the same businessman was asked about the meth business in Bangkang, he went on to say: "To be involved in the meth business, you need to have capital, expertise, machines, chemicals, and, most importantly, someone who can help you arrange an understanding with the [Wa] headquarters. Of course, if you have money, you can always find such a middleman. If you have all these qualifications, it won't be hard to find a Wa official to be your partner."[17]

In sum, many people in the Wa area, especially the young, are increasingly attracted to the meth business because it is an easy way to get rich quickly. A twenty-two-year-old man who was a heavy user and a retailer said:

> Here, if you want to get 20,000 yuan worth [$2,400] of speed pills for retail, a distributor will let you walk away with the drug without any payment. But if you want to start any other type of business, you might have a hard time getting a bottle of mineral water without paying for it. That's why so many people here can get into the methamphetamine business without a penny. Indeed, there are many young people here in Bangkang who appear to be normal, but once you get to know them, you would be amazed to find out that they are not only heavy meth users but sellers of meth as well.[18]

Wa Leaders' Involvement in the Methamphetamine Business

All my subjects suggested that any individual involved in the methamphetamine business had to have some connection to powerful figures in the Wa government. If not, the person could be victimized by other businesspeople or arrested by Wa authorities. For example, a businessman in Bangkang told me:

> A friend of mine is a real estate developer who built a 700,000 yuan [$85,000] house for a customer. After the house was completed, the customer was forced to turn it over to another person to whom he owed 2 million yuan's worth [$240,000] of methamphetamine. The customer was a man from Jiangxi Province, China, who did not have many connections here in the Wa area. The fact that he couldn't speak Yunnanese Chinese makes him an easy prey here. That's why he lost the 2 million yuan's worth of methamphetamine; someone took the drug and did not bother to pay him. This man from Jiangxi was also involved in retailing speed pills. He was arrested last year and released only after he paid the Wa authorities a large sum of money. You are vulnerable if you are involved in the drug business without good connections to government officials here.[19]

As to whether Wa officials are also involved in the speed pill business or are as active in the speed pill business as they were in the heroin business, I believe the answer is unquestionably yes. According to my subjects, Wa officials are heavily involved in the speed pill business. The businessman in Bangkang cited above said:

The Wa Central Authority (WCA) is definitely involved in the methamphetamine business. Under its control, there is a business unit which is allowed to conduct all kinds of money-generating businesses. The WCA does not care what businesses the unit is getting into as long as the unit pays the WCA a certain amount of money on a regular basis. In fact, the unit's working capital is provided by the WCA.[20]

Another subject supported the above viewpoint:

My former boyfriend was in the drug business. When we were going out, he told me he could see me only every two months. I said it had to be more often than that. He would not tell me what he did for a living; all I knew was that he worked for the WCA. After a while, when I pressed him about why he could not see me more often, he told me that he was working in a heroin and methamphetamine factory that was far away from Bangkang and he could only take a leave once in a while. He said he was in charge of the factory's financial matters. He told me to keep it a secret and not to tell anyone. He also would not tell me the name of his boss.[21]

Hedao is believed to be a center for the manufacturing of methamphetamine, and Wa leaders in the Hedao area, especially leaders of the notorious army regiment *jingweituan* (Security Regiment), are alleged to be heavily involved in the production of the pills. According to a government document dated October 8, 1999, three leaders in the Hedao area—Aitai (deputy chief of staff of the Security Regiment), Jiebei (the head of Division 519), and Yingxiang (the party secretary of Mengping District)—had been arrested for a long and varied list of offenses—including theft, robbery, assault, murder, and insolence—in what became known as the "Hedao Incident" (United Wa State Party 1999a). Although the three were not charged with methamphetamine production, all their victims were government officials and businesspeople who were involved in the methamphetamine trade. It was believed that the entire incident was about vying for control of the meth trade in the Hedao area.

On September 6, 1999, the three had been arrested, interrogated, and eventually beaten to death, presumably by soldiers in the Security Regiment. Bao Youhua, the leader of the Security Regiment who was alleged to have been very lenient with the three, was one of the four Bao brothers (Youyi, Youxiang, Youliang, and Youhua).[22] According to a key informant I interviewed while I was in Hedao,

> people have to be careful when they visit Hedao and Mengping because members of the Security Regiment are known to be reckless. Some officials in the central government like to call Youhua *tuhuangdi*, or local emperor. There are many methamphetamine factories in the two areas, and if strangers approach these factories, the guards, mostly members of *jinweituan*, will shoot to kill. Nobody in Bangkang, with the exception of perhaps Bao Youxiang, can control Youhua. The two brothers fought often in the past.[23]

Just like the heroin business, Wa officials and/or their close relatives were also involved in the production of speed pills independent from the Wa government's operation. According to a Wa official,

> we know that there are several major methamphetamine producers in the Wa, but we dare not arrest them because that could implicate a lot of powerful people here in the Wa State. Besides, this is Burma; no matter what activity you are involved in, as long as there are no 'accidents' [no publicity, no arrest, no violent incident] you are not going to be bothered by the authorities. Furthermore, we are not that clean anyway [meaning, the Wa is still involved in opium growing]. How can we be so strict with people who are producing or dealing meth?[24]

This was also confirmed by the top leader Bao Youxiang during my interview with him: "Just a few days ago, we arrested a family member of an official after we discovered he was transporting methamphetamine to the Thai-Burma border area. We confiscated the drugs and the car. This was quite unusual. We let the smuggler go free because of his family tie to the official. In the past, we would not have done anything if we found out that the smuggler was a member of an official's family."[25]

When I asked people in Bangkang about Wa leaders' involvement in the meth business, most believed that the majority of the leaders did participate in either producing or trafficking the drug. And it was evident that even those few leaders who were thought to be uninvolved in the drug trade nevertheless had family members who were involved. In a place like the Wa State, it is not reasonable for the head of a family to say that he is not responsible for any of his family members being involved in the drug trade, simply because he is *the* reason why a family member is a successful drug entrepreneur.

Wei Xuegang: The King of Methamphetamine

The discussion of the Wa leaders' involvement in the methamphetamine business is incomplete if I do not mention Wei Xuegang. According to the media and some law enforcement authorities, he has been considered Khun Sa's replacement in the Golden Triangle after Khun Sa surrendered to the Burmese government, and from his base in Mong Yawn near the Thai-Burma border, he has been responsible for the trafficking of hundreds of millions of speed pills into Thailand each year.

As mentioned in chapter 2, the Wa State is divided into Northern Wa and Southern Wa regions. Bao Youxiang is considered to be the number-one leader of the Wa State, and definitely the most powerful figure in the Northern Wa area. In the Southern Wa area, however, the most influential figure is Wei Xuegang, an ethnic Chinese who joined the Wa as recently as the early 1990s but rapidly climbed the power ladder to become one of the most dominant Wa leaders and probably the richest man in the entire Wa area, north and south. Wei, the general commander of the Southern Wa military region, is believed to be *the* kingpin of Burma's methamphetamine business.

Wei Xuegang, born in 1946, was alleged to be a key figure in the heroin empire of Khun Sa and responsible for the smuggling of 600 kilograms of heroin to the United States in 1987. When he was granted Thai citizenship in 1985, he changed his name to Prasit or Changchai Cheewin-nitipanya. In 1994, Wei was sentenced to life imprisonment by the Thai authorities for drug smuggling. He was granted bail during his appeal and fled to Burma.

In June 1998, the U.S. State Department announced a $2 million reward for information leading to his arrest or conviction (Pathan 2005). According to a subject in Mae Sai,

> when he was living in Mae Sai, Wei was an assistant of Khun Sa. After Wei established a name in the drug business, he could no longer stay in Mae Sai anymore because the Thai authorities were going after him; that's why he went to Khun Sa's place. After Khun Sa surrendered to the Burmese in 1996, Wei had no choice but to find a

new protector, and he became a partner of the Wa. If the Burmese wanted to do something to Wei, they would have to take into consideration the Wa's reaction.

I am convinced that Wei Xuegang is the kingpin of the speed trade. He is doing it big time in Southern Wa State and Bao Youxiang is protecting him. Bao is willing to support Wei because Wei is paying tribute to Bao with money from the drug trade. Basically, Wei needs the protection and Bao needs the money. If not for Bao, the Burmese authorities would have gone after Wei. Wei is not capable of protecting himself from the Burmese authorities on his own.[26]

Another subject in Bangkang explained the intricate relationship between the two Wa leaders:

Bao can eliminate Wei Xuegang but he also has to take into consideration Wei Xuegang's two brothers [Wei Xuelong and Wei Xueyun] of which one is a member of the central committee of the Wa government. Besides, Wei Xuegang's relationship with the Burmese authorities is an ambiguous one; if Bao attacks Wei, Wei might turn to the Burmese authorities for help and team up with the Burmese and turn against Bao. Besides, the money from Wei is extremely important for Bao's financial well-being.[27]

My key informants told me that they saw Wei with Bao in Bangkang on a number of occasions and that Bao showed a lot of respect for Wei in public. Nevertheless, not very many ordinary people in the Wa area have the opportunity to see Bao and Wei together because the meetings are always held in utmost secrecy.

Regardless of how he is related to Bao Yuoxiang, Wei Xuegang is viewed by the Thai media as the man who is most responsible for the yaba epidemic in Thailand (*Bangkok Post*, November 7, 1999). Yet, in 2001 when Wa leaders in Bangkang talked to me about Wei Xuegang, they tended to stress that Wei used to be involved in the drug business but no longer. Moreover, they prefer to talk about the large donations Wei made to support public works projects in the Wa area. For example, according to the Wa leaders, Wei had donated more than 100 million baht ($2.32 million) to build a high school and 1 million yuan ($120,000) to build a library for the middle school in Bangkang. According to the Wa leaders, Wei is the most generous philanthropist in the Wa State and he cares about the well-being of the Wa people. A Wa leader summarized how he felt about Wei: "Wei Xuegang was a major drug manufacturer in the past but he is doing a lot of good things now to redeem himself. You should not label a person a drug kingpin for the rest of his life."[28] Another Wa leader asserted that Wei is not directly involved in the drug trade anymore. However, he also believed that some of Wei's followers are still involved in the drug business.[29] Only one Wa leader I talked to was critical of Wei:

I know what is going on in the South. I reprimanded Wei Xuegang a couple of times, telling him to get his act together and get out of the drug business. His response was, "If you want, you can take the army back. I am a businessman, I am not interested in keeping your army [meaning he had to feed the army and he needs money to do that]." Anyway, it does not matter what I have to say to him; he won't listen.[30]

When I visited the Wa area for the third time in April 2005, the few Wa leaders I talked to were still adamant in suggesting that Wei Xuegang was a new person, as opposed to being the notorious drug lord of many years ago. One leader said this when I asked him about Wei's role in the drug business:

There is one person whom I really admire and that is Wei Xuegang. He may have been involved in the heroin business when he was with Khun Sa—that's because he was then the finance minister for Khun Sa and his job was to bring in money. However, now he is the one person in the Wa area who is serious about banning drugs. Look at what he did! He moved a large number of people from Northern Wa State to his area and these people are now living a good life without having to rely on drugs for a living. I can assure you that there is neither opium cultivation nor heroin production in his area. As far as methamphetamine is concerned, I can tell you that Mong Yawn [under Wei's control] is the center of methamphetamine distribution, not production. All the yaba that are produced all over Burma are being transported to that town to trade, and then the drugs are transported into Thailand. You see, there is a huge difference between being the center of production and being the center of distribution.[31]

Bao Yuoxiang also would like the West to see Wei Xuegang as a "former" heroin dealer who is determined to eradicate opium from the Wa area. Bao would like outsiders to give credit to Wei for financing numerous large-scale developmental and educational projects in the Wa State.[32] Jeremy Milsom, the head of the UN office in the Wa area, also suggested that "Wei Xuegang has done more to support impoverished poppy farmers break their dependence on the crop than any other single person or institution in Burma, and this has been done by putting past drug profits back into the people, as he perhaps tries himself to move into the mainstream economy" (Milsom 2005, 75).

For the Burmese authorities, even if Wei Xuegang is an active drug lord responsible for the booming methamphetamine trade, they are concerned that if they take action against Wei, they might antagonize Wa leaders in Bangkang and that is something they want to avoid if they can. According to a Burmese military intelligence officer,

> if we arrest Wei, we have to worry about the Wa. If the Wa decide to fight us to protect Wei, that would be a bigger concern for us than Wei, because the Wa are very strong. Besides, there is no hard evidence against Wei. Why did the Thai authorities let Wei flee Thailand after being sentenced to death? That's because there are many high-ranking Thai officials behind him. The meth epidemic in Thailand is not Wei's fault. It is the Thai government's fault. Besides, leaders are rarely directly involved in the drug business nowadays; they ask people around them to do it for them.[33]

The Role of Kokang in the Speed Trade

In the heroin trade, the Wa are still believed to be key players but many people, especially the Wa leaders themselves, suggest that Kokangnese are actually more active in heroin production and trafficking than the Wa. Similarly, the extent of Kokang involvement in the methamphetamine business is also an issue. In the Thai media, readers only learn about how active the so-called Red Wa are in the yaba business; rarely are the Kokangnese mentioned. According to Chartchai Suthiklom, deputy secretary-general of the Office of Narcotics Control Board of Thailand, people in Kokang are as active as the Wa in the meth trade:

> Between 1995 and 1998, we believed the Wa was responsible for 80 percent of the speed pills being smuggled into Thailand. However, starting from 1999 and until now, we believe that 40 percent of the pills are from the Wa, 40 percent from the Kokang, and 20 percent

from the SSA South [Shan State Army South] and other ethnic groups along the border. Even though many groups are involved in the yaba business, the Thai media only focus on the Wa because they do not know much about the Kokang. Whenever I talk to reporters, I always stress that the Wa are not completely responsible, but they never pay much attention to this point.[34]

However, Luo Xinghan, the "King of Opium" whom I interviewed in Rangoon in 2002, disagreed with Chartchai Suthiklom's statement: "To say that the Kokang is responsible for 40 percent of the yaba smuggled onto Thai soil is an overestimation. I will say the Wa are responsible for at least 70 percent and maybe up to 80 percent. The Kokang yaba does not have a good reputation; the Wa yaba is considered to be the better yaba because the Wa chemists are better than the Kokang."[35]

Interestingly, a Chinese businesswoman in Mae Sai thought that the Wa are responsible for only one-third of the yaba trade:

Out of one hundred pills produced in the Golden Triangle, ninety are from Burma. Of the ninety pills from Burma, the Wa produce thirty. However, because the Wa were the very first people to get into this business, and their pills are still considered to be of the best quality, most producers simply say that their pills are Wa pills. The Wa pills became, in a sense, name brand. There are other people who are also involved in speed pill production, including the Kokangnese, the Yunnanese, and the Burmese. Some individuals here in Thailand are also involved in producing the pills but most of their operations are small scale because it is impossible for Thai people to produce the pills in a large scale due to police crackdown.[36]

Again, as pointed out in the previous chapter on the heroin trade, it is not always easy to be exact about which area is responsible for what in the drug trade in the Shan State because people in the various areas or special regions are tightly linked and very often are involved in the drug trade as partners or maintain business relationships.

The Wa Leaders' Perspective

The Wa leaders have admitted that for a few years in the mid-1990s they allowed businessmen from outside to come to the Wa area and set up methamphetamine factories, and that they collected taxes from these producers. But they are adamant that this is no longer permitted. When asked why the Wa leaders once let outsiders produce speed pills in their area, a Wa official said,

> we did not have the precursor chemicals or the technical know-how to produce speed pills. The chemicals were imported from China and India and the techniques were transplanted here from Thailand. Speed pills were originally produced in Thailand; at that time the precursor chemicals were transported into Thailand via the Wa State. We stood to make some money from this arrangement, but someone suggested that we produce the pills ourselves here in the Wa State. That way, we could make more money. That's why we allowed businessmen from other places to come here to set up methamphetamine factories. At that time, we were not aware that our decision might have a major impact on our society [the spread of methamphetamine use among young people and soldiers in the Wa area]. At any rate, there are always pros and cons to a decision.[37]

Another Wa leader, however, suggested that there was never a decision made to allow people to set up speed pill factories. Instead, the "decision" was simply a reaction to the reality at that time: "The taxing of methamphetamine factories was not predetermined; we taxed the owners of these factories only after we discovered that they were already in existence and there was not much that we could do about it. We did not have a meeting and decide that we were going to allow them to establish drug factories here."[38]

To the Wa leaders who are tolerant of speed pill production, this Wa leader said,

> some of the leaders here are ignorant of the impact of methamphetamine use. They think that the influx of methamphetamines here is not really a big deal. They believe that this drug is not addictive and that it could actually help users remain awake and productive when necessary. Bao Youxiang once told these leaders that he was going to give them methamphetamines so that they could go and kill themselves by getting addicted to the drug.[39]

In the Wa area, methamphetamine tablets are called *mahuangsu* (the Chinese word for ephedrine) or *mayao* (ephedrine medicine). Regardless of what the Wa leaders had to say about the prohibition of methamphetamine production in their territory after 1999, my fieldwork and interviews in Bangkang suggested that the meth business was still the most lucrative trade in the Wa area in 2001.

Methamphetamine Distribution in Thailand

The main market for methamphetamine produced in Burma is Thailand (Greenfeld 2001).[40] In 1989, methamphetamine made its first recorded appearance in the Thai market and its production had exploded by 1993. By 2004, the Office of Narcotics Control Board, the Thai drug enforcement agency, projected that about eight hundred million speed pills were trafficked into Thailand from Burma. ONCB Deputy Secretary-General Chartchai Suthiklom explained how his agency conducted the estimation:

We estimate the amount of yaba smuggled into Thailand this way: first, we estimate the number of users, multiply it with an average of two tablets per day, and then multiply the amount of tablets with the number of days in a year. That's how we got our prediction of eight hundred million tablets a year being smuggled into Thailand. The estimated amount has increased from a low of a few million per year to eight hundred million now.[41]

After the pills are manufactured in the Wa area, they will be transported to either Tachilek or Mong Yawn (a Wa town in Southern Wa State situated not far from Mae Ai, Thailand) to be smuggled across the border into Thailand. Similar to the pattern with heroin trafficking, many Chinese and hill people living along the rugged border area of northern Thailand are actively involved in the transportation of methamphetamine. For example, Mr. Lee, the man who first introduced me to the Wa leaders, told me that

all sorts of people in northern Thailand are involved in the meth trade. There are more than thirty ethnic groups there and many of them are poor hill people. A person can easily carry about 160,000 speed pills. A drug trafficker might approach someone from a hill tribe and say that if you transport 160,000 pills across the border, I will pay you 1 baht (less than three cents) per pill. Think of it! That person may never, ever in his or her wildest dreams ever get to own 160,000 baht [$4,300]. Of course, when the opportunity comes, the person is going to take advantage of it. He may even recruit his wife, children, parents, and even grandparents to participate in the trade. Most of the people who transport the drug from Burma into Thailand are not Wa people.[42]

According to a businesswoman in Mae Sai, the person who approaches a hill person is more likely to be a middleman rather than the producer:

Most of the time, a producer will find someone to help him smuggle the pills. Let's say a producer had one million pills to be smuggled into Thailand. He will find someone to help him and that someone will find someone else for assistance. The producer will pay the middleman 2 baht [a little more than five cents] per pill, and the middleman will pay the courier 1 baht per pill.[43] Most of the time, the authorities only catch the couriers, not the second and third tier of traffickers.[44]

Unlike heroin, which passes through Thailand on its way to foreign destinations, meth pills are smuggled into Thailand for local consumption. Not only are there countless people involved in drug dealing in Thailand as a result of the meth epidemic but there many thousands more, many of them professionals and students unlikely to be attracted to heroin, who use meth or yaba (Pathan 2005). Because of this, the Thai government's relationship with the Burmese regime, and especially the Wa, began to deteriorate in the late 1990s as millions of speed pills continued to flow into Thailand. Not only was there a dramatic increase in the number of border skirmishes between the Thai and Burmese/Wa forces but by 2001 the Thai authorities had also begun to crack down on speed pill traffickers and dealers.

Many Chinese villages and hill tribe villages (the Ahka, the Lisu, the Lahu, and the Yao in particular) in northern Thailand were used as warehouses for speed pills destined for southern Thailand. Hill tribe people were hired to carry tens of thousands of speed pills across the border, and headmen of these villages were also often recruited by drug traffickers to be the middlemen between drug producers in Burma and key buyers in Bangkok. A subject from a Chinese village at the Thai-Burma border area said,

Our village head was involved in the meth business. He was a middleman for the Wa. He used to live in a big house, but after he was almost killed by a group of would-be assassins, he fled, and nobody knows where he is now. He is a Yunnanese Chinese, and after he fled, his drug operation collapsed. He had been ambushed by a group of gunmen armed with M-16 rifles, as he was on his way home. Some of his family members were killed in the attack. After he escaped, Thai authorities confiscated all his cars and houses.[45]

Another subject from the border area explained how the Thai authorities normally figure out which village head is involved in the drug trade:

Most producers and traffickers try to find a village head to assist them because these chiefs are the most powerful figures in the hill villages. But when a village head would start driving a brand new car with money from the speed trade, that's when the Thai authorities would notice him and conclude that the village head was involved in the speed business. Otherwise, how could he afford a new car that cost 700,000 baht [$18,000]?[46]

Many Chinese villages along the border are populated by the offspring of the KMT soldiers who were once active in the opium trade and by the Yunnanese Chinese from Burma who arrived in the early 1990s. According to a resident of one of those villages, people were well aware that their village had a reputation as being a center of the drug trade, and they had a good idea who was involved in the trade. He said people often came to the village to discuss drug deals.

Besides the Yunnanese Chinese and the hill tribe people, powerful Thai politicians and law enforcement officials are also alleged to be behind the speed business either as operators or as protectors (Chouvy and Meissonnier 2004). For example, a subject from Mae Sai said,

Just recently, a high-ranking politician was arrested near Mae Sai for smuggling millions of speed pills. His Cherokee jeep was stopped at the outskirts of Mae Sai as he was heading for Chiang Rai. He flashed his ID and said he was in a hurry. However, the police setting up the roadblock had already been tipped off and they would not permit the politician to drive off. They searched his car and found millions of speed pills. The police officers told the politician that they would let him go if he could come up with 3 million baht [$79,000] in cash. The politician called a village head to bail him out. The village head and his followers arrived with the cash after frantically raising the money, and the police arrested them all and confiscated the money and their cars. That's how the police cleverly rounded up the other conspirators. Eventually, the politician was sentenced to death and executed.[47]

Tachilek and Mae Sai: The Trade Centers of Methamphetamine

Tachilek, a town in the Shan State, is located across from Mae Sai, Thailand; the two towns are separated by the Mae Sai River. The river is so tiny that people can swim across it in certain parts. A large number of street vendors in Tachilek go to Mae Sai every day to sell their goods in the streets and many businesspeople in Mae Sai cross the border into Tachilek to deliver their products or work on large-scale construction projects. Tachilek is Burma's major trading post because most consumer goods from abroad are transported into Burma via Tachilek. For the Thai government, the border trade between Mae Sai and Tachilek is important for the well-being of the Thai economy, especially after the country was hit hard by the financial crisis of Southeast Asia in 1998.

As legitimate business activities between Tachilek and Mae Sai began to flourish in the 1990s, the cross-border methamphetamine trade also began to develop. According to the 2002 report of the Office of Narcotics Control Board of Thailand, the Mae Sai area became the region's largest smuggling point for methamphetamine. Meth tablets produced in Muse, Kokang, Wa, and other parts of the Shan State were transported to Tachilek to be smuggled into Thailand. Moreover, meth factories were established near Tachilek to avoid transporting the pills through Burmese-controlled territories. One subject told me that there are about nine yaba factories in Tachilek: five belong to the Wa and four are non-Wa. Thai authorities know where the factories are located, but without the cooperation of the Burmese authorities the Thai authorities cannot do anything about these factories.

A subject in Mae Sai characterized the drug business in Tachilek this way:

There are many people in Tachilek who got extremely rich over the past three years because of the speed business. Then they came to Mae Sai to buy houses. I know where their money is from, but because I am a real estate agent, I only care whether they have the money to buy my houses. My company developed a whole area in the suburbs of Mae Sai where the houses are mostly sold to foreigners (from Taiwan, Hong Kong, Malaysia, Singapore) for their mistresses. Some of the houses were bought by people from Tachilek. One of the

Tachilek buyers bought a 1.2 million baht [$32,000] house and said, "Can I give you 500,000 baht [$13,500] in cash and the other 700,000 baht [$18,500] in speed pills?" I said no. When the bridge over the Mae Sai River was closed in 2001 due to clashes between Thai and Burmese troops, the Thai authorities came to search some of the houses we sold. They told me, "You are selling houses to people who are involved in the speed business. Your firm is a construction company fueled by drug money." Some government officials warned me not to get too close to certain customers because they are suspected drug dealers.[48]

The same subject continued to explain how the drug business is conducted and the risks associated with it:

When I was with them, they always talked about their drug business, something like the *huo* [commodity] just arrived and they needed to go pick it up. Once a delivery arrived, the drug would be distributed to four or five middlemen. People in Tachilek got the drug on credit and did not have to pay the money collectors for three months.[Usually, producers in the Wa area would give the middlemen in Tachilek a three-month credit]. If, for some reason, the authorities seized the middleman's drugs, there was always suspicion. Did the deal really go wrong or was the middleman making up the story to avoid paying for the drugs?[49]

Yaba producers and traffickers on the Burmese side must rely on people on the Thai side not only to help transport the pills into Thailand but to distribute them as well. A long-time Mae Sai resident explained how a friend living in the Wa area once tried to recruit him into the meth business:

A good friend from Yingpan [in Northern Wa State] came to visit me in Mae Sai and after seeing that I was living a modest life, asked me whether I would be willing to sell speed pills for him. He said no start-up money was needed and that the drug would be delivered to Mae Sai; all I needed to do was to find buyers here. I told him that I didn't want to have anything to do with drugs. When he brought up the idea a second time, I said, "Well, let's say I need money and I want to be involved. But I don't want to be in it for a long time because you never know when you are going to run out of luck. You may make millions of baht after a few successful deals, but if you get caught in the next deal, whatever you made before could be lost overnight. Could I just do it once and make some money and quit?" My friend listened to me intently, but did not utter a word and never brought up the idea again. I guess once you are in, there's no way out in this business. Many people here are killed when they try to get out. Hired gunmen are sent to kill you—to keep you quiet.[50]

But, unlike the above subject, many Mae Sai residents, especially those who were already involved in the heroin trade, could not resist the temptation of the lucrative meth trade and became key players in the process of moving yaba from northeastern Burma to Bangkok, the final destination for the majority of the tablets. Meth tablets are normally transported to Bangkok from northern Thailand by car instead of by air because, according to a subject in Mae Sai,[51] "it is a lot more risky by air. With cars, unless the authorities are tipped off, it is highly unlikely the pills would be detected."[52]

Were the Wa Leaders Responsible?

Methamphetamine production in the Wa area began in the mid-1990s because the market was lucrative, production costs were low, and the manufacturing process was less complicated than converting opium into heroin. Ephedrine, the main ingredient used in the production of methamphetamine, was readily available from sources in China and India. The finished methamphetamine tablets were primarily destined for the Thai market, and their manufacture provided a golden opportunity for leaders in the Wa and the Kokang areas to achieve three important goals at the same time: generate a large sum of money for infrastructure projects, gradually decrease their reliance on opium in response to the enormous international pressure to ban opium cultivation, and placate the Chinese government by reducing the amount of heroin entering China.

As indicated by some of the Wa leaders I interviewed, the arrival of a group of "businessmen" from Thailand and China in Bangkang in the mid-1990s was the turning point in the shift from heroin to methamphetamine production in the Wa area. After methamphetamine production was legalized and taxed by the Wa authorities in 1996, it was inconceivable for powerful leaders (and their families) not to take advantage of the opportunity to benefit themselves to the fullest extent by joining businessmen from abroad as partners. As long as their meth factories were paying the Wa government the so-called *jiagongfei* (manufacturing fee), their involvement in the drug business was considered perfectly legal and perhaps expected.

To what extent were the Wa culpable for the meth epidemic? Should the Wa be fully responsible for the hundreds of millions of speed pills being smuggled into Thailand from Burma every year? Certain reporters from the West have characterized the "Wa tribe" as Asia's most dangerous drug cartel and the United Wa State Army soldiers as the "world's most heavily armed narco-traffickers" (Marshall and Davis 2002). On the other hand, sympathizers of the Wa argued that their leaders and, especially, the Wa in general were unfairly blamed for the yaba trade, which was actually dominated by international crime syndicates made up of ethnic Chinese. According to Jeremy Milsom (2005, 76–77), the UNDCP's representative in the Wa State,

> Media reports have regularly attributed 80 percent of ATS [amphetamine-type stimulant] traffic to the Wa. Such accounts are misleading and display a general ignorance of the nature of this trade. The manufacture and trafficking of ATS is undertaken by many small criminal groups, most of whom are linked ultimately to transnational crime syndicates and trafficking networks that operate across Asia. The raw materials, equipment, and expertise for this trade must be brought into Burma, where the complex economic and ethnic factors, and comparatively weaker law enforcement capacity make it easy to produce and conceal. It quickly replaced heroin in many areas and was an easy way for local groups and militias to make money in the same manner as they had in the past with opium and heroin. . . . ATS production and trafficking is a commercial criminal activity linked to greed that is driven by transnational criminal syndicates that operate across Asia and for whom borders are relatively meaningless. Putting the bulk of the blame onto the ethnic Wa has detracted from a more balanced understanding of the industry as a whole and has led to misguided efforts to curb it. The vast majority of ethnic Wa are poor hill farmers and as such do not profit from ATS production.

A high-ranking Burmese narcotics official also suggested that the majority of the ATS producers are ethnic Chinese and that most drug syndicates are made up of Chinese (Kramer 2005). A Wa leader explained how and why the Wa are exploited by ethnic Chinese from China and Kokang, the key players in the yaba trade:

> Let me tell you what I think about this drug business. The people in the Wa area, including ethnic Wa and ethnic Chinese who were born in the Wa area or live here for a long time, are easy to control and they will take our orders seriously. It's those Chinese from mainland China and people from Kokang who come to our area and get involved in the drug business. People in the Wa area may receive some money from these outside drug dealers, but it is the Wa who will be blamed by the world community. People in the Wa area are easy to exploit, and they do not know that the small amount of money they receive from the drug dealers entails a huge sacrifice [a bad reputation].[53]

To fully answer the question of who should be primarily responsible for the booming methamphetamine trade in Southeast Asia, we need to understand the different roles a person can play in the trade:

1. Precursor chemical and machine importer/trafficker: This person is responsible for locating and transporting precursor chemicals (mainly ephedrine) and machines from China or India into Burma.

2. Organizer/investor/producer: This person is the one who initiates the process, invests money in the business, and oversees the whole operation.

3. Protector/partner: This person functions as someone whom the above person can go to for protection. This person often not only provides sanctuary and a factory location for the producer but also invests a certain amount of money in the operation so that he or she will have a stake at the business.

4. Transporter: This person is responsible for the movement of the pills from the factories inside the Wa and the Kokang territories to the Thai-Burma border area. If the pills are transported from the Northern Wa area (as opposed to the Southern Wa area) and Kokang, they must go through areas controlled by the Burmese authorities.

5. Wholesaler in Burma: This person is the one who buys and sells speed pills on a wholesale level on the Burmese side.

6. Trafficker: This person is in charge of the movement of speed pills across the Thai-Burma border area. He or she is not directly involved in the transportation of the pills.

7. Courier: This person carries the yaba across the border.

8. Distributor in Thailand: This person is responsible for the distribution of the speed pills on a wholesale level inside Thailand.

9. Retailer: This person is the one who sell the pills to the users. Retailing is carried out both in Burma and Thailand.

The majority of the Wa people living in the remote mountainside villages are highly unlikely to play any roles in the yaba trade. Ordinary Wa people living in the major Wa towns like Bangkang or Nandeng are also unlikely to be involved because they have nothing to contribute to the trade. Of course, Wa officials, regardless of whether they are Wa or Chinese, could play the role of protector/partner and their families or relatives could be the organizer/investor/producer. Other roles associated with the production sites are dominated by Chinese from China and roles near the consuming markets are associated with Thai, Chinese, or certain hill tribes in Thailand. I think there are good reasons for us not to blame only the Wa for the yaba epidemic. However, it is also true that Wa leaders and their families and relatives are not as innocent as they or certain observers would like us to believe.

Wei Xuegang is considered by Western authorities to be the king of methamphetamine in the Golden Triangle and was indicted by a U.S. federal court in 2005 for heroin and methamphetamine production and trafficking. However, in the Wa area, and especially among the leaders in Bangkang, Wei is viewed as the most generous of persons when it comes to donating money to build schools, roads, and other major infrastructure projects. Many people I interviewed told me that Bao Youxiang relied heavily on Wei Xuegang to finance the many ambitious public works projects the Wa Central Authority implemented throughout the Wa State in the late 1990s and early 2000s. Wei is undoubtedly a good example of a state builder who generates large sums of money from the drug trade while simultaneously contributing enormously to the development of the Wa State. Of course, for Wei (and for many other Wa leaders) this dual role of being a drug kingpin and a state builder is probably performed out of necessity rather than out of pure benevolence. Donating money to the Wa cause is a prerequisite to being considered a good Wa leader and therefore worthy of the opportunities to join in the many money-generating activities.

Chapter Six

Drug Use

Most articles and books on the drug trade in the Golden Triangle have focused on the cultivation of opium and the production of heroin and methamphetamine for the world market, and have paid little attention to the negative impact of these drugs on the local population. In this chapter, I will discuss the problem of opium, heroin, and methamphetamine use in the Wa State, Burma, Thailand, and China. Data for this chapter came from my fieldwork in the Wa State, Rangoon, northern Thailand, and the Yunnan Province of China. When discussing the social processes and patterns of drug use in the region, I will rely heavily on interviewers with fifty-two drug users in the Wa area and twenty-five heroin users in Kunming City in Yunnan Province. The interviews were conducted with the aid of two standardized questionnaires, one for the drug users in the Wa area and one for heroin users in Kunming.

The Wa State

Opium

There are no reliable statistics about the extent of opium use in the Wa State. The Wa authorities do not systematically collect this type of information and opium users are reluctant to identify themselves as such because of the stigma attached to being a drug user and also the possibility of being penalized by the authorities.[1] According to the Wa Basic Law, if an opium smoker is under fifty, he or she has to enroll in a drug detoxification program for three years. That means that the individual will be forced into confinement in a prisonlike compound for three years. An opium user who is fifty to sixty years old is required to quit within a time limit set by the local authorities and failure to do so means enrollment in a forced detoxification program. An opium smoker above the age of sixty is left alone by the authorities.

In an interview in 2001, a public health official with the Wa government told me that "about fifteen years ago, there were twenty thousand to thirty thousand opium smokers in the Wa area. Over the past ten years, about ten thousand people were arrested for smoking opium and approximately four thousand quit. Now there are only about ten thousand opium smokers. We began to arrest young opium smokers in 1989."[2]

In the interviews with three hundred opium growers, we asked them whether they used opium; only twenty-four (8 percent) said they smoked opium. This figure may not be reliable because we are certain that some subjects denied their opium use out of shame or fear. The United Nations 2005 opium survey in Burma indicated that the average level of opium addiction in the Wa area was only 0.83 percent (United Nations Office on Drugs and Crime 2005a), an estimate the UN believed is highly unreliable. According to the data I collected, opium growers living some distance from the border area with China (i.e., Nankangwu, Denge, Yingpan, Hedao) were more likely to admit smoking opium than those who lived close to China (i.e., Longtan, Nandeng, Shaopa, Aicheng). In fact, none of the subjects interviewed in the border area with China said they smoked opium. The twenty-four subjects who said they smoked opium were predominantly married Wa males in their fifties. Most of them said they smoked opium once or twice a day.

INITIATION INTO OPIUM USE

In addition to questioning opium growers in the hilltop villages about their opium use, we also interviewed twenty-five opium users in Bangkang. In the face-to-face interviews conducted using a standardized questionnaire, we asked the subjects about their backgrounds, their initiation into opium use, their patterns of use, and the impact of opium use. The twenty-five opium users interviewed in Bangkang were mostly Wa males in their forties or fifties, married, unemployed, and had no or very little education.

Many opium users told us that the main reason for their initiation into opium use was to cure illness, as a forty-year-old Wa woman, married with five children, explained:

> At one point, I was afflicted with a very serious and strange disease and the pain was unbearable. I wanted to die. My whole body, from head to toe, felt like it was on fire. I went to China for treatment, but the doctors there said I was dying and told my family to just take me home. My mother explored all kinds of ways to cure my illness, but to no avail. Eventually, she prepared some opium and told me to smoke it. I did and I felt much better after that.[3]

Other subjects said they began to smoke opium because they were not happy. According to a sixty-nine-year-old Wa widow with six children,

> I had been a widow for two years. My eldest daughter was taken advantage of by a man who promised to marry her. He took her to Bangkang, but then married another woman. After that incident, I felt like I had lost all face. That, and my husband had died. I was very unhappy. One day a friend of mine invited me to smoke opium with her. I did; that was the first time.[4]

Other subjects began to use opium simply because their friends or neighbors were smoking and when they were asked to give it a try, they did. A fifty-two-year-old Lahu man noted: "One day, I was visiting my friend and I saw him smoking opium. He said it is fantastic and told me to try it. When he said that, I was very much tempted and I smoked it for the first time."[5]

My subjects reacted differently to opium after they smoked it for the first time. One subject, the woman who said she tried opium because she felt bad after her daughter was deceived by a man, stated: "After I had a couple of puffs, I felt very good. My body began to float; it was a wonderful feeling. Right then, I decided I am going to keep on smoking. I forgot all my troubles."[6] Others did not feel good after they first tried opium. "I did not feel very well after my first and second puff," a male opium user said. "The smell was awful and it made me dizzy. I could not eat. I did not want to continue, but because I was sick and my doctor insisted that I should continue smoking, I had no choice but to keep on smoking."[7]

OPIUM ADDICTION

At the time of the interviews, my subjects had been using opium for an average of sixteen years (see table 9). Regardless of how they reacted after they tried it for the first time, most smoked it again within one to five days. Most thought that they had become addicted to opium within one year after initial use, although a few said that they were hooked a few days after their first experience with opium. The woman who was sick with a serious and strange disease said she felt she was addicted to opium after three months of continual use: "After I recovered from my illness, I went back to work in the field again. When I stopped smoking, I felt very uncomfortable. Sometimes I felt hot; sometimes I felt cold. I also lost my appetite. When that happened to me, I was very concerned. So I went around and asked people about this, and they told me I was addicted to opium."[8] A twenty-four-year-old Wa male who began to smoke opium with his friends out of boredom believed he was addicted to opium five months after initial use:

One day, all of a sudden I got cold, then feverishly hot. It felt like there were ants crawling all over my body. The symptoms were similar to flu. I took some medicine, but it did not help. After five hours, the quilt was damp from my sweat. I had a runny nose and teary eyes. People said: "Maybe that 'dry cow shit' [opium] is causing this!" They then prepared some opium for me. Right after I took a few puffs, I felt better, and an hour later I was completely back to normal. That was when I knew I was addicted.[9]

It took other subjects longer to become addicted to opium. A forty-six-year-old Wa officer who began to smoke opium when he was working in the countryside, and was often offered opium by villagers as a sign of respect, said he realized he was hooked only after smoking it for two years: "After I came back to the military base from the hills, I had no strength at all. I was thirsty, but drinking water did not help me. After I ate something, I felt sick. I ran to a local person's home and asked for a little opium to smoke. I just laced the opium on top of a cigarette and smoked it. After I had done that, I felt all right and my mind became clear."[10] The woman whose daughter made her lose "face" and caused her to smoke opium said she felt addicted about four years after her initial use, a significant departure from the two subjects cited above: "Later, I was thinking about opium all the time, and felt like I can't live without opium. If I did not smoke, I couldn't open my eyes or get out of bed. Then I realized that I was

Table 9. Characteristics of Opium Use in the Wa Area

	Mean	Mode	Median	Minimum	Maximum
Length of use (in years)	16	20	10	2	53
Subsequent use after first use (in days)	58	1	5	1	360
Addiction after first use (in days)	539	360	360	1	2,520
Number of times smoked per day	2.8	3	3	1	5
Amount of opium consumed monthly (in *qie*)[a]	30	20	15	1	330
Monthly expense for opium (in US$)	81	24	24	1	487

Note: N=25
[a]100 *qie* = 10 *kang* = 1 *joi* or viss

hooked on opium."[11] One subject said he was addicted to opium only after seven years of use. However, our data suggests that opium users in the Wa area are most likely to be addicted within a year of their initial use (see table 9).

KICKING THE HABIT

At the time of the interviews, most subjects were smoking about three times a day. On average, each smoker consumed about 30 *qie* (equivalent to 3 *kang* or .3 *joi* or viss) a month. Because these users lived in the town of Bangkang and had no access to farmers' opium, most of them had to rely on local opium retailers for their supply. According to my subjects, it cost them an average of 668 yuan ($81) per month to support their habit, a formidable amount of money for most people in the Wa area (see table 9).

Most of my subjects wanted to kick the habit because it was expensive, and because family members disapproved of it. Of the twenty-five opium users we interviewed, half of them had tried to stop and the other half said they had not. Of the ones who tried, they either did so voluntarily or were forced to by the authorities. Regardless, the process of quitting was never easy. The fifty-two-year-old Lahu man who picked up the habit after being associated with an opium-smoking neighbor remembered how he tried and failed to stop smoking opium on his own:

> I did that for my wife and children, and for my family's economic well-being. We are a poor family because we do not know how to conduct business. I was afraid that if I kept smoking, one day we might have to beg to survive, so I wanted to quit. To do so, I began to eat a lot. I also spent most of my time working in the field and staying away from home. Sometimes, I even slept in the field. I tried my best not to go home, nor visit the friends who smoked opium. At the end, I failed. Without opium, I had no strength to work and my whole body ached. I went home and started smoking again because I could not bear it anymore.[12]

A young widower who began to smoke opium after her husband died described how she stopped for seven years and then relapsed:

> After my husband died, I wasn't making any money. My children were still small, and nobody could take care of them. My parents did not live with us. I wanted to quit opium for my children. When I went to the hills to cut firewood, I threw away all my opium-smoking utensils. After I sold the firewood in the market, I bought some meat and rice, so that I could regain my health by eating well. I kicked the habit for seven years; my children grew up and I did not have to worry about them anymore and, as a result, I started to smoke again. That's because whenever I thought of my husband, I always cried and felt very sad. Smoking opium helped me to forget all my problems and gave me happiness.[13]

Other subjects began to kick the opium habit because they were forced to do so. An army officer recalled:

> The authorities told me to enroll in a drug treatment program. According to them, if I did not go, I would be locked up for two months and ten days. Actually, I gave up using opium by myself. The authorities just gave me a time frame to control myself. They did not

give me any medications. I just went cold turkey and endured the pains for ten full days. Eventually, I quit. If you abstain from opium for seven days, you are considered to have quit it. After I did, I realized smoking opium is not a good thing to do. However, when I was smoking, all I thought about was opium.[14]

Some opium smokers were actually detained by the Wa authorities and forced to quit. A forty-year-old Wa man, who began to smoke opium after his two sons died abruptly, explained how he was forced to stop:

For several years now, the Wa government has not allowed people to smoke opium, so they sent someone to tell me that if I did not quit, I would be locked up. In the end, I was jailed for five months. While I was imprisoned and deprived of the drug, my whole body hurt; it felt like the pain had penetrated into my bones. I did not take any medication. After one month, I regained my health. My mood also changed for the better. I realized I had let my family down. Eventually, I quit. I don't want to be locked up again. I want to be a good person for the rest of my life, and I will not use any drug anymore.[15]

THE IMPACT OF OPIUM USE

Opium users in Bangkang were asked to reflect how opium smoking had changed their psychological, physical, and economic well-being. Some had ambivalent feelings about smoking opium, including a forty-year-old Wa woman who smoked opium to deal with a painful illness: "When I was young and healthy, I was a beautiful, attractive woman. After I became addicted to opium, I looked like a piece of rotten wood. I admit that, without opium to ease the pain, I might have died many years ago. Though I did not accomplish anything in my life, at least I am still living to nurture my children."[16]

Most subjects, however, thought that their lives, even the lives of their loved ones, were shattered by their opium dependency. A sixty-one-year-old Wa man who picked up the habit from his friends commented that "opium ruined my life. Because I was an addict, my wife committed suicide by taking rat poison. My children are not living with me; they stay with relatives rather than stay with me. I live alone right now."[17] Other subjects felt that opium had completely destroyed their minds and bodies. A forty-six-year-old Wa army officer noted that "opium has completely affected my body. My wisdom, intelligence, analytical ability, and communication skills were all taken away by opium. If I was sick, I would smoke opium first instead of visiting a doctor. Opium has become an important part of my life and controlled my world and my imagination."[18] One subject summed it up succinctly by saying that opium "sucked my blood, ate my flesh, made me miserable, and separated my beloved ones from me."[19]

Other subjects thought that the negative physical impact was a trade-off for the positive psychological effect, including a forty-three-year-old Wa woman, married with four children: "Smoking opium affects my health in a negative way, but it also keeps me in a good mood. I am addicted to it and if I don't smoke for even one day, I will yell at my husband and children for no reason. If I smoke every day, I will feel very good, even though I am losing weight day after day. At this point, I don't care about anything, I am just hanging in there."[20] Another subject, a fifty-year-old widowed female who followed her parents' footsteps by trying to use opium to cure her illnesses, said, "If I don't smoke opium, I become very uncomfortable and tired. I also lose my appetite and the desire to work. Smoking opium did affect me. I have smoked opium for a long time, and I feel that it is not good for my health. I am addicted, and it is very hard for me to stop."[21]

Some subjects stated that they were very fond of their opium-smoking experience. A sixty-nine-year-old Wa woman, who began using opium after her husband died and her daughter was exploited by a con artist, did not hesitate to say how much she enjoyed the drug: "I believe smoking opium does not have any negative affect on my health. Actually, it makes me happy. To me, opium is good stuff. It not only cures diseases, but also helps me to forget all my troubles. I really like opium."[22] However, the impact of her opium habit on her, her children, and grandchildren was hard to ignore, according to the interviewer who spoke to her:

Her clothes were all worn out and extremely dirty. She was thin, unkempt, and smelled bad. It seemed as though she had not had a shower for months. When I interviewed her, she was answering my questions while smoking opium; she was in a good mood. She was in bed, lying on an old, dirty blanket. Beside her was her eight-month-old grandson. The baby boy was sweating and coughing while inhaling his grandma's opium smoke. I felt really bad for the baby. But what can you do? There's nobody else to take care of the baby.[23]

According to my subjects, the impact of opium use on one's family relationship and family financial status was unequivocally negative. Almost all my subjects said their relationships with their spouses and children deteriorated, they were ridiculed by friends and neighbors, and the financial well-being of their families was seriously compromised because of their opium habit.

Heroin

In the Wa State, most people either smoke opium (mainly farmers in their forties or older) or methamphetamine (mostly young people living in towns or serving in the army). As a result, we were not very successful in finding heroin users to participate in our study. Of the fifty-two drug users we interviewed in Bangkang, only two were heroin users. The first subject was a thirty-year-old Wa man who was born in Cangyuan County, Yunnan Province, China.[24] The single man had no formal education or a steady job. He said he began to smoke heroin when he was a twenty years old and living in Kokang and was wrongly accused of thievery—when people questioned his innocence, he was devastated. He had been smoking heroin for a while when a friend told him to inject the drug instead because it would have more of an impact. According to the subject, "After I injected it a few times, I felt like it could get rid of all my troubles and unhappiness. After that, I just kept on injecting the drug."[25] He said he kicked the habit for two years, but relapsed after he ran into troubles he could not solve.

The second subject was also a young Wa male in his twenties who had smoked heroin for three years. He said he began to smoke heroin while he was working in a ruby mine; the first time he tried it was with his colleagues. He did so because he was not finding any rubies and he was frustrated. After smoking heroin for a month, he knew he was addicted because he could not concentrate on his work and did not have the energy to do anything unless he smoked some heroin. He kicked the habit a couple of times, but relapsed when his father died and when he was in a car accident and a number of friends were killed.[26]

Both subjects said they also smoked methamphetamine occasionally, but their primary drug was heroin. They thought methamphetamine smoking was not good for their physical well-being but heroin gave them a very pleasant feeling.

While I was in Bangkang, I also heard that people from China who came to Bangkang to work or do business were often involved in heroin use because of its availability. A key informant from Lancang who had been doing business in Bangkang for several years told me that "there are not very many heroin users in the Wa Hills. Most of them are here in Bangkang. Heroin users in Bangkang are mostly from China because it is cheaper and easier to find here. However, this is a small town and users could be arrested and locked up in those horrible jails. That is why the users maintain a very low profile."[27] The same informant described how his brother-in-law had died a few years ago of a drug overdose:

> I asked my brother-in-law to move to Bangkang because he had nothing going on for him in Lancang, China. Not long after he arrived in Bangkang, he was injecting heroin. I believe he started it in Lancang, but the problem got worse after he came here. After I found out about it, I sent him back to Langcang because at least it is a little more difficult to find the drug there. One day, my wife, who was living in Lancang, called me and said that her brother had passed out in his bathroom and was being taken to a hospital. I rushed to Lancang [about two hours' drive from Bangkang]. By the time I got to the hospital, he was dead. He was only twenty-one when he died.[28]

Heroin use is probably a more serious problem in China than in the Wa State. I will discuss the problem of heroin use in China later in this chapter.

Methamphetamine

Most people I talked to in Bangkang believed that methamphetamine use among young people, especially by students and soldiers, was rampant in the Wa area. One of my interviewers observed that teenagers in Bangkang, some of them as young as thirteen or fourteen, were smoking speed pills. Another interviewer commented that many students in Zhenxing Middle School, the highest and best education institution in the Wa area, were smoking methamphetamine. According to both interviewers, a Wa leader once made a speech on TV that left a long-lasting impression on the Wa people because of his somewhat dramatic characterization of the problem. The interviewers characterized the leader's words as follows:

> What the hell are you people at the *zhengfabu* [Political Legal Bureau, the unit that was responsible for maintaining law and order] doing? You guys see those methamphetamine dealers walking back and forth in front of you and you do nothing! You guys not only won't arrest them, when they ask you to smoke the tablets along with

them, you do. In the past, when we went to a friend's home, the friend gave us tea and cigarettes; now the friend gives us methamphetamine tablets. When you see elderly people walk by carrying a bag, don't assume that they have money in their bag. It is a water bottle [a water bottle is needed to smoke the tablets]. When you see students with their schoolbags, don't imagine they have books in their bags; they have water bottles.[29]

In the hotel where I stayed, I saw young people or truck drivers smoking speed pills inside their rooms. At one point, I asked a young woman to show me the process of preparing and smoking the tablets and she did. The woman brought out the following items from her bag: a water bottle, a knife, a lighter, a candle, a toothpick, a piece of tinfoil, a straw, a damp facial tissue, and several tablets. She opened the water bottle and poured out half the water. She then made a hole above the water line in the water bottle and inserted the straw into the bottle. One side of the straw was underneath the water and the other side was sticking out of the bottle. She also cut a hole in the bottle cap with the knife. She then put the damp facial tissue on top of the bottle mouth and put the cap back. She then put two tablets on top of a piece of tinfoil and held it underneath the straw's mouth. She also stuck a piece of the toothpick into the mouth of the lighter so that the flame coming out of the lighter was compressed and concentrated. She then held the lighter underneath the tinfoil and put her mouth on the bottle cap. When the flame was burning underneath, the two tablets started to jump around and melt as the smoke came out. The woman then inhaled the smoke that went through the straw, into the water, and then was filtered through the wet facial tissue. The candle was used to light the lighter so that there would be no sound when striking the lighter, presumably to avoid detection by the authorities.

According to the woman who showed me how to smoke methamphetamine,

> I asked a friend of mine to go buy the tablets and he came back with twelve tablets. I gave him 30 yuan [$3.60], but he bought only 20 yuan [$2.40] worth of speed pills. I know, because you can get twelve pills for 20 yuan here. There are many brand names for these tablets, like Double Dragons, OK, Five Sisters, Four Sisters, etc. The tablets from Kokang are considered to be of inferior quality because they can cause the user to go crazy. Besides, Kokang tablets are more addictive; a person who uses the pills from Kokang has an insatiable

desire for more. Normally, a user smokes two or three pills at a time, but heavy users may consume up to eight pills in one shot. Users have the urge to use the tablets whenever they see a water bottle and, especially, a lighter.[30]

The twenty-five methamphetamine users interviewed were significantly different from the twenty-five opium users interviewed in terms of age, marital status, education, and ethnicity. The meth users we interviewed were mostly young, single, better educated Chinese.

INITIATION INTO METHAMPHETAMINE USE

Reasons for initiation into methamphetamine use were relatively similar to opium use. Some of my subjects said they started to smoke methamphetamine because they were with their friends and having a good time and smoking methamphetamine occurred spontaneously. Others stated that they tried it for the first time because they were curious about it, like this twenty-six-year-old single man:

I went to visit a friend in Hedao in 1998. He told me there was a new kind of pill that tasted better than alcohol or cigarettes. The price at that time was 5 yuan [60 cents] per pill. He went out and bought some. I knew right then that it was not a good thing to do, but we human beings are inherently devilish anyway. Even though it is a bad thing, as long as it is something new, we men are very likely to want to give it a try. We started to smoke, but I smoked only half a pill; afterwards, I didn't sleep at all that night.[31]

Other subjects began to smoke methamphetamine when there was a need for them to be alert and energized, as a twenty-four-year-old Shan male recounted: "Once I went to Kokang with several friends to have fun. After driving for several hours, everyone felt very tired. It was dark and we were almost falling asleep while driving. Then our car broke down. At that point, someone said that we should smoke some speed pills to energize us. My friends always had speed pills with them."[32] A thirty-year-old Burmese car mechanic said he smoked methamphetamine the first time because of his boss: "When I was working in a car repair shop, one night my boss asked us to work overtime. It was very late and we were all tired and sleepy. My colleagues said that we should smoke some speed pills and heroin to keep us awake. I said I would smoke speed pills, but not heroin."[33]

Some of my subjects said they smoked methamphetamine because, like some of the opium users cited above, they were depressed. A nineteen-year-old Chinese woman, single, was lovesick when she first tried the drug: "I started to smoke speed pills out of love. I broke up with my boyfriend because he said I did not understand him or care about his well-being. I had a friend who was smoking pills, so I asked her to bring me a few pills. That's how I got started."[34] Two other subjects said they began to smoke the drug because they were working in a methamphetamine factory, as a twenty-five-year-old Wa who was single noted: "When I was living in Kokang, I used to work in a methamphetamine factory. Because we produce these pills, I also began to smoke them. Later, I smoked every day. I would occasionally stop smoking for two or three days to recover my strength and then start smoking again."[35]

Initiation into opium or methamphetamine could be due to the function of the drug (to cure an illness or to remain alert), the need to socialize (socializing with friends or neighbors and having a good time), the urge to try something out of curiosity, or the desire to alleviate psychological pain.

REACTIONS TO METHAMPHETAMINE USE

Most subjects did not feel good when they smoked methamphetamine for the first time. The nineteen-year-old Chinese woman who tried it because she broke up with her boyfriend recalled: "I felt awful. It tasted bitter; I thought it was disgusting. I almost threw up."[36] A thirty-one-year-old Wa woman, who was an aunt of the baby boy left with an opium-smoking grandmother, said: "When I tried it the first time, I felt dizzy and sick. I wanted to throw up, and my hands and feet became limp. I felt like ants were crawling all over my body. I did not want to smoke it again."[37]

Other subjects found it somewhat more pleasant than the subjects cited above. Two subjects stressed how much they enjoyed the smell of methamphetamine when they first tried it. A twenty-nine-year-old Chinese female, divorced with two children, described the experience of using the drug for the first time: "After I smoked it, my mouth was bitter. However, the smoke out of my mouth smelled very good. After I smoked one pill, I sweated a lot. I felt very warm. It was like I had had a drink, though drinking makes your face hot and speed won't do that to your face. When I smoked another pill, I felt a little excited, like I was falling in love for the first time."[38] A twenty-three-year-old Shan woman who admitted to being a sex worker had the following to say about her initial use: "I really wanted to keep on smoking nonstop; I wanted to smoke until I had had enough. However, I was also worried that if I smoked too much, I might lose my mind. That's because when you smoke speed pills, the smell is really captivating."[39]

Most of my subjects had been smoking methamphetamine for two or three years when we interviewed them (see table 10). According to a key informant, even though methamphetamine production was rampant in the Wa area in 1997 and 1998, people in the Wa area did not begin to use it until 1999. Even though the majority of the subjects (68 percent) said they were not addicted to speed pills and they did not think the drug was addictive, the few subjects (32 percent) who thought they were addicted to speed pills said it happened relatively quickly for them.

Those who thought they were addicted told us how they first realized it. The Wa woman whose mother was an opium user commented: "When I was not smoking, I was lazy. I just wanted to sleep and had no desire to work. I had no strength at all. After I smoked meth, I was awake and alert. That's when I knew I was hooked."[40] A young Wa female explained why she

Table 10. Characteristics of Methamphetamine Use in the Wa Area

	Mean	Mode	Median	Minimum	Maximum
Length of use (in years)	3	3	3	1	4
Subsequent use after first use (in days)	95	1	10	1	1,080
Addiction after first use (in days)	258		120	7	1,200
Number of times smoked per day	2.4	2	2	1	4
Amount of methamphetamine consumed monthly (in tablets)	162	200	175	35	400
Monthly expense for methamphetamine (in US$)	31	0, 6, 48	24	0	122

Note: N=25

thought she was addicted: "If I did not smoke it, I had no strength at all. I could not even open my eyes. As soon as I sat down, I fell asleep. My body, my hands, and my feet were useless. I often felt hungry. Even after I ate something, I was hungry an hour later as though I had not eaten anything at all. I thought I might be addicted."[41] Another subject, a twenty-two-year-old Chinese man from Hedao, found out his drug dependency unexpectedly: "I went to Kunming with my girlfriend for sightseeing and I did not smoke any pills for only a couple of days. My whole body was uncomfortable and I felt extremely tired. I became very sleepy. My bones were aching—it was as though ants were biting my bones. I knew I was addicted."[42]

On average, my subjects smoked the pills about twice a day (see table 10). Some subjects smoked only once a day and some took the pills four times a day. My subjects smoked an average of 162 pills per month and spent an average of $31 a month on speed pills. A few subjects said they did not need to spend any money on the drug because they either work in a meth factory or are meth dealers.

KICKING THE METHAMPHETAMINE HABIT

Those who thought they were addicted to methamphetamine have tried to kick the habit on their own. The twenty-year-old Wa woman who started smoking for the fun of it told how she stopped:

I love my parents very much and that's why I decided to quit the pills by any means. My parents did not know I was taking drugs. When my friends were going to Kunming, I told my parents I wanted to go, too, because I had never been there. They let me go. They love me very much, and they have never said no to me. I stayed in Kunming for three weeks. I went out every day and had fun and enjoyed the food. I tried my best to make myself happy and to forget about speed pills. The result was very good. I now have no desire to smoke again.[43]

Another subject, a twenty-two-year-old Chinese man from Hedao, also adopted the same method, though with a different result:

I began to think that I was still young and it isn't a good thing to keep on smoking. I wanted to marry and start a family. If I continued with my drug use, I may not find a wife because of my drug habit. So, I went to Kunming, Jinghong, and Ruili for sightseeing because it is hard to find drugs there. It worked. I did quit. However, after I came back to Bangkang, within a year the place was saturated with speed pills and many people were smoking meth. When I saw them smoking, I could not control myself and I started smoking again. If I were not living in Bangkang, maybe I would not be smoking again.[44]

A Shan man who was an army officer said he was able to kick the habit by gradually decreasing the number of pills he used every day:

I did not quit it completely, all at once. During the first month, I tried to decrease my dose from ten to five pills to one to half a pill per occasion. It was unbearable. So, almost every day I tried to go out and meet my close friends and do enjoyable things with them. I felt time pass quickly this way. To quit, I think the most important thing is to control yourself. After I maintained half a pill per occasion for a week, I woke up one morning and smoked one last puff and threw away the rest. Now, I can go to work, and I am not troubled by it anymore. When I see the drug now, I just look at it like it is garbage.[45]

THE IMPACT OF METHAMPHETAMINE

When asked whether methamphetamine use had any impact on their physical and psychological well-being, some subjects said the drug had a major, negative impact on them. According to a young female user, "Smoking speed pills affects me in many ways. I am like a different person. My throat hurts so much that I have almost lost my voice. I have lost a lot of weight. I also have a bad temper most of the time. Many friends don't like the kind of personality I have now."[46] Another young Chinese woman noted, "It had a major effect. After you smoke a few pills, you don't want to sleep or eat. After spending several days trying to recover your health, you smoke a few pills and all your efforts go down the drain. Speed pills also affect your brain; they cause you to think of only crazy things."[47]

Some subjects, on the other hand, had only positive things to say about the drug. A twenty-four-year-old Shan man commented, "Actually, smoking speed pills does not really have much impact on your mind and body. When you are tired, you smoke a few pills and you will be immediately energized and lighten up. All you have to be concerned about is that you don't let yourself get addicted to it."[48] The young sex worker also thought smoking methamphetamine was good for her line of work:

After smoking the pills, my smiles are more attractive to my sex-crazed customers and I am better able to communicate with them. Besides, these pills keep my body in good shape. I am not a heavy user. But if I smoke three pills, I do not feel tired at all even if I have to have sex with a customer the whole night. I cannot imagine how I would survive without speed pills. When I started to work as a sex worker, I was always tired. Right now, I do not feel that way anymore. After I began to smoke speed pills, more and more customers fall in love with me because I can give them much more satisfaction.[49]

Unlike opium and heroin users, some speed pill users were able to hide their drug habit from their families. A young woman whose parents were not aware of her drug use reflected how the use of speed pills had ruined her relationships with people around her:

Taking drugs has changed my relationships with my family members a lot. My elder sister does not talk to me anymore. My brother and I have become estranged. Sometimes, my relatives refuse to talk to me and treat me like a stranger. Up until now, my parents do not know I use drugs, otherwise they would send me to prison.[50]

Those subjects who could not hide their methamphetamine habit from their families encountered strong, negative reactions from family members. A forty-one-year-old Wa woman who was a widow said,

Smoking speed pills had a major impact on my family. When my husband was alive, after he learned that I was smoking this stuff, we argued every day. Because we were a poor family, we occasionally would have a problem making ends meet. Under these circumstances, it was really unforgivable of me to spend 60 to 70 yuan [about $8] a month on speed pills.[51]

A twenty-three-year-old Chinese woman, married with two children, was still smoking speed pills at the time of the interview, and she was candid about what the drug has done to her and her family: "Taking drugs has had an impact on my family. My kids cannot eat good food or wear beautiful clothes. My family has no other financial resources. However, if I had 10 yuan, I would go out and buy speed pills right now. I do not care about whether my family has money to buy food. I have no choice. I simply cannot quit."[52] She also said her mother smoked both opium and methamphetamine, her sister smoked methamphetamine, and her sister's husband used both heroin and methamphetamine.

WA LEADERS' RESPONSES TO METHAMPHETAMINE USE

In the late 1990s, when the Wa leaders allowed outsiders to produce methamphetamine tablets in the Wa territory, they were thinking that the drug would simply be exported to neighboring countries. If a small proportion of the drug was consumed in the Wa area, they reasoned, it would be relatively harmless. Asked why the Wa leaders approved of foreigners manufacturing methamphetamine in the Wa area, Zhou Dafu of the Wa Central Authority, who had ambivalent feelings about the drug, replied: "We hoped the methamphetamine tablets would flow out of the Wa, but we were wrong; we caused a lot of harm to ourselves. But, in fact, methamphetamine is good for energizing a person. We thought it would be all right to use it occasionally, especially if you needed to work overtime to meet a deadline."[53]

Early on, Bao Youxiang told me he was aware of the dangers of methamphetamine:

> So far, seventy to eighty people here have died due to meth tablets and we have arrested about one thousand people for using or dealing the tablets. I am afraid of meth tablets. I told my people if you want to smoke the tablets, you might as well come ask me for a gun and commit suicide. The danger of methamphetamine is much more serious than an armed enemy.[54]

A health official with the Wa government commented on how methamphetamine was a youth fad in the Wa area and how the authorities' response was inadequate:

> Young people here have no idea of the danger of smoking meth tablets. They are heavily influenced by Hong Kong films and they also like to show off. When they are with their methamphetamine-using friends, they are under a lot of pressure to smoke as well. We are only involved in arresting methamphetamine smokers and have never really developed any plans to educate the young people about the dangers of smoking the drug.[55]

A consequence of this widespread use is that most Wa leaders send their children to China or Rangoon to attend school, mainly to prevent them from smoking methamphetamine.

METHAMPHETAMINE USE AMONG PRODUCERS AND DEALERS

According to my subjects, methamphetamine producers and dealers are vulnerable to the very drug they are producing or trading. Some of them were believed to be addicted to methamphetamine because they were required to smoke the drug to determine its quality. Most opium traders, however, were able to tell the quality of opium by examining it with their eyes or by smelling it. A key informant revealed how the son-in-law of a high-ranking Wa leader was addicted to both heroin and methamphetamine:

> The second daughter of a Wa leader married a man from China last year. This is her second marriage. The daughter's ex-husband was a drug addict; he used both heroin and methamphetamine—that's why they divorced. If you are in the drug business, after all, there are plenty of drugs around and you may have to test the quality of the drugs by using them.[56]

The daughter of another leader was a major methamphetamine dealer and she, too, was addicted to methamphetamine. Even though there is no statistical data to verify that methamphetamine use in the Wa area is a serious problem, it is clear from my fieldwork that a substantial number of people in the area, especially young people and those who are involved in the methamphetamine business, are smoking the tablets.

Burma

Drug use in Burma has a long history. Cannabis and opium were widely used in Burma before the British colonized the country in 1885, and opium production and use increased significantly in Burma under British rule (Maule 1992). Burmese documents and newspapers admitted to a narcotics problem in Rangoon, particularly with heroin (Renard 1996). According to Renard (1996, 9), expatriate Burmese students and graduates estimated that "perhaps 50 percent of the student body of Rangoon University has tried heroin, while over 80 percent have tried or are using marijuana."

The Transnational Institute (2006, 1–2) reported that "international NGOs put the number of drug users in Burma at between 300,000 and 500,000" and that "the increasing number of injecting drug users (IDUs) and the growing HIV/AIDS epidemic in Burma presents one of the most serious health threats to the population in the country, and also to the region at large."

When I was in Rangoon interviewing Burmese officials, I had an opportunity to meet an old schoolmate who grew up with me in the same neighborhood. He is a Muslim whose grandparents migrated to Burma from India in the early twentieth century. He told his story of how he was initiated into heroin use:

> Around 1970, heroin began to show up in Rangoon. During that time, you could get a penicillin-size bottle of heroin from a Chinese lady in Chinatown for 250 kyat. Normally, we shared the drug; two or three friends got together and used it. We mixed the heroin with the tobacco from a cigarette and smoked it. At the very beginning, people from the neighborhood across the street, people we called *mingmaniang* [tough men who couldn't be controlled, even by the king] came over to our apartment complex and smoked heroin in the stairways. They offered us the opportunity to smoke with them, and after the first time, there was the second time.
>
> The first time I smoked it, it was quite unpleasant; I felt like throwing up. I was also sweating. However, after smoking it three to four times, I felt great. You got the feeling of the drug and you felt very relaxed, very talkative, and not afraid of anything. A 250-kyat worth of heroin would enable a group of users to smoke for two days. At that time, there was no law against heroin smoking. The group of people I smoked heroin with included Chinese, Burmese, and Muslims, all male. As far as I know, very few females smoke heroin except for some movie stars and musicians. The group had about fifteen users, and over the years, four have died because of heroin overdoses. Those who got hooked were smoking heroin not because of the good feeling anymore but because of the dependency. They have to continue to smoke just to feel all right. I was never addicted because I never went on a binge; after a few days of use, I stopped.
>
> In 1976, the government began to ban heroin use and that caused the price to increase to 1,200 kyat per penicillin-size bottle. Even so, the price was not as formidable as it is now. Now, in 2002, a half bottle costs about 9,000 kyat. As a result, a buyer would simply tell a

dealer he has 3,000 kyat only and ask the dealer to give him any amount of drug he sees fit. After 1976, not only were the Chinese selling heroin, all ethnic groups were involved in it. The Chinese lady was arrested later.

After 1992, I stopped smoking heroin on a regular basis and used it only occasionally, like every three to four months. I remember when we met in 1998 and you said I looked sick. That was the time when I was using heroin heavily. I did not look normal, and my face became dark and distorted. Some of my friends went cold turkey after heroin was almost impossible to get. It wasn't easy, but there was no other way to do it. I was never arrested for drug use because I was extremely careful. I rarely smoked in public and was quite conscious with whom I smoked.[57]

Although it is not clear how many people in Burma use methamphetamine, the 2003 INCRS report stated that "in 2003 there were troubling signs that a nascent domestic market for ATS [amphetamine-type stimulant] began to emerge in Burma, although deteriorating economic conditions will likely stifle significant growth in consumption" (U.S. Department of State 2003, 273). According to the friend quoted above:

When yaba, called *ming* or horse in Burmese, became more available, someone once offered me half a tablet and I swallowed it. I did not like the experience because I did not feel the effect of the drug. All I could remember was that I became greatly energized. I just wanted to go out and move around. I did not want to sleep. I liked the high heroin gave me, but not the energy deriving from yaba. Here, in Rangoon, most people swallow yaba although some may also smoke it. A tablet costs about 600 kyat.[58]

Most young people in Burma are not attending school (mainly high school and college) because the schools have often been closed since the 1988 crackdown on student demonstrations. The unemployment rate is extremely high because of Burma's stagnant economy. As a result, many young people there are idle, spending most of their time sipping tea in teahouses or drinking beer in bars while silently waiting for the military regime to collapse. For these youths, taking a mind-altering drug is an appealing thing to do because it helps them temporarily forget their dire existence (Renard 1996).

Thailand

In a March 2, 2002, article in the *Bangkok Post*, it was estimated that there were 2.6 million addicts in Thailand, of which 91 percent or 2.3 million are believed to be addicted to methamphetamines, about eighty thousand people to marijuana, twenty-three thousand to heroin, and twenty thousand to opium. A year later (March 1, 2003), the same newspaper reported that Thai health officials estimated that three million Thais—roughly 5 percent of the population—were addicted to methamphetamines. Methamphetamine cases have jumped from 1.8 percent of drug-related court cases in 1990 to 67.3 percent in 2000 (*Bangkok Post*, April 14, 2000) and to 81.6 percent in 2001–02 (Office of Narcotics Control Board 2002). Methamphetamine is the number-one drug of choice for many young people in Thailand nowadays, and a matter of great concern to government officials (United Nations Office on Drugs and Crime 2005b). According to an editorial in the *Bangkok Post* (April 14, 2000, 6), "A decade ago methamphetamines were used almost exclusively by truck drivers to stay awake on long hauls. Today they have found their way into our schools and an alarming number of Thai children and youths have become hooked."

Similar to the situation in the meth-producing Wa area, methamphetamine tablets became very popular in Thailand because, according to Chartchai Suthiklom, deputy secretary-general of the Office of Narcotic Control Board of Thailand, "It is cute, smells great, and energizes you. Many young people are attracted to the pills because it is a very different type of drug in comparison with opium or heroin."[59] Moreover, the tablets are not as expensive as heroin, as an informant in Mae Sai said: "One yaba tablet costs between 15 to 70 baht in Mae Sai, depending on the quality. Even so, it is still a lot cheaper than heroin. That's why some heroin users have switched to speed pills."[60]

As the yaba epidemic engulfed Thailand, Bangkok's Klong Toey community, home to twelve thousand poverty-stricken families, became the country's central market for methamphetamine pills. According to one source, more than half the people living there were thought to be involved in drugs (Nanuam 2002). An article in the *Christian Science Monitor* (Murphy 2002, 6) described the drug scene in Thailand:

> Five years ago, just a trickle of methamphetamines were reaching Thailand. Today it's a torrent. About 70,000 Thais were convicted

for methamphetamine-related offenses last year, up from 16,000 in 1997. . . . In a new report on Thai drug use in 2001, the Thai Narcotics Control Board stressed the way the drug cuts through class distinctions and age groups: "Never before has narcotics reached out to all levels of Thai society like methamphetamine does," the report stated.

The impact of the meth epidemic on Thailand in the early 2000s was quite similar to the impact of the crack epidemic on the United States in the mid-1980s (Belenko 1993; Bourgois 1996). The meth epidemic in Thailand created a whole new generation of drug users, clogged the criminal justice system with a dramatic increase in drug cases, overwhelmed the service sector with a large number of impoverished drug addicts, and damaged the country's relationship with an important neighboring country because of numerous border clashes. No wonder that the Thai media has often claimed that the meth epidemic should be considered the country's number-one security threat and that Thailand should not hesitate to go to war with Burma, if necessary, to stop the drug scourge.

China

Opium

Before the Communist takeover in 1949, opium use in China was rampant (Booth 1997; Dikotter, Laamann, and Zhou 2004; Ting 2004). Opium was not only widely cultivated and trafficked internally, but it also was imported into China on a large scale (Meyer and Parssinen 1998). Moreover, opium grown in Yunnan was "transported along caravan routes to the Shan States, Burma proper, northern Siam and Laos by Chinese Muslims known as Panthays" (Maule 2002, 217). According to Fiskesjo (2000, 193–94), "much of the *yuntu*, Yunnan 'mud' or opium, famous in China, actually came from the Wa areas."

According to one source, there were more than twenty million drug users in China (about 4.4 percent of the population) at the dawn of the Communist takeover in 1949. In Yunnan Province, about a quarter of the population used opium. More than three million people (about 21.4 percent of the population) in Guizhou Province smoked opium (Ma 1994). Nowadays, opium use in China is believed to be restricted to hill people living in the border areas with Burma, Laos, and Vietnam (Ma 1994).

Heroin

According to Chinese authorities, the number-one drug problem in China is heroin (Sun 2001; Yunnan Province Narcotics Control Committee 2003). Not only do large amounts of heroin from the Golden Triangle pass through China on their way to international markets, since the late 1980s new heroin markets have sprung up all over China itself. Of all the provinces in China, Yunnan is the most affected area due to its proximity to the Golden Triangle (Luo and Liang 1999; Luo, Liang, and Yang 2004). Because heroin is easily accessible and relatively cheap in Yunnan, the province is populated not only by homegrown heroin users but also by users from other parts of China. For example, Ruili, the town just across from Muse, Burma, is one of the popular hubs for heroin users from the inland areas of China.

In subsequent research conducted not long after I finished collecting data in the Wa area, I and my colleagues interviewed twenty-five heroin users in Kunming in 2004. The majority of the subjects were single or divorced males who were born in Kunming, although only half of them considered themselves to be Yunnanese. Most of them were ethnic Chinese in their thirties with much more education than drug users in the Wa area.

INITIATION

Many subjects said they started to smoke heroin after they were urged by their friends to give it a try, and out of curiosity, they did. A thirty-four-year-old Chinese male in Kunming who was unemployed and had been using heroin since 1991 recalled: "I used the drug for the first time at a social gathering among friends. It was after work. At that time, I had many friends and colleagues who were using heroin; it was a cool thing to do then. At the gathering, my friends asked me to give it a try. It wasn't like they were trying to ruin me by asking me to smoke heroin; they were just eager to share with me their pleasant experience with heroin."[61]

Other subjects said there was a reason for their initiation into heroin use. A thirty-one-year-old single male from Kunming, unemployed with little education, said: "I smoked it for the first time after I was unable to persuade my girlfriend to quit smoking it; I tried for two years to help her kick the habit. As a result, I became curious about the drug myself and I tried it. The first time I used it, I felt very uncomfortable because I got a headache, had blurry eyesight, I wanted to vomit, got thirsty, and my whole body was itchy. However, when I woke up the next day and saw my girlfriend smoking it, I joined her and smoked for the second time."[62]

A thirty-eight-year-old male from Shanxi Province said a variety of factors were at play when he first tried heroin: "A friend of mine brought the heroin from Ruili and he said that I should use it and that it would help me with my sexual performance. I was curious, so I tried it. Besides, I was just about to divorce my wife, and I wasn't in a good mood. After I used it, I threw up and my head went dizzy. I slept very well that night, and I had that good feeling of hallucination and happiness."[63]

A forty-two-year-old male from Beijing stated that he smoked heroin because it was considered a very cool thing to do:

> I started it because it was a fashionable thing to do at that time. I was working in a government unit, my girlfriend owned a hair salon, and I also had a taxi in my name. You can say I was doing very well then. At that time, if you didn't use heroin, you couldn't really hang around with the people (*wanbuchulai*). I visited my friends, and they were all smoking heroin with their cigarettes, and there was no public service information about heroin dependency so we did not know heroin smoking was addictive. I was, of course, curious to give it try. After I tried it, I thought it was the most absurd thing to do because I felt very uncomfortable.[64]

Generally, most of the heroin users we interviewed said they were doing relatively well when they stumbled into heroin use by chance or by their desire to be with the "in" group in Kunming—the heroin users. Easy access to heroin and the lack of knowledge about the addictiveness of the drug also played a role in the process of creating a large number of heroin users in Kunming. Only a very small percentage of our subjects said their initiation into heroin use was associated with depression or despair.

ADDICTION, MAINTENANCE, AND CHANGING PATTERNS OF USE

Most of my subjects have used heroin for more than ten years. After their first experience with heroin, it did not take long for them to try the drug again, often within a few days. Some subjects found out that they were addicted to heroin not long after their first use (see table 11). A businessman in Ruili who thought he was not going to be addicted to heroin said he was surprised to find out he was hooked after only three days of continuous use:

Table 11. Characteristics of Heroin Use in Kunming, China

	Mean	Mode	Median	Minimum	Maximum
Length of use (in years)	11.4	10	12	1	16
Subsequent use after first use (in days)	32	1	6	1	180
Addiction after first use (in days)	137	15, 40, 105	55	5	730
Number of times used per day	4.4	3	3	1	12
Amount of heroin consumed daily (in grams)	0.81	1	1	0.2	2
Daily expense for heroin (in US$)	17	12	14.6	6	42.6

Note: N=25

Three days later, I traveled to Baoshan [a nearby town which is a few hours' drive from Ruili] and after I got there, I became very sick because I had not had a chance to smoke heroin. My stomach ached and I felt awful. I realized that I needed to smoke some heroin to make me feel better, so I found a heroin dealer in Baoshan and smoked the heroin. Right after I smoked it, I felt fine again. At that point, I realized that I was addicted to heroin.[65]

A subject who was working for a construction company also found out about his heroin dependency the hard way:

After a month of smoking heroin, I took a business trip to a place about a hundred kilometers from Kunming. I went there with a group of visitors from out of town. After we arrived there, I became very uncomfortable in the evening. I felt awful and had all the symptoms of heroin withdrawal. The next morning, I abandoned my guests and came back to Kunming to look for heroin. When a heroin dealer handed me the drug, I was ready to pay him whatever he asked. That was 1997.[66]

A subject who was urged by his friends to try heroin after work noted: "A week later, I tried it again and three or four months later, I was completely hooked. All day, I was only concerned with getting the money, buying the drug, and going home and using it. I used it two or three times a day, half a gram per day, and it cost me about 80 to 100 yuan [$15 to $17] every day."[67]

After the subjects were addicted to heroin, they switched from smoking to injecting heroin if they could not afford to smoke the drug anymore. Some of them also began to use the drug in public places as well as at home, including a Sichaunese male who was born in Kunming: "At the beginning, I smoked heroin by laying it on cigarettes. Later, I began to inject it because then I won't waste any of it. In the beginning, I used it at home, but later I used it wherever I had an urge for a fix, including public restrooms and the sidewalk. When there is a craving, it doesn't matter where you are, you've got to inject it."[68]

The Beijingnese who thought using heroin was a cool thing also started as a smoker and ended up being an injector: "I started in 1991, and at that time I smoked heroin with cigarettes. After two or three months, I began smoking the drug by burning it on tinfoil. After a year, I began to inject. The quantity of heroin also increased from 0.2 gram to 1 gram per day. In March 2003, I passed out in a public toilet after I injected myself."[69]

Another subject told how he learned to inject heroin:

When I first used heroin, I smoked it. I put the heroin on top of tinfoil paper and burnt it with a lighter underneath. However, when I spent some time in a drug rehabilitation center, I became friends with another patient at the center. After we both came out, he taught me how to inject heroin. I went into a coma the first time I injected it, and that guy just ran away when that happened. After that incident, I couldn't go back to smoking heroin anymore; I had to inject the heroin in order for me to have the feeling.[70]

The same subject described his level of use after full addiction:

When I was using heroin, I ate only once a day because I often threw up after I ate. I could not stand the smell of liquor, either. I would be injecting heroin all day long, and after each injection, my whole body would have the smell of apples, and it smelled great. I felt dizzy and the only thing I wanted to do was to find a place to lie down. Good quality drugs will keep you high for a longer period of time; poor quality drugs make you feel good for only about fifteen minutes.[71]

Those who could afford the drug said they smoked it and never thought of injecting it. According to a subject who was a businessman, "I only smoked heroin and never injected it because I could afford it. Injecting is only for those who cannot afford to smoke it. The way I smoked it was to mix heroin with cigarette tobacco. I took all the tobacco out of a cigarette, mixed four or five layers of heroin with the tobacco, and then rewrapped it."[72] He went on to describe how he spent a typical day when he was a heroin addict:

> Every day, the first thing I did when I opened my eyes in the morning was to smoke heroin. I put some heroin into a cigarette and smoked it. After that, I lay down and enjoyed the high. It would last for a few hours and then I would go out and look for No. 4. Once I got it, I would come home and smoke another cigarette. Normally, I needed to smoke three or four heroin cigarettes a day. One gram normally would be enough for two heroin cigarettes. Of course, if I was short of heroin, I tried to put less heroin into a cigarette. Usually, the drug was in a pressurized crystal form, and I had to break it up into powder form. When I was smoking, that was pretty much what I did every day.[73]

As shown in table 11, most heroin users I interviewed in Kunming smoked or injected heroin three or four times a day, consuming about one gram every day. They said it cost them an average of $17 a day for drugs, an enormous amount of money for people living in a city where many people earn less than $4 a day.

CESSATION

In China, if a person is arrested for heroin use, he or she is required to go to a drug detoxification center for at least a month. Family members of a heroin user may also enroll the user in a voluntary drug treatment center. If a person is arrested a second or third time for heroin use, the authorities may send the person to a *laodong jiaoyang* or *laojiao* (education-through-labor) camp (essentially a jail) for one year.[74] Most heroin users in China have spent some time in a mandatory or a voluntary rehabilitation center or both, and those individuals who both use and sell heroin are very likely to have been imprisoned in a labor camp during their heroin careers.

Most heroin users we interviewed do not think the drug detoxification centers in China work. A thirty-four-year-old male commented: "I was sent to a mandatory drug detoxification center four different times. The first two times, I spent forty days each visit. I stayed for six months on my third trip to the center, and a year on my last enrollment. It did not work. I am sure more than 90 percent of the people who come out of the center relapse."[75] A businessman who went to Ruili from Kunming and came back to Kunming after he was addicted to heroin during his stay in Ruili observed:

I will say the relapse rate for people who have received help in the detoxification centers is 98 percent. Only two out of one hundred drug users who come out of these centers might quit, most likely because they were shocked and scared by their experiences in the centers and had the will to quit. It is a mess in these drug centers; the staff will train certain patients to control other patients. We were never allowed to walk together normally; we always had to walk single file, like ducks in a line. It was very humiliating to be a patient at the centers.[76]

A thirty-eight-year-old male who was divorced twice because of his heroin addiction explained how his experience in a drug detoxification center transformed him into a dope fiend:

On one occasion, I was arrested while looking for drugs. Before I went to that detoxification center, I knew only a few drug users. At the center, I came to know more drug users and learned new techniques to use the drug. Before I went in, I thought I would kick the habit after being in that center; however, it was just the opposite. After I came out of the center, I felt like I was more embedded into the drug subculture. Once I got out of that center, I ran into the drug friends I knew at the center and then I went to *lioaxinyuan* (fulfill a wish).[77]

Some of my subjects said they stopped using heroin after they were sent to a labor camp for a long period of time. A forty-year-old divorced male said: "I was once sent to a compulsory rehabilitation center and once to a voluntary treatment center. Later I was sent to a reeducation-through-labor camp for two years. I was released after serving eighteen months. I came out of the labor camp in the year 2002, and I have not smoked heroin for almost three years."[78]

Another subject, a thirty-year-old single male who was born in Kunming, recalled what prompted him to quit: "A young niece once said to me: 'Uncle, what is the point of smoking this thing? Every day, you are searching. You first search for money, then you search for the drug, and then you are busy searching a quiet place to inject the drug. Then you search for a good spot in your veins to inject the drug, and finally, you search for the feeling. To live like this is so tiresome.' When I heard that, I was shocked. I decided to quit."[79]

IMPACT

The majority of the twenty-five active or former heroin users I interviewed were unemployed, divorced or still single, and needed to rely on someone else for financial support. Most of them spent a substantial amount of their time at the drop-in centers for heroin users in Kunming. These centers, funded and managed by overseas organizations, provide community-based treatment programs to former and active heroin users. Like the heroin users studied by Johnson and his associates (1985) in New York City, some of my subjects characterized their heroin lifestyle as active and meaningful. According to a thirty-three-year-old single male who was born in Kunming, "When I was using heroin, I felt like I was living a solid life. Every day, I was looking for money and then looking for the drug. I was busy. When I stopped using heroin, I felt like my life was so hollow; I didn't know what to do."[80] Even so, most subjects thought that their dependency on heroin had basically ruined their lives and brought enormous suffering to their loved ones. A forty-year-old divorced man recalled how his wife and son left him:

My wife divorced me because of my heroin habit. When I was smoking heroin, she and I got along because I was functioning. What scared her and our son was when I was trying to quit. It was then that she realized how terrible I looked. When I went cold turkey, I was awful: I lost a lot of weight and I had teary eyes and a runny nose. I was miserable. That's why they left me. After the divorce, I just spent every day smoking heroin. I really regret the whole thing. I threw away my life, my family, and all my money. I was looked down on by friends and relatives, and I felt really lonely because nobody wanted to be near me.[81]

The man who began to use heroin with his girlfriend was also guilt-ridden when he talked about his parents: "Because of my heroin habit, my parents began to worry and they often got sick and did not have time to take care of my little brother. My whole family was deeply affected by me. Now, whenever they see me, they cry. They are deeply saddened by my heroin addiction."[82]

Amphetamine and Other Drugs

A growing number of people in China, especially young men and women in urban centers who are students, professionals, or businesspeople, are being attracted to a variety of the so-called *xinxingdupin*, or newly emerged drugs, including ecstasy, amphetamine, and ketamine powder. In general, young people consume these drugs collectively in a nightclub, a dancehall, or a karaoke lounge where there are special rooms for customers to use drugs. Employees of these entertainment centers normally work closely with drug pushers to satisfy the customers' demands for drugs. Some of the dealers are reported to be local gang members.

Interestingly, methamphetamine is not a popular drug in China yet. According to authorities in Yunnan, Sichuan, Guangdong, Guizhou, Guangxi, and Fujian, there is no evidence to suggest that methamphetamine tablets from the Golden Triangle are flowing into China on a large scale.

Unintended Consequences

The literature on the drug problem in Southeast Asia focuses mainly on drug producing activities in the region and rarely pays much attention to the impact of illicit drugs on people living in the region. This chapter shows that opium, heroin, and methamphetamine are not only produced in the region but are also heavily consumed by people there, regardless of whether they are involved in the drug trade or not. The damaging effects of drug use on individuals in the region are as devastating as they are on their counterparts in Western societies.

In the Wa area, many opium farmers are addicted to opium and some of them are seriously affected by their addiction. My study shows that opium use in the Wa area is not as well integrated into highland life as many Western observers have suggested and that its use does disrupt and ruin individuals and their families. Some of the Chinese who travel to the Wa area from China to work or do business are reported to be at risk of becoming heroin addicts because heroin is easily accessible in the area. Young people in the Wa area, especially those who are involved in the methamphetamine trade, are highly vulnerable to methamphetamine use. Because drug treatment programs are nonexistent in the Wa area, people who become addicted to opium, heroin, or methamphetamine are forced to deal with their addictions on their own.

The explosion of methamphetamine trafficking and use in Thailand in the late 1990s was very similar to the crack cocaine epidemic in the United States in the late 1980s. Methamphetamine tablets became the drug of choice for a whole new generation of drug users in Thailand and corrupted a large number of Thai officials and law enforcement authorities. Violence associated with yaba, be it the result of the pharmacological effect of smoking yaba or the business aspect of dealing yaba, became a constant feature in the Thai media almost on a daily basis. As a result, in 2002 the Thaksin Sinawatra administration declared war on yaba and carried out the extrajudicial killings of thousands of suspected yaba dealers in Thailand. Thailand's relationship with yaba-producing Burma also hit an all-time low, and on a few occasions serious border skirmishes broke out, leading to the closing of the border by both sides for many months.

After China adopted its open door policy in the late 1970s and began to encourage economic reform and social development, the problem of drug use, especially heroin injection, reemerged. People who inject heroin in China are reported to be at risk of HIV/AIDS for sharing needles with other users. A thirty-four-year-old subject who had been using heroin since 1991 said: "On a few occasions, I risked my life sharing a needle with other drug users. During those times, the urge for a fix was so strong that you really did not care about the consequences. On the other hand, we also fight among ourselves to decide who will be the first to use the only clean needle that is there."[83] Chinese authorities are now extremely concerned with the increase in the number of drug addicts in China and the problems associated with drug use.

In sum, when a group of people are involved in the production and trafficking of drugs, these activities have unintended consequences, including the consumption of these drugs by the very people who are in the drug trade and by those who live around them. Many drug users we interviewed were initiated into drug use simply because they were producing or dealing the very drug they later became addicted to. In the Golden Triangle, the impact of drug addiction is very similar to what we have observed in the developed world, and probably more devastating due to poverty and the lack of treatment facilities in the border areas of Burma, Thailand, and China.

Chapter Seven

Drug Control

The drug trade in the Golden Triangle has been an international problem for more than half a century (McCoy 1972, 1991; Lintner 1994b; Renard 1996; Boucaud and Boucaud 1998), with the drug under scrutiny evolving from opium to heroin and, most recently, to methamphetamine (Phongpaichit, Piriyarangsan, and Teerat 1998; Takano 2002; Chouvy and Meissonnier 2004). Key players in the ongoing drug trade have included China's Kuomintang soldiers in the 1950s and the 1960s, Burma's Luo Xinghan and Khun Sa in the 1970s up to the mid-1990s, now Wei Xuegang and the United Wa State Army (Jelsma, Kramer, and Vervest 2005). Drug transportation routes in the area have changed as drug traffickers adjust to new political and economic conditions (Ting 2004; Finckenauer and Chin 2006). As I will demonstrate in this chapter, a number of countries, but especially Burma, Thailand, China, and the United States, have devoted substantial amounts of energy and resources in an effort to transform the area into a drug-free zone or, at the least, to diminish the flow of drugs from the area.

The Wa State

Opium growers in the Wa State were ambivalent about their government's plan to ban opium cultivation in 2005. Some supported the plan and believed they would be able to get by without the income from opium, while others thought they would suffer enormously if they are deprived of the meager income from opium sales. Of course, in the Wa area, what the opium growers think or feel is of little significance because, as one grower said, "tens of thousands of words that come out of our mouths are no match to one bullet."[1] In a society like the Wa, it is what the leaders think or feel that matters the most because they are the ones with the power.

When I talked to Wa leaders about the drug business in their territory, their reactions varied. Some refused to talk about it and did not care what outsiders had to say about them. An official with the Public Relations Bureau said, "I don't want to clarify anything about the Thai media's accusation that we are the biggest drug trafficking organization in the world. Let people in the West and Thailand say whatever they want to about us. It will not get us sick."[2]

Other leaders liked to point out that Westerners (the British) were the ones who first brought opium to the area and taught the Wa how to grow opium.[3] The thinking of an official from the Wa Central Authority was typical of that of many Wa leaders:

When we talk about the current opium trade in the Wa area, we must understand that opium cultivation was imported into this area from the West. No one can deny that many Western capitalists have gained their fortune through the opium trade. You cannot blame us for making money through opium while completely ignoring the fact that Westerners did the same thing in the past. Why is it all right for them to grow opium but not us?[4]

Bao Youxiang, the top leader, thought that, even now, foreigners were the aggressive perpetrators and the Wa were the passive collaborators in the drug trade. Whenever he was interviewed by journalists about the drug business in his territory, this was what he usually said:

You see we Wa people, we don't have any culture or education. Where would we get the chemicals or the machinery for this [drug processing]? It must come from more developed countries, including

Thailand. I think business people—foreign business people—use our territory or hide in our territory and then re-export these things to Thailand, China and elsewhere. . . . It's all these businesspeople, including Thais who come here, maybe Thais and Burmese working together, and it is always the Wa who get the blame. I really can't accept this. I really can't accept this anymore. (Jagan 2004, 6)

Regardless of how they viewed the drug problem in their territory, all the Wa leaders I talked to said that they decided to get rid of drugs not long after they dissociated themselves from the Communist Party of Burma and signed a cease-fire agreement with the Burmese government in April 1989. In an interview with Li Ziru, an ethnic Chinese who was one of the Wa's influential leaders before he died in early 2005, Li explained what the Wa authorities had been working on since 1989:

Now that we have announced that we are going to eradicate opium growing in the Wa area in 2005, we must accomplish this; it would hurt our reputation if we fail to do so. Right after we parted ways with the Communist Party of Burma, we had a meeting of local and central authorities in July 1989 to discuss drug prevention and economic development. We launched the first five-year plan [1990–94] in 1990. The main goal of that plan was to rebuild our society, with special attention to schools and hospitals. The main goal of the second five-year plan [1995–99] was the completion of various infrastructure projects, with the focus on the construction of power plants, roads, and communication systems. In both five-year plans, we did not receive any assistance from foreign countries, only some financial support from the central [Burmese] government. The ultimate goal of the second five-year plan was drug eradication. During those five years, we established a drug investigation unit. Its goals were to (1) prohibit the buying and selling of opium and other drugs, (2) gradually eliminate opium growing, and (3) prohibit drug use. We also tried to prevent foreigners from coming here and setting up drug factories. We sent our troops to destroy heroin factories and arrested many government officials, including a key figure in the central government.[5]

Discussions on how to reduce, and eventually stop, opium cultivation in the Wa area occupied a prominent space in most of the Wa government documents dating from this period (Milsom 2005). Bao Youxiang also repeatedly asserted in public that he was willing to bet his life that the Wa area would be drug free in 2005, an announcement that was first made in December 1996 (Marshall and Davis 2002). For example, Bao once said in a sobbing voice in public, "I don't want to be the leader of a bunch of drug addicts. When I see my people use drugs, I want to kill myself. However, I don't want to go down like this. That's why I want to get rid of opium growing, a practice that has been with us for so many generations. The tragedy that was created by our ancestors has to be eliminated by this generation" (Ting 2001, 58).

According to the 2003 version of the Wa Basic Law (United Wa State Party 2004, 163–64), drug-related laws are as follows:

- Opium cultivation will be banned starting in the year 2005.
- Anyone arrested for drug production will have all drug-producing machines, transportation tools, and illegal assets confiscated, and the offender will be imprisoned for three to ten years.
- Anyone arrested for providing a place, capital, or other assistance to a drug producer will receive the same criminal penalty as the drug producer.
- Anyone arrested for entering the Wa area with drugs will have all drugs, assets, and transportation tools confiscated. If the crime is serious, the offender will be sentenced to prison for five to seven years.

For some reason, the 2003 law made no mention of punishment for people who smuggled drugs into China from the Wa area, although the 1993 version had stipulated that a person who smuggled five units of heroin into China would receive the death penalty.[6] A high-ranking police officer whom I interviewed in April 2005 explained why, according to the 2003 law, drug offenders are not executed anymore: "We don't sentence people to death for drug offenses anymore because, after all, this is still a place where people are allowed to grow opium. [The ban on opium cultivation was to take effect later, in October 2005.] Now, even if a person is discovered with hundreds of kilograms of heroin, the maximum sentence is seven years."[7]

In a speech at a workshop on drug prohibition in 2001, the head of the Political Legal Bureau[8] pointed out quite frankly the difficulties of enforcing the drug law:

In general, there are a few reasons why we have gotten lax in the fight against drugs over the past two years. First of all, we did not fully understand the nature of the drugs we were dealing with. Second, there was no coordination among the various official units. Third, our officials themselves, as well as their relatives, were often involved in drug use, production, or trafficking. As a result, our law enforcement units were afraid to act, and even when they did, they were ineffective. Eventually, we just stood by and watched. Consequently, the problems of drug use and drug dealing have gotten worse. If we don't make some changes, our plan to completely eliminate drugs in the Wa State is going to fail. (United Wa State Party 2001e, 4)

Xiao Mingliang, deputy commander of the UWSA, summarized the difficulties of opium eradication this way:

We have to implement the opium eradication plan no matter how difficult it is going to be. There are three main obstacles. One, opium growing has been a custom here for more than a hundred years, and if we ask our people to give up this custom, it will take time. Two, without opium people are going to have problems surviving. Here, opium is the only real money that circulates freely. You see people buying a bowl of noodles, a bottle of cooking wine, and a bag of rice, and they are doing all these things basically with money from selling opium. Local farmers may also become desperate and may decide to join an uprising against government officials. These people may also move to places where opium growing is still allowed. Three, local governments may not follow the central government's order to eliminate opium.[9]

Programs Implemented by the Wa Government

Since 1989, the Wa authorities have implemented a number of crop-substitution programs to reduce opium cultivation. For example, farmers were encouraged to grow tea, sugar cane, rubber, longan, and other crops, instead of opium. However, due to the lack of planning, technology, and cash support, most of these programs either failed or were on such a small scale that their impact on the area's widespread opium culture was insignificant. Finally, the outcomes of these programs were often affected not only by economic factors but by political factors as well.

Besides crop-substitution programs, the Wa government also embarked on many legitimate business endeavors, presumably to diversify its sources of income. Many of these were joint ventures with Chinese firms, including liquor and cigarette factories, granite and tin mines, gem mines, and other businesses. According to my informants, most of these enterprises were either losing money or making very little due to poor management and the lack of a market for the products. Take the tobacco company, for example. The Wa government invested a large amount of money in this project, only to discover that there was no market for the cigarettes the company produced. In 2001, when I asked a key member of the Wa State Tobacco Company about the prospects for his company, he expressed his frustration:

> I was originally with the Chongqing Tobacco Company in China. We [the Chinese side] invested 20 million yuan [$2.4 million] and the Wa government about 40 million [$4.8 million] in this new tobacco company. The factory was established in 1999. The main purpose of the Chinese was to help the Wa get rid of its reliance on poppy cultivation. We gave all the profits to the Wa government. The establishment of the factory was approved by the Burmese government, though initially they were reluctant to do so. But, under pressure from UNDCP [United Nations Drug Control Program], they eventually gave in. Our main problem now is that we don't have a market in Burma for our products. The Burmese authorities allowed us to sell the products in Burma, but the tax is very high. You cannot really expect us to compete in the Burmese market with that kind of tax on our products. That is the irony in all of this. The Burmese government expects the Wa to stop growing opium, but they will not allow a manufacturing industry to grow here as an alternative. If they let us truly compete in the Burmese market, the profits from the tobacco industry could be quite formidable. This would help the Wa economy tremendously.[10]

This situation, and the rumors that some of the business endeavors in the Wa area were set up specifically to produce drugs or firearms or to launder drug money, have prompted many outsiders to suspect that the Wa government is still predominantly reliant on drug money to survive. A Thai army general asserted that the income of the United Wa State Army comes directly from the illicit drug trade, dismissing the UWSA claim that its main income derived from trading in mineral ores, gemstones, and other natural resources (Kasitipradit and Nanuam 1999b).

In the early 1980s, a large number of Chinese from China moved to the Wa area to become involved in a variety of legitimate businesses. When

Wa leaders began to invest heavily in infrastructure projects in the late 1990s, the number of Chinese businessmen, technicians, and laborers increased dramatically. As the Wa economy began to slow down in the early 2000s, many Chinese returned to China, and their departure further reduced the amount and scope of economic activities in the area. Even though Chinese entrepreneurs did play a key role in the development of the Wa area in the past fifteen years, their lack of professionalism and commitment to the Wa society also contributed to the development of a weak and primitive economy. Jeremy Milsom (2005, 71), the representative of the United Nations Office on Drugs and Crime (UNODC, formerly UNDCP) in the Wa area, also observed that

> Wa leaders placed high hopes on cigarette, liquor, and paper factories, as well as a tin smelter at Longtan. It was hoped they would bring employment opportunities for former poppy farmers and trigger other commercial developments in the region. These ventures have failed to meet their goals due to marketing problems, export restrictions in both China and Burma proper, and lack of technical expertise, with benefits going to Chinese immigrants or people from outside the region rather than to poppy farmers.

Wa leaders also took pride in discussing their so-called Drug Prevention through Migration. In 1999 and 2000, tens of thousands of villagers from prime opium-producing areas of Northern Wa State were forcefully transported to Southern Wa State, under the assumption that these opium farmers would not have to grow opium to survive in their new environment but, instead, could grow other crops in the lowland area. Many observers were skeptical of the Wa leaders' real motives. For example, according to Steinberg (2001, 59), an expert on Burma,

> the attempts at the close of the century to resettle some 140,000–150,000 Wa in other areas of the Shan State closer to the Thai border, although explained as an effort to eliminate opium production by creating new agricultural and rural-based employment, may in fact be an effort by the Wa (with the consent of the Rangoon authorities) to expand their territorial reach so that by the time a new constitution is formed, the "autonomous" area of the Wa will be vastly expanded at the expense of the Shan.

The United Nations' Wa Alternative Development Project (WADP)

The United Nations Office on Drugs and Crime (UNODC) had an on-going project in the Wa area. Known as the Wa Alternative Development Project (WADP), the project was a five-year, $15 million program intended to introduce economically viable alternative crops to replace reliance on opium poppy cultivation (U.S. Department of State 2000). According to Jelsma, Kramer, and Vervest (2005, x), "The purpose of the project is to improve food security, promote alternative livelihoods and the basic improvement of living conditions, health care, and education in four townships." The UNODC office was first set up in Mengbo in 1998, and in 2004 a second office was opened in Bangkang.

Most Wa leaders were reluctant to publicly criticize the UNODC, afraid that this might jeopardize their chance of receiving help from one of the two viable international organizations (the other is the World Food Program) active in their area. On the other hand, UNODC was frustrated when Wa leaders were only interested in receiving money, roads, and electricity. The essence of the WADP project, from the UNODC's viewpoint, was to establish a sustainable, community-based approach to the reduction and eventual elimination of the supply of and demand for opium in the Wa region. To achieve this mandate, the six main components of the project included institutionalizing a system that involved the local community in planning and implementing development, establishing an accessible and culturally sensitive primary health care delivery system, improving infrastructure, developing ecologically sustainable and financially attractive alternative income sources for local people, and installing a poppy cultivation monitoring program. The WADP was more interested in community empowerment and awareness, and was never intended to be a program that delivers money to the doorsteps of the opium farmers or the Wa leaders.

Burma

Anyone who takes a cursory look at what Burmese authorities have done to combat the drug problem in their country would be impressed with the many suppression measures undertaken by the *tatmadaw* (the Burmese army) over the past five decades (Central Committee for Drug Abuse Control 2000, 2001). Wave after wave of military attacks have been carried out against drug-trafficking insurgent groups, and hundreds of Burmese soldiers have been killed in these battles. Unfortunately, these measures have not been effective, and drug production and trafficking in the northeastern part of Burma continues to be a major problem.

When the Burmese authorities signed cease-fire agreements with many former CPB groups in 1989, people in the West suspected that the two sides had struck a deal: the insurgent groups would end their fight with the Burmese government so that the latter could concentrate on the bigger problem of the democratic movement in Rangoon and other parts of Burma. In return, the Burmese authorities would turn a blind eye to the insurgents' involvement in the drug business (Thant Myint-U 2006). Some observers in the West thought that 1989 was the turning point in the development of the drug trade in the Golden Triangle because, from that time onward, some groups in the Shan State began to turn all their attention to expanding their drug business (U.S. Department of State 1993).

After 1989, Burmese authorities did not conduct any major campaigns against drug trafficking organizations. Only low-level heroin traffickers with a kilogram or so of heroin were arrested, while major heroin traffickers were left alone. In the meantime, the shift from heroin to methamphetamine production had upset the Thai government because, unlike heroin, which was just passing through Thailand, the methamphetamine tablets were for the Thai drug market (Dupont 2001).

When I interviewed Burmese officials in Rangoon, most of them were relatively defensive, especially when they were informed of the Thai accusations of the Burmese authorities' inaction against the yaba business. A Burmese drug enforcement official responded bluntly:

> If we wish only bad things for the Thais, we would not be concerned with the yaba problem at all. Besides, it is more of a Thai problem than a Burmese problem because the tablets are transported and distributed by the Thais, not the Burmese, and most of the profits belong to the Thai transporters and distributors, not the producers in Burma. The Thai are screaming now with the yaba problem because this time it hits them in the mouth; in the past with heroin, Thailand was just a transit point.[11]

According to the 2001 INCSR Report, in 2000 the Burmese authorities finally shifted from their passive drug policy and resumed their efforts to curb drug production and trafficking:

In 2000 and 2001, the Burmese government launched its first serious campaigns against trafficking by former insurgent groups. In November 2000, the GOB [Government of Burma] took advantage of a mutiny within the Mong Ko Defense Army to seize Mong Ko and put that band and its leader, Mong Sa La, out of the narcotic business. It also sharply stepped up its pressure on the Kokang Chinese, who missed their 2000 target date for establishing an "opium free" zone throughout the Kokang Chinese Special Region No. 1 and the arrest of major traffickers. The Burmese government has also made clear to the Kokang Chinese that this campaign will continue. According to Burmese police sources, Secretary 1 Khin Nyunt has flatly told the Kokang leadership that they must be out of the narcotics business by 2002 or else the Burmese government would take "all necessary measures." (U.S. Department of State 2001, VIII–10)

The following year, the 2002 INCSR Report concluded that both the Kokang and the Wa were continually pressured by the Burmese authorities to do something about the drug trade in their territories:

In 2002, the Burmese government continued its crackdown in the Kokang region controlled by Peng Jiasheng's Myanmar National Democratic Alliance Army (MNDAA), which had pledged to be opium-free by 2000. The government modestly increased pressure on the Wa in 2002, closing down Wa liaison offices along the Thai border and arresting several Wa traffickers. . . . The government also took a more aggressive stance on traveling in the Wa territory, informing UWSA officials of such visits rather than seeking their permission in advance . . . During January, Kokang based trafficker, Liu Ming, was found after an engagement, dead. . . . The Kokang Chinese missed their opium-free target (scheduled for the year 2000), but have paid a heavy price for that failure in terms of increased attention from both the Burmese and the Chinese police. (U.S. Department of State 2002, VIII–7)

When it comes to combating drugs, Burmese officials also thought that the Wa were more likely to be successful than the Kokang. According to a high-ranking drug enforcer in Rangoon, "We are more optimistic with the Wa efforts than the Kokang efforts because the Wa leaders are more sincere about drug elimination and they are better organized. When the

Wa leaders talk, their people listen. Whereas in the Kokang, the Pengs' [Peng Jiasheng and Peng Jiafu, the two brothers who are the top leaders of the Kokang] words may not be followed strictly by people there and the Kokang government is somewhat in disarray."[12]

The fact that so many Wa and Kokang leaders and former drug kingpins like Luo Xinghan and Khun Sa were allowed to invest in major business ventures throughout Burma had observers in the West wondering about the sincerity of the Burmese government's intention to fight drugs. According to various sources, the Burmese economy is kept afloat almost entirely by drug money coming from drug lords. To this, the Burmese drug enforcer quoted above responded by saying that "drug money represents only a small portion of the total capital in Rangoon. Besides, from our point of view, involving drug lords in legitimate businesses is the best way to lure them away from the drug scene."[13]

In other words, drug control for the Burmese government is more than the straightforward implementation of drug prevention and suppression measures. Very often, drug control in Burma is politicized, and political considerations probably play a more important role than any other concerns.

Thailand

In the late 1990s, as Thailand became a major market for methamphetamine tablets produced in Burma, the Thai authorities made a concerted effort to stop the flow of these tablets across the Thai-Burma border. In many Thai border towns, the Thai authorities established a large network of informants. For example, one of my subjects estimated that there were three hundred informants in Mae Sai alone, acting as taxi drivers, food vendors, or bus drivers. The subject believed that most drug arrests occurred because the authorities were tipped off by informants.

Moreover, Thai authorities began to routinely check cars leaving Mae Sai for Bangkok. Initially, police officers in charge of the roadblocks did not check buses, especially tourist buses transporting foreign visitors. But after they found out that tour guides were taking advantage of the situation and were moving yaba pills, even tour buses were searched. Buses for local passengers would most definitely be searched.

Nonetheless, the influx of methamphetamine tablets from Burma into Thailand overwhelmed the Thai government. Between 1999 and 2000,

methamphetamine trafficking across the border reached an unprece-
dented level and prompted an editorial in the *Bangkok Post* (January 18,
2000, 10) to conclude that

> since their arrival, the UWSA [United Wa State Army] have proved to
> be far more ruthless, more efficient and far more dangerous drug
> traffickers than their predecessors. They have been named, quite cor-
> rectly, as the greatest single threat to Thai national security. Placing
> this Wa group in charge of eradicating the heroin problem seems very
> much like putting the wolves in charge of the cattle ranch. The UWSA
> have taken to the drug trade like a duck to water. They are the greatest
> producers of methamphetamine tablets in the world.

In the year 2000, the Thai Farmers Research Center estimated that illegal sales of methamphetamines had reached 50 billion baht ($1.28 bil-
lion) per year, and when medical costs and other programs were included,
the total cost to the Thai society had been more than 100 billion baht
($2.56 billion) annually (*Bangkok Post*, April 17, 2000).

Conflicts between Thailand and Burma

After Khun Sa and his troops surrendered to the government in Rangoon in 1996, some of his followers, mostly Shan, remained behind and
later became known as the Shan State Army South (SSA South), led by
Colonel Yawd Serk. According to reports in the *Bangkok Post*, an English-
language newspaper that is anti-Wa and pro-SSA South and has long
been banned in Burma, the SSA South became a nuisance to the Wa
when they began to routinely inform Thai authorities about drug trafficking activities in the border area. This also irritated the Burmese army
because they, too, were benefiting from and protecting the Wa drug trade.
A *Bangkok Post* article (November 14, 2000) stated that on November 11,
2000, the SSA South ambushed a group of Burmese soldiers who were
delivering speed pills to Thailand from a drug plant in Burma. The attack
was part of the SSA South's antidrug drive targeting the UWSA and Burmese troops. Thai authorities praised the SSA South for its antidrug efforts. Burma believed it was the work of Thai soldiers and that a clash
between Burmese and Thai troops ensued in which two Thai rangers
were wounded and a Burmese soldier was killed (Khuenkaew and Nanuam 2000). Two months later, Burmese forces attacked positions held by
the Shan at Tachilek, just across from Mae Sai in Chiang Rai (*Bangkok

Post, February 12, 2001). Several mortar shells and grenades hit Mae Sai, killing three Thais, wounding civilians and soldiers, causing damage to buildings and a vehicle, and forcing residents to flee their homes (Ashayagachat 2001). The Friendship Bridge between Mae Sai and Tachilek was closed, forcing merchants on both sides of the bridge to shut down their businesses between February and June 2001, which led to severe economic losses estimated at around 3 billion baht ($66 million) (Kumtita and Tunyasiri 2002). The trafficking of methamphetamine tablets across the border also came to a halt.

After the border was closed, Thai officials conducted a systematic investigation in Mae Sai, looking for businesspeople suspected of being involved with drug dealers on the Burmese side. Thai authorities also took the opportunity to clean up some of the Chinese villages in the border areas that were considered to be hot spots for the drug trade. A subject in the Thai-Burma border area stated that "the Thai authorities, during the time the Friendship Bridge was closed, surrounded Huai Khrai and Ban Yang. In Ban Yang, they searched each and every household, and once surrounded by the authorities, there is no way out for villagers. Yunnan Chinese in Thailand are very much stigmatized by Thai people as drug dealers."[14]

Four months later, the Burmese reopened the border with Thailand. Once border crossings between Thailand and Burma resumed, the methamphetamine trade also returned with a vengeance. As hundreds of millions of speed pills continued to pour into Thailand, the Thai authorities, out of desperation, began to come up with many unconventional measures to cope with the problem. For example, some Thai politicians suggested that their government should engage in methamphetamine production and sell it for 1 baht a pill to drive the Wa pills out of the Thai market (*Bangkok Post*, October 28, 2000). In another instance, a Buddhist-Brahmin ceremony was conducted to curse all those involved in the production and trafficking of methamphetamines, and anyone else who benefits from the trade. Dry chilies and salt were burned together, in the traditional belief that those cursed would suffer burning heat and pain (Assavanonda 2001). Thai authorities also went after Wei Xuegang's money and assets in Thailand. By early 2002, the Money Laundering Office of Thailand had frozen 342 million baht ($7.8 million) in assets belonging to Wei and his close aides after a series of drug sweeps (Charoenpo 2002). Moreover, a tougher drug law was proposed by Thai lawmakers under which drug offenders found in possession of fifteen methamphetamine pills or more would be forced to serve prison terms as dealers, rather than be treated for addiction at rehabilitation centers. Some of the Thai police who were involved in the yaba business were arrested and jailed, and Klong Toey, the drug trading slum in Bangkok, was targeted by law enforcement authorities.

On May 2002, less than a year after the first border closure, another skirmish occurred when Thai and Wa troops traded artillery fire across the border. Thai authorities claimed that their troops fired warning shots after stray shells from fighting between the SSA South and the Wa fell on Thai territory. Burmese authorities, on the other hand, accused the Thai forces of supplying heavy artillery support to antigovernment SSA South rebels who then attacked military positions held by Burmese and Wa forces. Two days later, in protest against a military exercise conducted by the Thai army in the border area, Burma shut its entire border with Thailand. The closure put a stop to joint efforts in a wide range of economic ventures along the border, and cost local traders about 30 million baht ($700,000) per day in lost business (Khamthita 2002).

Under pressure from the Thai business community to reopen the border, Prime Minister Thaksin Shinawatra of Thailand, whose family had many business ventures in Burma, abruptly ordered his army in the north to stop the military exercise immediately, pack up, and leave (Khuenkaew and Nanuam 2002). Thaksin also instructed his troops in the north not to "overreact" if stray shells from fighting inside Burma landed in Thai territory and to fire only flares as warning shots. Moreover, he decided that Thailand should give up the "buffer state" policy against Burma and stop supporting the anti-Rangoon Shan State Army. In return, Thaksin asked Burma to control the UWSA and do something about the UWSA's drug trade. In the meantime, Burma, with the full support of the Wa, conducted a major military offensive against the SSA South after Thai troops stopped supporting the SSA South. Moreover, Thaksin also removed some of the anti-Rangoon generals from the Thai army and rounded up Burmese dissidents living in Thailand to appease the Burmese generals.

Regardless, speed pills continued to enter Thailand via Laos as some of the pill factories were reported to have moved to Laos from the Southern Wa area. The Burmese economy also took a nosedive, and the Burmese kyat plummeted. After the border was closed for five months, the Burmese government reopened the checkpoints with Thailand on October 15, 2002.

The 2003 Drug War

Numerous conflicts between Burmese/Wa and Thai/SSA South over the past decade had resulted in the deaths of many soldiers. Subsequent border closures along the Thai-Burma border also took a huge economic toll on people living on both sides of the border. Yet these incidents did not have a significant impact on cross-border drug trafficking, as hundreds of millions of speed pills flowed into Thailand after Burma reopened its border with Thailand on October 2002. A Thai army general warned on November 2002 that one billion speed pills would be smuggled into Thailand during the following year. There were also reports that the SSA South, long considered by the Thais to be an antidrug force, had also begun its own involvement in the drug business, now that it was no longer being supported by the Thais.

Against this backdrop, a report in the January 15, 2003, *Bangkok Post* announced that

> Prime Minister Thaksin Shinawatra has given authorities till April 30 to rid "every square inch" of the country of drugs. . . . The prime minister told yesterday's briefing of national strategies against drugs for more than 1,000 governors, police and military personnel and state officials, that he would no longer tolerate drug problems. He also vowed to match cruelty with cruelty. "Drug traders are unkind toward our children so we will be unkind towards them," he said. . . . The nationwide drug campaign will start at 9am on Feb. 1 and continue until 9pm on April 30. (Tunyasiri and Charoenpo 2003, 1)

By then, it was clear that Thaksin was prepared to take drastic measures to cope with the methamphetamine epidemic that had had such devastating effects on the country for so many years. Ten days after the *Bangkok Post* report, Interior Minister Wan Muhamad Nor Matha issued an ultimatum to drug dealers—quit the drug trade or prepare to face harsh state action that could be lethal: "Tell them to stop selling drugs and leave the communities for good, or they will be put behind bars or even 'vanish without a trace.' Who cares? They are destroying our country" (*Bangkok Post*, January 25, 2003, 1).

The Thai government launched its three-month crusade against drugs in grand style, with Prime Minister Thaksin Shinawatra opening the campaign at a ceremony at the Royal Plaza, a popular shopping area in Bangkok (*Bangkok Post*, February 1, 2003). Soon afterward, there were reports that drug suspects had been shot dead on their way home after being questioned by the police at local police stations. The reports also hinted that many drug suspects had been killed by the police or military personnel in extrajudicial killings with no thought to observing legal niceties. The police, however, denied that they were responsible and implied that "the deaths stemmed from infighting within the drug trade as prominent figures moved to eliminate the risk of being exposed by potential stool pigeons" (*Bangkok Post*, February 2, 2003, 1). The price of speed pills in the Klong Toey slum community reportedly shot up to 200 baht ($4.60) each, a sharp increase on the 70–80 baht (about $1.70) a pill before the crackdown began (Tunyasiri and Ngarmkham 2003).

Within days after the crackdown, authorities arrested fifty-seven hundred drug suspects, seized 3.8 million speed pills, and froze 129 million baht ($3 million) in assets. Human rights groups, on the other hand, voiced concern about the rising number of deaths among alleged drug traders, believing many were victims of summary executions by police (Santimetaneedol 2003a). According to the police, one hundred suspects had been killed within a few days of the campaign's onset. The police also emphasized that fewer than twenty were killed by the police, and always in self-defense. The others had been killed by drug traffickers who turned against each other, according to the police (Hutasingh and Bangprapa 2003).

When human rights groups in Thailand began to question the use of extrajudicial killings by the Thai government, Prime Minister Thaksin urged

> Thailand not to pay so much attention to the rising death toll that they lose sight of the "big picture." . . . You should ask yourselves if you're concerned about your children. You have been caring for them since they came into this world. Now they are innocent victims who are dying slowly because of drugs; yet you are talking about the statistics of those who are silenced by people of their own kind," he said. . . . "In war we cannot sympathise with our enemies. If we do, they will come back and do us in," he said. (Tunyasiri and Ashayagachat 2003, 1)

In response, the Asian Forum for Human Rights and Development (Forum-Asia) issued a statement saying that it was "alarmed by Prime Minister Thaksin's comment that murder is not an unusual fate for wicked people and the public should not be alarmed by their death. This statement might be interpreted as endorsement for the use of violence in ongoing drug suppression campaigns" (Ruangdit 2003, 2).

By March 4, 2003, it was reported that 1,282 people had died in drug-related killings, an average of forty-six deaths a day. Unyielding, the Thai government ordered all provinces to aim for a 25 percent reduction in the number of blacklisted drug pushers (Tunyasiri and Traisophon 2003).[15] The price of yaba in Bangkok was reported to have increased to about 500 baht ($11.70) per pill (Charoenpo 2003). By the time it was over, the *Bangkok Post* (May 1, 2003, 1) reported that

> all 75 provinces exceeded the target of reducing the number of drug traders and users set at 75%, with 10 of them achieving a perfect 100%, 40 provinces more than 90%, and many others more than 80%. The worst was 78%. . . . Chartchai Suthiklom, deputy secretary-general of the Narcotics Control Board, said the campaign netted a total of 1,765 big-time drug traders and 15,244 small dealers. A total of 280,207 pushers and addicts surrendered and were sent for rehabilitation, while 15.5 million speed pills were seized.

Some sources estimated that as many as three thousand drug suspects were killed during the campaign (Ngamkham 2003). While it was not clear what long-lasting effect this might have on the yaba trade, human rights groups were outraged that so many had died without knowing why. An editorial in the *Bangkok Post* (August 21, 2003, 10) also criticized the Thai government's ruthless approach:

> The justification of harsh authoritarian measures in the name of national security is a delicate undertaking. The concept of universal human rights, of the sanctity of the rule of law, and the right to fair trial are not idle constructs, but rather values which must be preserved and supported for all, by all. All too many governments have justified the use of force against their citizens in the name of the public good. By all means take the firmest action against drug traffickers, but even the guilty deserve their day in court.

An op-ed in the *New York Times* by Pasuk Phongpaichit and Chris Baker (2003, A15), a Thai professor and a U.S.-based researcher, also questioned whether the Thai government unjustifiably went after low-level drug dealers while ignoring the fact that so many Thai police, politicians, and government officials were implicated in the drug trade. U.S. drug officials in Thailand, on the other hand, hailed Thailand's war against drugs as a success. William J. Snipes, the regional director of the U.S. Drug Enforcement Administration, said the war on drugs had been effective, even though he was not sure whether it would have a lasting effect (*Bangkok Post*, November 27, 2003). A subject familiar with the Wa drug business in

Thailand told me that "among those thousands of drug dealers in Thailand who were killed, about half of them were somehow related to the Wa. That's why it was so detrimental to the Wa's drug business."[16]

Prime Minister Thaksin Shinawatra announced that his next step in the war against drugs would be to set up a committee to suppress influential people and officials who were involved in illegal businesses (*Bangkok Post*, May 9, 2003). The police also had compiled a list of eight hundred gunmen and gangsters to be investigated (*Bangkok Post*, May 15, 2003). "If we can solve the police problem, we can solve most problems because police have a hand in every illegal business," a Thai official remarked (Santimetaneedol 2003b). Unfortunately, the campaign to suppress influential figures ended abruptly and quietly without gaining any momentum, and it is not clear why.

Tension between Thailand and Burma will persist as long as drugs from Burma continue to flow into Thailand and it could trigger serious regional strife by dragging neighboring countries into the conflict. From the Thai perspective, Burma is only serious about stopping opium cultivation and not methamphetamine production and trafficking, and consequently Burma is a national security threat that must be dealt with promptly and decisively (*Bangkok Post*, October 9, 2002).

Besides blaming its neighbor for the yaba problem, many Thais also thought that social inequality and lack of economic development in the border areas were also contributing factors to the persistent involvement of Chinese Haw (Muslims) and hill tribes in the drug trade. According to Sanitsuda Ekachai (2002, 1), writing in the *Bangkok Post*,

> a large number of hillpeople are indigenous to this land or are long-time migrants who have lived in Thailand for decades. Yet, they are considered illegal aliens. Robbed of education and job opportunities, many of them are being pushed by state discrimination to join the underground economy backed by corrupt authorities. Unless crooked officials are punished and ethnic people in Thailand receive their rights as citizens and the chance to live a normal life, fighting drug trafficking is a pipedream.

China

As mentioned above, China had a major drug problem before the Communists defeated the Kuomintang in 1949:

After their takeover of the country in 1949, it took the [Communist] party a mere three years radically to eliminate all illegal substances; a dense network of police institutions, resident committees and mass organizations were used to crush drug offenders, some even being denounced by their own family members. Public trials and mass executions dealt a final blow to narcotic culture, while tens of thousands of offenders were sent to prison, often for life. (Dikotter, Laamann, and Zhou 2004, 208)

Communist authorities reported that "between 1950 and 1953, over 80,000 drug criminals have been brought to justice and 20 million addicts were rehabilitated" (National Narcotics Control Commission 1999, 3). According to various sources, drug-related crimes almost did not exist between 1954 and the late 1970s, when China adopted an open door policy and instituted a series of economic reforms.

In the 1980s, when border trade between China and Burma began to flourish, opium and heroin from Burma also began to flow into China. During that time, Chinese authorities were not overly concerned with the emerging drug problem, because they were mostly preoccupied with promoting trade and accumulating wealth. However, by the mid-1990s, because of the dramatic increase in the number of drug users in China and the international perception that China was becoming a major transit country for heroin, Chinese authorities began to pay attention to drug use and trafficking. Consequently, the Chinese government developed the working principle of "simultaneously promoting the 'four prohibitions' (prohibition of drug abuse, trafficking, cultivation, and manufacturing), eradicating the sources of drugs and obstructing their trafficking channels, enforcing the law strictly and solving the problem by examining both its root causes and its symptoms" (Ting 2004, 28–29).

To obstruct the flow of drugs, the Chinese authorities set up three lines of defense. The first line was the border area where any exit or entry was subject to strict examination. The second line was composed of checkpoints in inland regions, and the third line consisted of checks on vital communication lines, airports, railway stations, and harbors (Ting 2004). According to the National Narcotics Control Commission (2001, 46), "The first line is in Yunnan Province, the frontier of the infiltration of drugs from the Golden Triangle; the second line is Guangxi, Guizhou and Sichuan adjacent to Yunnan; and the third line is in Chongqing Municipality and Guangdong, Fujian, Ganshu, Ningxia, Hunan, Hubei, Henan and Anhui Provinces, which are the important drug trafficking routes."

Local or First Line of Defense

Yunnan Province, the first line of China's drug defense, is adjacent to three countries: Burma, Laos, and Vietnam. The border stretches over 4,060 kilometers: Yunnan-Burma, 1,997 kilometers; Yunnan-Laos, 710 kilometers; Yunnan-Vietnam, 1,353 kilometers. Even though drugs have been smuggled into China via the Yunnan-Laos or Yunnan-Vietnam border areas, Chinese authorities are mostly concerned with drug trafficking along the China-Burma border, especially in the areas of Dehong Prefecture, Baoshan District, Lincang District, Dali Prefecture, and Kunming City.

DEHONG PREFECTURE

Dehong Prefecture is a semiautonomous region of two ethnic minorities: the Dai and the Jingpo. Its proximity to the drug-producing areas of the Kachin, the Kokang, and the Wa on the Burmese side makes it one of the most important battlegrounds in the war against drugs. Ruili, a wild frontier town in the prefecture, is also located just across from Muse, the Burmese town that is the center of drug production and trafficking. Because of the increase in border trade and the aggressive development of Ruili as a tourist attraction by the local and provincial authorities, it provides many people a chance to use border trade and sightseeing to cover their drug trafficking activities. A police officer in Luxi, where the only airport within the prefecture is located, estimated that

> in 2003, of all the drug dealing-related arrests, 46 percent were local people, 20.6 percent from other parts of Yunnan, 31.5 percent out-of-province people, and 1.1 percent from abroad. You can see outsiders were the majority. Local people are more likely to be involved in small-scale trafficking, like a few grams to a few hundred grams and they are doing it to support their drug habit. Out-of- province people are bringing heroin to the inland areas; they are more likely to be involved in large quantities of drugs, like 10 kilograms or more.[17]

Drug enforcers in Yunnan Province often suggested that one of the unique aspects to drug trafficking in their jurisdiction is *liangtouzaiwai*, or "the two 'heads' are outside." A drug enforcement officer in Ruili noted:

> Very often, the two 'heads' are located outside of our jurisdiction. Drug producers operate their business in Burma, and they hire border area residents or unemployed, out-of-province people in Ruili to

move the drug for them. They hide the drugs in goods, people, or liquid commodities. In general, the bosses abroad and the bosses in the inland provinces are highly organized, but the people who are actually involved in the trafficking and transportation are hired on a temporary basis.[18]

As a result, the authorities were frustrated that they were only catching and punishing the drug mules and not the big bosses.

Most drug enforcers in the area were not optimistic about winning the war on drugs, as this police officer in Ruili explained:

The drug problem in this area is going to get worse. First of all, drug trafficking is going to increase because the border is now patrolled by the army, not the armed police. The army patrols in a certain way; they patrol according to a schedule, and they conduct high profile—highly visible—patrols. When the armed police were in charge, they patrolled irregularly and quietly. Drug dealers are now in a better position to evade the authorities than in the past. The change was made last year, in 2003, and since then, more drugs are being trafficked across the border. Secondly, there is a problem with increased drug abuse. There is an increase in the number of drug addicts in this area. Drug use has spread to the Dai villages. Many young Dai are unemployed and have no future, so they get involved in motorcycle racing and drug use.[19]

The same subject went on to explain why it was so challenging to catch drug traffickers:

No doubt, there are big drug dealers living in this area and we know who they are. However, we cannot just go out and arrest them because we do not have the evidence against them. Nowadays, big drug dealers rarely touch the drugs. They hire someone to help them. Besides, they are getting better and better at evading us. For example, they like to conduct so-called trial trafficking. The big boss will organize a major drug trafficking scheme, but only he knows that the whole thing is fake. Everything will be carried out as if they are trying to smuggle drugs into China, but in actuality it is a way for the big boss to see whether the information is leaked to the police, if there would be problems, or if someone in his organization is unreliable, etc. After a few trials, then the big boss will actually move the drug.[20]

According to the officer, the lack of resources was probably the most discouraging aspect to drug enforcement:

> Last year [2003], Beijing designated Ruili as a drug disaster area. Even so, the central and provincial governments did not do anything to deal with the problem. There was no funding, no additional manpower, or new laws to help us to fight against drug trafficking. It is no use to just say this is a disaster area and then do nothing about it. Our main problem is the lack of funding. We have to rely on the money we confiscate from drug dealers or the money we get from selling the drug dealers' cars and furniture. The fixed, regular budget from the government is very limited.[21]

BAOSHAN DISTRICT

After drugs from Burma are smuggled into Dehong Prefecture via the Muse-Ruili checkpoint or the Bangsai-Wanding checkpoint (another pair of trading posts located only a few miles away from Muse-Ruili), they will be moved to Luxi and then to the town of Baoshan in the district of the same name. As a result, the checkpoint in Mukang, a small town between Luxi and Longling of Baoshan District, is one of the most important checkpoints for drugs in Yunnan Province. Tenchong, another major town in the district, is also a key transit point for drugs heading for Baoshan.

DALI PREFECTURE

After Baoshan District, drugs are moved through Dali Prefecture, a semiautonomous region of the Pai ethnic minority, to arrive in Kunming, the center of drug trafficking in Yunnan Province. The Chinese authorities consider the area a frontline in the drug war because a large number of the Muslim minority live there and they are very active in drug trafficking. Weishan County is the home of numerous Muslim drug traffickers who have been apprehended.

LINCANG PREFECTURE

Lincang Prefecture is adjacent to both the Kokang and the Wa areas. Chinese from Zhenkang County (located just across Laukkai in Kokang) and the Wa from Cangyuan County (located just across Kunma in Northern Wa State) are very active in cross-border drug trafficking. A drug expert in Kunming analyzed the situation in Lincang by saying that along the entire border area of China and Burma, the police force at Lincang is the most important enforcement unit because that's where most heroin comes in. Kokang people are unlike Wa people; the Wa mostly kept their promise when they said they will not smuggle drugs through China. That's not the case with the Kokang people. There are many powerful groups in Kokang and they are not all controlled by Peng Jiasheng [the top Kokang leader]. Kokang people are very active in the production of heroin, much more so than the Wa. The Wa are more likely to smuggle their drugs through Thailand. The Kokang people are very good at claiming that they are not involved in the drug trade anymore, but we all know they are still involved.[22]

KUNMING CITY

Kunming City is the capital of Yunnan Province and it is where most of the drugs that go through the above-mentioned four areas accumulate and then continue to flow to other parts of China or to the international market. Over the past two decades, about 80 percent of the heroin-related arrests in China occurred in Yunnan Province (Ting 2004), and the bulk of these arrests were in the vicinity of Kunming. "Kunming plays an important role in the heroin trade," a drug expert in Kunming said. "Many drug traffickers from abroad have to rely on people here in Kunming to establish a drug route to facilitate the flow of drugs from Burma through the border areas and through Kunming."[23]

In addition to the five areas mentioned above, drugs from Burma can also be smuggled into China via the Simao District and the Xishuangbanna Prefecture. Simao District is located between Bangkang and Kunming, and Jinghong City of Xishuangbanna is not far away from the No. 4 Special Region (Mengla) of Burma.

Along with the Muslims from Weishan County in Dali Prefecture, Muslims from the town of Pingyuan in Wenshan Prefecture, located south of Kunming, are also active in heroin trafficking. Some of the drug dealers I interviewed in Kunming said that their suppliers were from Pingyuan. However, it is believed that drug trafficking in Pingyuan has dramatically decreased ever since the Chinese government sent troops and tanks into Pingyuan in 1992 to wipe out the arms and drug dealers who had congregated in the town. Scores of suspects were believed to have been killed by the Chinese army and hundreds more were arrested (Ting 2004).

Regional or Second Line of Defense

After drugs from Burma pass through Yunnan, they are then transported through the adjacent provinces of Sichuan, Guizhou, and Guangxi. According to an interview with a drug expert in Chengdu City, the capital of Sichuan Province:

> Chengdu is mainly a distribution and transit point; the majority of the heroin comes in and goes out. We also think that the bulk of the heroin is for the Chinese market, as the amount of the drug diminishes by the time it arrives in the coastal areas. Some of this heroin may be smuggled into Hong Kong. The other thing unique about Chengdu is that it plays a key role in the smuggling of ephedrine from China into Burma. It is transported to Chengdu from Xinjiang and then into Burma. There are also a large number of chemical plants in this city. Many people in Xichang and Liangshan [of Sichuan Province] are involved in heroin trafficking.[24]

Guizhou is another province where drugs from Yunnan pass through to reach the coastal areas of China (Guizhou Police College 2004). According to Chang Ting (2004, 57), "Some drug traffickers have long used Guizhou as a transit route and have opened trafficking markets along this line, and as a result, many people in Guizhou have suffered greatly from drug addiction." A drug expert in Guiyang, the capital of Guizhou, described how authorities in Guizhou paid close attention to drug mules using public transportation to move drugs:

> One out of three drug couriers may be arrested on his or her first try. Drug enforcers here are now pretty good at guessing who among the passengers on a bus or a train are involved in drug transportation. They look for clues such as: the person is not eating anything (to prevent themselves from having to go to the bathroom because they have swallowed heroin bags), they look nervous, they are from certain areas in Guizhou (the five places where drug dealing is rampant), they wear similar clothes (because the person who hired them to move the drug bought the same clothes for all of them), they carry very little luggage, etc.[25]

After Guizhou, drugs must go through Guangxi Province to reach Guangzhou City, the capital of Guangdong Province. As a result, drug enforcement authorities in Guangxi are always alert to large consignments of heroin passing through their jurisdiction. However, authorities have been frustrated by their inability to conduct controlled delivery to go after the big dealers outside of their province:[26]

> There is no way we can conduct a controlled delivery when we are tipped off that there is a drug consignment passing through our jurisdiction. First of all, we are never sure there will be heroin inside the truck that was tipped off to us, so we are not going to make fools of ourselves by informing authorities in another province only to find out later that the intelligence was wrong. Secondly, we can't go over to another province to arrest drug suspects, so this means we are out of the ballgame. Thirdly, we want to confiscate the drug ourselves so that we will be monetarily compensated by our provincial authorities later. Fourthly, we want to have the credit for the arrest. Finally, if we were to allow drugs to go through our territory and authorities in another province discover the drugs, then we are doomed. As a result there is not much cooperation between us and authorities from other provinces.[27]

National or Third Line of Defense

From the Chinese authorities' viewpoint, Guangzhou City is the heroin distribution center of China outside of the three provinces of southwest China (Yunnan, Sichuan, and Guizhou). One drug expert I interviewed estimated that more than 80 percent of the heroin consumed in China went through Guangzhou. The city is also the last and most important link between China and Hong Kong, an international center for the heroin trade (Ting 2004).

Chongqing City, the largest industrial and economic center in southwestern China, is the fourth provincial-level municipality, after Beijing, Shanghai, and Tianjin.[28] Chongqing is now the biggest city in China, with a population of about thirty million. According to a drug enforcer in Chongqing,

> Chongqing was originally a drug consumption area (*xiaofeidi*) for heroin that was smuggled here via Guizhou, Chengdu, and Xuanwei [in Qujing District of Yunnan]. By the year 2000, this city became a transit point for heroin for the drug market in Shanghai, Suchow, and other places in the delta of the Changjiang River. That's because

Chongqing is a transportation hub and the Sichuanese have good connections to drug producers in the Golden Triangle.[29]

In November 1990, the Chinese government established the National Narcotics Control Commission (NNCC), which was charged with the task of formulating major drug policies and specific drug control measures. In August 1998, the Ministry of Public Security set up the Drug Control Bureau, which also serves as an operational agency of the NNCC (National Narcotics Control Commission 1999; Ting 2004). The bureau has a staff of fifty. There are about seventeen thousand specialized antinarcotic officers nationwide.

International Cooperation

To fight cross-border drug trafficking, the Chinese government has been active in establishing good working relationships with neighboring countries such as Burma, Laos, Vietnam, and Thailand (Yunnan Province Narcotics Control Committee 2003; Sheng 2006). Chinese drug authorities meet frequently with their counterparts in those countries, and numerous joint operations have led to the arrests of drug lords and the confiscation of huge consignments of drugs. Moreover, Chinese authorities also provide training to drug enforcement agents from Burma and Laos in a police college located in Kunming.

The working relationship between Chinese and American drug enforcement authorities hit a low point because of the "Goldfish Case." In 1988, authorities in Shanghai intercepted a shipment of about seven pounds of heroin stuffed in condoms that were tucked inside the bodies of 140 living large goldfish. Because the goldfish were to be sent to the United States, the Chinese informed the DEA; a short time later three Chinese living in San Francisco were arrested. When the case went to trial, a suspect arrested in Shanghai, a Chinese citizen, was sent to the United States to testify. After the suspect arrived in the United States, he applied for political asylum on the grounds that the Chinese authorities had tortured him to obtain a confession. When the U.S. government accepted his application, five Chinese police officers who had accompanied the witness to the United States left the court in protest and flew back to China. Consequently, the judge for the case declared a mistrial.

In the aftermath of the Goldfish Case, the Chinese and the American authorities worked very hard to improve their relationship. In 1999, the DEA established an office in Beijing, and in 2003 the arrest of a major heroin trafficker in Fuzhou City by Chinese and American authorities signified that both sides had came a long way since the Goldfish Case. However, political considerations often interfere with drug enforcement decisions. According to Dong Sheng, the deputy director of the Yunnan Provincial Anti-Narcotics Bureau in Kunming,

> the biggest problem with international cooperation is the difference of opinion in understanding the big political picture. The U.S. government views the Burmese government as a military regime that denies human rights and political freedom to its people, so Americans are not willing to cooperate with Burma. The Chinese government, on the other hand, has another point of view. Beside the complicated problem of drug control, the Burmese government is also one of our neighbors, so political stability in Burma is one of our main concerns.[30]

U.S. Role

In Burma

From the early 1970s until 1988, the United States funded an antinarcotics program in Burma and provided over $80 million in assistance:

> In 1972, the United States began to provide material assistance to what had been a unilateral Yangon effort against its drug-trafficking insurgencies. Yangon accepted Washington's offer of helicopters, fixed wing aircraft, communications equipment, and other non-lethal items to be used against the drug trade. United States–Myanmar counternarcotics cooperation continued until 1988, when Washington terminated its support in retaliation for human rights violations and the suppression of Aung San Suu Kyi and her democratically elected National League for Democracy by the *Tatmadaw's* State Law and Restoration Council (SLORC). (Gibson and Haseman 2003, 6)

In September 1988, the United States suspended assistance to Burma because of the government's violent crackdown on student demonstrations. U.S. authorities concluded that "despite 15 years of U.S. assistance for an anti-narcotics program, Burma's opium production has continued to increase" (United States General Accounting Office 1989, 17), and decided not to certify the Burmese government as cooperating in narcotics eradication. After the U.S. government cut off its drug enforcement support, the Burmese government signed cease-fire agreements with various armed groups in the border area, and drug suppression activities in Burma slowed down significantly.

In the spring of 2002, the Burmese antidrug czar, Col. Kyaw Thein, came to Washington, D.C., to urge the U.S. government to certify Burma as cooperating in the fight against narcotics. The rules had been changed recently to ensure Mexico qualified. However, "lobbying from the U.S. Senate and House of Representatives, highlighting human rights abuses committed by the SPDC [State Peace and Development Council, the successor to SLORC] and the political impasse in the country, was a key factor in the final decision to deny certification once more" (Transnational Institute 2003, 23). A certification that Burma had cooperated with the United States to reach minimum anti-narcotics benchmarks would have cleared the way for U.S. antinarcotics funding. According to Steinberg (2006, 116), "Not only was an opportunity to improve relations lost, but those within the *tatmadaw* who had worked toward that end (and may have been potential reformers) lost considerable status."

Wei Xuegang, the leader of Southern Wa State, was one of the first individuals designated by the United States in June 2000 as a "drug kingpin" pursuant to the 1999 Foreign Narcotics Kingpin Designation Act. In 2002, in the aftermath of 9/11, the United States declared that the United Wa State Army, as a so-called heavily armed drug trafficking organization, was an important target in the war on terrorism (Dawson 2002). Three years later, in January 2005, the federal court in the Eastern District of New York and the New York Field Division of the Drug Enforcement Administration announced the indictment of eight Wa leaders in absentia on charges of heroin and methamphetamine trafficking: Wei Xuegang and his two brothers, Wei Xuelong and Wei Xueyun; Bao Youxiang and his three brothers, Bao Youyi, Bao Youliang, and Bao Youhua; and an unrelated Bao Huaqiang. The indictment was a result of a long-term international initiative led by the DEA's Asian Heroin Task Force (also known as Group 41) in cooperation with several branches of the Royal Thai Police, including the Narcotics Suppression Bureau, the Office of Narcotics Control Board, and the Anti-Money Laundering Office. The initiative, code named Operation Warlord, was intended to stop the flow of illegal drugs at their source.

According to the indictment, "The United Wa State Army was a criminal narcotics trafficking organization operating in a large semi-autonomous region of the Shan State of Burma (Myanmar). This organization has engaged in: (1) the collection, transportation, and taxing of opium; (2) the manufacturing and distribution of heroin and methamphetamine; and (3) the laundering of narcotic proceeds" (U.S. District Court 2005, 1). DEA records showed that since 1985 the defendants have exported from Burma over a ton of heroin with a retail value of $1 billion into the United States alone. To this, a DEA agent clarified that the defendants may or may not have been directly involved in the transportation, but as long as they were the suppliers, they were guilty of being part of a conspiracy with the investors, the transporters, and the buyers to export heroin to the United States.[31]

The indictment also charged the eight Wa leaders with trafficking methamphetamine into the United States because over twelve thousand methamphetamine tablets labeled with the UWSA logo had been seized at mail facilities throughout the United States. When a DEA agent with Group 41 was asked about the indicted Wa leaders' involvement in the smuggling of methamphetamine into the United States, he appeared startled and said so far that he had not encountered any methamphetamine trafficking case against the Wa leaders.[32]

If convicted, the defendants each face mandatory prison sentences and fines. The indictment seeks a forfeiture money judgment of $103 million, for which all eight defendants are jointly and severally liable. The indictment also seeks forfeiture of the defendants' directly traceable assets, including the Hong Pang Group holding company and affiliated businesses, operating in Thailand, Burma, Hong Kong, China, and other countries.

The U.S. indictment caught the Wa leaders by surprise, as they only learned about the indictment through the television news programs from China and Hong Kong that were aired in the Wa area. The Wa leaders promptly issued a five-page statement: "The U.S. court's indictment of the Wa leaders is an irresponsible act and we would like to express our strong displeasure and regret. Over the past fifteen years, we have been working very hard to eliminate drugs, and we have achieved a certain level of success. At this crucial juncture in our efforts to ban drugs, certain Thai institutions and political bosses provided false information about us to the U.S. authorities. We suspect that there is a political motive behind this whole episode" (United Wa State Party 2005b, 1).

Regardless of the fact that U.S. authorities may never be able to bring the eight defendants to trial in the United States, the impact of the indictment was felt in Bangkang. Now that the authorities and the businessmen in China have to think twice before they set foot in the Wa area because they do not want to be viewed as associates of indicted drug traffickers, few people from China are willing to venture over to the Wa side.

In Thailand

To prevent Southeast Asian heroin from entering the United States, the U.S. government has maintained a strong presence in Thailand, a country that has been one of the strongest U.S. allies in Asia. Annually, since 1974, the U.S. government has provided financial support to narcotics control activities in Thailand. In 1998, U.S. authorities established the International Law Enforcement Academy (ILEA) in Bangkok "to support criminal justice in Asia by putting emphasis on rule of law and law enforcement, to strengthen partnership among Asian countries to address problem of narcotic and other transnational crime, to provide training and assistance to promote mutual legal assistance and extradition to combat transnational crime, and to strengthen cooperation among the law enforcement communities of the U.S. and others" (Office of Narcotics Control Board 1999, 65–66).

In the early 1990s, Operation Tiger Trap, a joint operation between U.S. and Thai authorities, resulted in the arrests and convictions of more than a dozen of Khun Sa's core associates in the heroin trade. Thai officials and American DEA agents in Bangkok also played a key role in the dismantling of Wang Jianzhang's heroin trafficking organization, which had bases in Fuzhou City and New York City. The DEA not only maintains an office in the U.S. Embassy in Bangkok but it is also very active in drug intelligence gathering in northern Thailand, especially in the cities of Chiang Mai and Chiang Rai. According to a high-ranking Thai drug enforcement official,

Right now [in 2002], we have an extremely good working relationship with the American authorities. However, at the very beginning in the late 1990s, the U.S. authorities were reluctant to get involved in the war against yaba because yaba did not directly affect the U.S. They were only interested in the suppression of heroin. Only after we insisted that the U.S. should help Thailand fight against yaba did the U.S. authorities comply.[33]

Drugs as Commodities

Some experts have been critical of the warlike approach to the drug trade in the Golden Triangle, especially when authorities in the region went after one drug kingpin after another without realizing that the removal of a drug lord had little or no impact on the supply and demand of drugs (Mc-Coy 1999b). In fact, aggressive law enforcement tactics can backfire and result in increased production:

> When the blunt baton of law enforcement is brought down upon such an elaborate commerce, drug merchants usually react in ways not foreseen by the enforcement agencies. Indeed, the history of Nixon's drug war indicates that intensified repression produced an increase in narcotics supply. Treating the global narcotics trade as if it were a localized vice such as pornography or prostitution, Washington has applied repression without awareness of the complex global marketing systems that sustain the international drug traffic. Confronted with repression, the global narcotics trade has reacted by expanding both demand and supply, elaborating trafficking routes and making them less susceptible to control. Instead of reducing or eradicating narcotics, repression can become another market stimulus. Even under optimum circumstances, bilateral repression can actually increase, rather than reduce, the global supply of narcotics. (McCoy 1992, 270)

It is McCoy's contention that we should treat illicit drugs as a global commodity with its own supply and demand mechanisms that cannot be easily altered by law enforcement measures or by the removal of a drug kingpin.

Other scholars have argued that the drug problem in Burma was, more than anything else, the consequence of ethnic conflict and political instability in the region. They thought that the tensions between the majority Burmans and the minority ethnic groups such as the Wa and the Kachin played a key role in the development of the drug trade. For them, addressing ethnic minority political aspirations and providing economic development to minorities in the border communities must be key components of all comprehensive programs dealing with drugs in the region.

The Wa leaders' intention to ban opium cultivation in 2005 was welcome news, but the world community is still uncertain whether the Wa leaders are going to go after methamphetamine production in their territory with the same intensity. Some experts thought that the Wa leaders are simply replacing opium cultivation and heroin production with methamphetamine manufacturing and trafficking. For them, if Wa leaders are serious about establishing the Wa area as a drug-free zone, they must also stop producing methamphetamine tablets.

Even though authorities in Burma, Thailand, and China vowed in public that they were going to work together to fight against drugs, they also blamed one another in private for the problem. For example, the Chinese authorities blamed the Burmese and the Wa for the inflow of heroin into China, but Burma blamed China for smuggling precursor chemicals into Burma (Fabre 2005). The Burmese and the Wa insisted that, if chemicals from China were not so easily transported into Burma, the heroin industry in Burma would not have been established. A Chinese from Yunnan who had been working for the Wa leaders for many years told me that

> from the Chinese authorities' viewpoint, it is no big deal if people want to move precursor chemicals from China into Burma, as long as there is no heroin leaving Burma via China. As long as the transporters are willing to bribe the Chinese authorities, they have no problem moving chemicals for heroin and methamphetamine production. In fact, some Chinese authorities are actively involved in the transportation of chemicals from China to Burma. I mean, there is an abundance of these chemicals in China, and the opportunity to export them only pleases the Chinese authorities.[34]

A Wa official also thinks that the Chinese authorities are as responsible for the heroin problem as are the Wa leaders:

> If anyone from other countries criticizes us for heroin production, I won't be offended. But if the person is a Chinese official, I will tell him that we don't have any machines and precursor chemicals in the Wa area to produce heroin. These all come from China, and if they want to blame us, they better take a look at themselves in the mirror. They should stop the flow of these precursor chemicals into the Wa area.[35]

A Burmese official in Rangoon also argued that (Hkam Awng 2002, 226) "as far as Myanmar is concerned, if no precursor chemicals were easily trafficked into the border areas of Myanmar, there would be no production of stimulants in our borders. The solution is very simple: no chemicals, no drugs."

In sum, the attempts to combat the drug problem in Burma must take into consideration the fact that illicit drugs are commercial commodities more likely to be affected by the supply and demand of the market than by law enforcement measures. Moreover, the removal of a few drug kingpins, a tactic traditionally used by drug enforcement, has little impact on a drug market that is not controlled by a few top people. Finally, it might be equally effective to stop the flow of machines and precursor chemicals into the Golden Triangle rather than to simply interdict the drugs coming out of the area. Without the machines and the chemicals from the outside, the people in the area could not possibly produce drugs like heroin and methamphetamine.

Chapter Eight

The Business and Politics of Drugs

In this final chapter, I will focus on two issues: the question of who runs the drug trade, and how politics affects it. Many individuals or groups have been blamed for the drug trade in the Golden Triangle. I will examine the roles of several groups and suggest which groups of people are particularly active in the Golden Triangle's drug business. The second question will examine how the drug business is closely related to politics and how politics often comes into play in the course of dealing with narcotics.

Supply and the Internal Dynamics of the Supply Region

There are two parts to the drug problem: supply and demand. Supply involves the cultivation, production, and trafficking of drugs in the drug producing and transit countries; demand concerns the consumption of drugs in the receiving countries. There is a continuing debate as to which side of the drug problem should be of primary concern in the effort to reduce drug use. Most people would agree that both supply and demand are important, and that we should try to reduce both supply and demand simultaneously.

More effective measures to reduce supply require more information about the important players on the supply side as well as the dynamics of supply. McCoy (1992) and Yawnghwe (1993) have suggested that not knowing exactly who the participants in the global drug trade are, who benefits the most from the drug trade, and how the drug trade reacts to drug suppression measures may lead us to develop ineffective and, worse, counterproductive programs in the war against drugs. According to U Win Naing (2001, 4), a Burmese pro-democracy activist,

> So who is responsible for the drug scourge? The farmers who grow the poppies? The laboratory workers who turn raw opium into heroin? The traffickers who transport the drugs to foreign markets? The wealthy people who run the drug syndicates? The countries that produce chemicals for drug refineries? Government officials who are involved in drug trafficking? And there are many more who are involved in this dirty business one way or another. . . . Countries like China, India, and Thailand are equally responsible for the booming drug trade. They provide basic chemicals such as acetic anhydride, ephedrine and caffeine that are the vital ingredients in refining the opium. Special manufacturing tools and equipment are also made in these countries. Without these chemicals and manufacturing tools, the raw opium could not be developed into saleable drugs. The world should hold these chemical producing countries responsible as well—no more, no less.

In this concluding chapter, I will examine the level of involvement, and the extent of culpability, of the Wa (and their leaders), the Burmese government, and organized crime groups in the drug trade of Southeast Asia.

The Wa and Their Leaders

To what extent the Wa people and their leaders are responsible for the drug trade in the entire Golden Triangle is hard to ascertain, even though there is no doubt that they are involved in it. Do they deserve the current level of concern from the world's drug enforcement agencies? Are they responsible for the bulk of the drugs produced in the region?

At the time this study was conducted, the United States viewed the Wa regime or the United Wa State Army as the most powerful drug-producing organization in Southeast Asia. Even in 1989, U.S. officials thought that "the lack of government control of the border regions has helped trafficking organizations to flourish, and insurgents groups have become increasingly involved in narcotics trafficking to finance their activities. It is possible that the political motives of some insurgents may eventually dissipate, as happened with the Nationalist Chinese, leaving Burma with additional well-armed, battle-hardened opium gangs" (U.S. General Accounting Office 1989, 27). In the 1996 U.S. Department of State report, the U.S. government concluded that "to equip and maintain its military force, UWSA [United Wa State Army] depends on funds generated from taxes on opium that Wa farmers cultivate and produce" (U.S. General Accounting Office 1996, 11).

Most reporters and freelance writers in the West also viewed the UWSA as primarily a drug trafficking organization—albeit a heavily armed one—and its leaders, drug kingpins. The work of Marshall and Davis (2002) is a good example of how Western reporters usually depicted the Wa leaders and their army. The front page of their article in *Asia Times*, a weekly English-language magazine widely circulated in Asia, was enlarged and prominently displayed at the press conference where U.S. authorities announced the indictment of eight Wa leaders in January 2005. From the DEA perspective in 2005 the Wa leaders were the most powerful and the most active drug producers in Southeast Asia.

Over the course of three research trips to the Wa area between 1998 and 2005, most of my informants thought that virtually all the Wa leaders and their families were involved in the drug trade; they could not think of one leader who was not involved. They also believed that the Wa and their leaders were decisively more active than any other groups in Burma and benefited significantly more from the drug business; the occasional arrest and punishment of drug offenders in the Wa area was just a farce. These insiders also believed that only a few leaders reaped the bulk of the drug profits, as one subject I talked to in Bangkang said:

> It [the drug business] is basically a family business. Bao [Youxiang] is perfectly clear who is doing what, but he needs money to develop the Wa State and to maintain his power. Here, money talks and it is everything; if you don't have money, you cannot be the top leader. Bao is the most powerful leader mainly because he knows how to make money. He can also ask businessmen here for money as a donation or investment for a public works project. These businessmen have no choice but to give him money because they know they can conduct their drug business mainly because Bao allows them, and

he provides his army for protection and transportation of their drugs.[1]

Wa leaders I interviewed, on the other hand, thought they were being singled out simply because they had become the largest organization in the Golden Triangle after Khun Sa surrendered to the Burmese in 1996. They also believed that their inability or unwillingness to "package" themselves was a key factor, especially when leaders in the Kokang and Mengla areas conducted high-profile ceremonies to announce that their areas had became drug-free and to open drug museums in their territories.

Bao Youxiang also complained to Bill Curtis of A&E that he should not be the main culprit because there were so many other groups involved in the drug business:

> More than a dozen groups have reached peace agreements with the Burmese government, but there are also more than a dozen groups still fighting the Burmese government. I, Bao Youxiang, am being blamed for all those [drug] businesses actually run by a variety of groups. I am not so powerful as to operate all those businesses. It's a shame! All these unfair accusations are made by those who do not understand what is really going on here. (United Wa State Party 2001d, 17)

Luo Xinghan, the former King of Opium, also thought that the drug trade in Burma was not dominated by the Wa, nor the Kokang or the Mengla for that matter. He said that many other little-known groups in other parts of Burma were also involved in the drug business: "As far as heroin production is concerned, there is no doubt that there are heroin factories in the Kokang area. However, the majority of the heroin factories are located west of the Salween River, in the Burmese territory."[2]

Chao-Tzang Yawnghwe, a Shan prince and a fighter who later became an academic in the West, felt that no ethnic minority group in Burma, let alone the Wa, should be held responsible for the global drug trade: "To say that the 'minorities' of Burma are behind the multi-billion dollar global industry is like saying that teenaged hamburger flippers are responsible for the billion dollars, globe girding, McDonald's empire" (Yawnghwe 1998, 1). In his opinion, there were many other more important players outside of the hilly areas who benefited the most from the illicit drug industry.

My research findings in the Wa area indicate that nearly everyone in the Wa region is involved in the drug trade. For people trying to survive in an isolated and impoverished area the drug trade has proved to be the most viable way to make a living. In the Wa Hills, the question of whether a person is a drug lord or a political leader, a drug producer, or a businessman, are all irrelevant. According to Luo Xinghan,

> In the West, you view heroin production as a crime and an evil thing to do, but there [in the Kokang and the Wa areas] it is perfectly legal and normal. People in the area see the production of heroin as simply another type of business, and for the local authorities it is just another way to generate income. No matter where you are from— China, other parts of Burma, Thailand, or Taiwan—as long as you are willing to pay a certain amount of money to the local authorities, they are willing to allow you to get involved in heroin production. You would get into trouble only if you do not pay. The same is true with yaba production.[3]

Even though it is true that most people in the Wa area are involved in the drug trade one way or the other and that they are probably the most influential group of the several drug-producing groups in the region, it is also true that they are being unfairly targeted by the world community.

The Burmese Government

Besides the Wa, the Burmese government is also viewed by the world community as a main culprit in the Southeast Asian drug trade. As Yawnghwe (1993, 313) suggested in his analysis of the many actors in the drug trade,

> There are political-military actors who loosely and fluidly control the physical space in which the production area and communication networks are situated. These political-military actors can be divided roughly into two categories. One category serve under internationally recognized flags—i.e., they are officials of recognized states. . . . The second category of political-military actors are local or locally based men who are in command of 'armies' and armed units, who fight, or claim to fight for various causes.

In his viewpoint, the Burmese government fits the first category, and the Wa, the second.

The question is what role the Burmese government plays, and to what extent Burmese authorities are involved in the drug trade. Some observers have concluded that the Burmese government is directly and systematically involved (Dupont 1999; ALTSEAN-Burma 2004). A 1998 report by the Southeast Asian Information Network (SAIN), a nongovernmental organization, observed that when the SLORC seized state power in 1988 and opium production then doubled over the next ten years, it suggested high-level junta involvement with the export of these narcotics: "Testimonies given to SAIN from dealers, carriers and users in Burma consistently point to the regime army, the *tatmadaw*, as playing a central role in the distribution of heroin from opium producing areas to the international market" (Southeast Asian Information Network 1998, 21).

Desmond Ball (1999, i), an Australian drug expert, concluded that

whatever the semantics of 'matter of policy' and 'government as a whole,' the State Peace and Development Council, which rules the country, is very dependent on drug trafficking for economic and strategic reasons, and that the whole regime is infused with corruption. . . . Khin Nyunt, the No. 3 man, probably has the most extensive drug connections. . . . In addition to his heroin interests, Khin Nyunt has recently acquired shares in five amphetamine laboratories in areas controlled by Lin Min-shing [Lin Mingxian] near Mong La [Mengla]. (Ball 1999, 6)

Some high-ranking Thai officials also thought that the Burmese military was instrumental in the methamphetamine business. A Thai official with the National Narcotics Operation Centre told the Thai media that

the Burmese military has played an active role behind the UWSA's production of speed pills along our common border. They have set a target to produce 200 million amphetamine tablets for export to our country this year. Burma is being two-faced, giving us a pledge during a meeting that it will help suppress narcotics along the border area, and then acting otherwise. The drug problem along the border area is getting very serious because Burma is not sincere. (Kasitipradit and Nanuam 1999a, 1)

Senator Kraisak Choonhavan, chairman of Thailand's Senate Standing Committee on Foreign Affairs, also publicly declared that the "Burmese government is directly involved in producing narcotics, and drug trafficking has been integrated into the economy" (Eads 2002, 57).

Some of the subjects I interviewed in Rangoon also thought that Burmese authorities were directly implicated in the drug trade. A former KMT drug trafficker said that "it is obvious that the Burmese government is either directly or indirectly involved in the drug trade; otherwise where else can they generate money to support its troops and build the infrastructure. Many banks in Rangoon are owned by drug traffickers and that's the best way to launder their money."[4] A schoolmate of mine, a Muslim born in Burma, also believed that

> even though the Burmese authorities did arrest some drug offenders, most of them are small-time dealers. The big fishes are pretty much left alone. The Burmese government has very few legitimate channels to make money and it is our understanding that they are relying on narco-dollars to finance their various public works projects. Under pressure from the world community, they might burn some drugs and arrest some drug dealers, but it is pretty much just a show.[5]

On the other hand, U.S. officials tend to believe that the Burmese government is unlikely to be directly involved in the drug trade, even though some officials, especially lower level officials in the border area, may have been bribed by drug traffickers to look the other way. According to the 1995 INCSR report,

> Despite widespread rumors, there is no strong evidence that the Burmese government is directly involved in or directly profits from the drug trade. . . . While direct government complicity in the drug trade does not appear to be a problem among senior officials, narcotics corruption is a problem among lower level officials. It is widely believed that lower level Burmese officials in the field, particularly in the Shan State, profit from drug trafficking for personal gain. This often takes the form of taking bribes for looking the other way. (U.S. Department of State 1995, 244)

Since that assessment in 1995 about the Burmese government's unlikely complicity in the drug trade, U.S. authorities maintained the same position for the next ten years:

Officials of both the U.S. Department of State and the U.S. Drug Enforcement Administration (DEA) have confirmed to the authors what they say publicly—they know of no evidence to support charges of state-sponsored drug trafficking in Myanmar. . . . Military and police officers are certainly in positions from which they can profit, either by simply looking the other way or by actively participating in the drug trade. . . . On the other hand, Yangon clearly tolerates the drug trade in order to maintain an uneasy peace with armed drug-trafficking insurgent groups. The government also welcomes financial investment from those same organizations, with few questions asked about the origin of the money. (Gibson and Haseman 2003, 4)

Burmese officials I talked to were annoyed to hear that some Westerners believe that their government is directly involved in the drug trade. A government official in Rangoon shot back when the issue was raised: "Foreigners always use all kinds of problems to denigrate Burma: from opium to heroin to human rights. Now it's forced labor, child exploitation, and other stuff."[6]

Over the course of three visits to the Wa area, I do not recall anyone ever mentioning the Burmese government's direct involvement in the drug trade. They often talked about the many shortcomings of the Burmese authorities and they certainly despised them, but no one ever accused the Burmese authorities of involvement in drug production, trafficking, or distribution. None of my subjects mentioned bribing the Burmese authorities to allow their drugs to go through the Burmese- controlled areas either. Leaders and businesspeople in the special regions of the Shan State no doubt often gave money or expensive gifts to the Burmese military officers working in the border areas in order to cultivate a good relationship, but the money or gifts were not given in exchange for the promise to provide protection to their drug businesses.

Organized Crime

There is also the question of whether organized crime groups of Chinese origins, such as the triads and the tongs, are involved in the drug trade. It is no secret that there are organized crime groups in Thailand, China, Hong Kong, and Taiwan, and that these crime groups are well connected and always looking for opportunities to make money. It is reasonable to assume that these well-entrenched organized crime groups in Asia might also try to make money from the lucrative drug trade.

The complicity of Chinese organized crime groups in the Southeast Asian drug trade has been well publicized in popular books written by Bresler (1981), Posner (1988), Black (1992), Dubro (1992), Booth (1999), Sack (2001), and Gould (2004). All of these authors have suggested that the triads in Hong Kong, the Chiu Chau (an ethnic Chinese) group in Thailand, the organized gangs in Taiwan, the Big Circle organized crime group in China, and the Chinese gangs and tongs in the United States have all played a role in the manufacturing, transportation, and distribution of heroin. For example, Brookes (1990, 11) concluded that "the people growing rich on this trade belong to international Chinese organized crime syndicates, many based in Hong Kong, which maintain connections in Chinese communities in cities from Bangkok to Los Angeles to Amsterdam."

U.S. law enforcement agencies have also alleged that Chinese organized crime groups were responsible for the trafficking of heroin from Southeast Asia to the United States (President's Commission on Organized Crime 1984; U.S. Senate 1992). As soon as Chinese were discovered to be active in importing heroin into the United States in the early 1980s, American authorities began to suggest that Chinese street gangs in the United States were responsible for the dramatic upsurge in heroin trafficking (U.S. Senate 1986). Law enforcement authorities charged that gang members, along with tong and triad members, were the main actors in promoting the heroin trade (Powell 1989). The media simply accepted the perspectives of the law enforcement authorities and blamed Chinese gangs and tongs for the upsurge in the heroin trade (Seper 1986; Seper and Emery 1986; DeStefano and Esposito 1987; Penn 1990). Journalists often accused Chinese drug traffickers of being members of gangs, tongs, or triad societies, insinuating that there was a conspiracy among these groups to flood the United States with heroin.

The United Nations International Drug Control Programme (1997, 133) also promoted the idea that organized crime groups were active in the drug trade: "Large-scale international movements of cocaine and heroin are entirely controlled by transnational organized crime groups, for whom drugs are consequently a primary source of revenue." When the influx of yaba into Thailand reached its peak in the early 2000, the media in Thailand also began to spread the assumption that the Hong Kong-based triads were cooperating with the Wa to expand their drug operations (*Bangkok Post*, December 22, 2000).

But there were others—myself and other researchers—who thought the link between global drug trafficking and organized crime was tenuous at best. In a 1990 book on the emergence of Chinese organized crime in the United States, I made the following observation:

We are observing the development of a subculture of drug trafficking among the Chinese in the United States, Hong Kong, Canada, Australia, Europe, and other parts of the world. Members of this subculture include import-export businessmen, community leaders, restaurant owners, workers, gamblers, housewives, and the unemployed. It is extremely difficult to penetrate this subculture because members have no prior criminal records, no identifiable organization, and no rigid structure and norms and values. They can conceal their criminal activities through their involvement in lawful business activities. Their involvement in criminal activities is sporadic rather than continuous. (Chin 1990, 153)

After that comment was made, I conducted a study on Chinese street gangs in the United States, and I again concluded that

gangs, tongs, and triads do not play a leading role in the American heroin trade. Rather, I find evidence which suggests that a new generation of Chinese criminals is emerging on the American crime scene. They appear not to belong to gangs, tongs, or triads; are responsible for the bulk of the heroin imported into the United States; and are more likely than tong and gang members to infiltrate the larger society through drug trafficking, the smuggling of aliens, and money laundering and other types of white-collar crime. They are wealthy, sophisticated, and well connected with associates outside the United States. Further, they are not committed to the rigid triad subcultural norms and values and thus can assemble quickly when criminal opportunities arise and dissolve a criminal operation upon its completion. (Chin 1996, 156)

In 2003, I studied the changing patterns of organized crime in Taiwan and I made the point that organized gangs there did not play a major role in the drug trade (Chin 2003). Most drug traffickers and distributors in Taiwan were businesspeople who were active in the business communities of China and Southeast Asia and took advantage of their connections and legitimate business operations to carry out the international transportation of drugs from the source countries into Taiwan.

When I interviewed Chinese law enforcement officials in 2004, most of them also argued that the rapidly expanding organized crime groups in China were not active in the narcotic business.[7] A drug expert in Chongqing City said,

So far, we have not encountered a single drug trafficking case involving an organized crime group. According to Chinese laws, in order to be considered an organized crime group, the group must have a protective umbrella [a government official who is protecting the group]. Corrupt officials are willing to protect these organized crime groups simply because these groups are primarily involved in prostitution, gambling, construction, transportation, and other activities that are considered less harmful to society than drugs. But if these organized crime groups are involved in the drug business, no government officials would be willing to be affiliated with them.[8]

The same argument was made by almost all the people I interviewed in the Wa area, in Yunnan Province, and other parts of China. None of the drug dealers who participated in this study indicated that they were members of a gang or organized crime group.

Other researchers have also argued that Chinese organized crime groups did not dominate the heroin trade in Southeast Asia. Chao-Tzang Yawnghwe (1993, 312–14), the Shan prince and scholar, for example, argued that

these commercial-economic actors, entrepreneurs, are not, strictly speaking, "criminal elements" in the sense of New York mafia or urban underworlds are. Their dealings in the opium-heroin business constitute only one facet of their entrepreneurial activities. Most of them are legitimate shopkeepers, jade and gem dealers, restaurant owners, bank managers, commodity brokers, hotel owners, and/or are active in respectable trade business associations, religious or social organizations, Rotary clubs, chambers of commerce, etc.

Jeremy Milsom (2005, 79), the UNODC representative in the Wa area, characterized the Southeast Asian drug trade as follows: "Almost all of the legitimate businesses [in the Wa area] are run by ethnic Chinese. However, most of the illicit drug manufacturing and trading is also controlled by local and overseas ethnic Han Chinese, usually under the cover of legitimate business fronts. It is a well-established fact that the bulk of the illicit drug trade in Asia is controlled by overseas Chinese networks today as in the past."

In sum, there is little evidence to suggest that traditional Chinese organized crime groups such as the triads, tongs, and gangs in Asia and the United States dominate the Southeast Asian heroin business (Chin 1990, 1996, 2003; Chu 2002). According to Zhang and Chin (2003, 479–80), the hierarchal structure and turf-based activities of Chinese street gangs and tongs in the United States, triad societies in Hong Kong, and organized gangs in Taiwan

> render these groups ineffective in expanding into uncharted territories where contingency, situational fluidity and legal constraints are the norm rather than the exception. The hazards of unreliable service providers, difficulties in developing and maintaining stable official collusions and the risk of being detected in foreign territories may be perceived by triad societies as too high. . . . Their organizational structure, chain of command (i.e., hierarchy) and secretive operations are effective only in territories where patron-client relationships are stable, police-community relationships cozy and long-term profit obtainable.

There is no question that some of the members of these groups are involved in the narcotics trade, but they do not play a dominant role and their participation is not sanctioned or protected by their groups. As a result, their organized crime backgrounds do not have much impact on the social organization and transaction patterns of the drug business.

China adopted the open door policy and engaged in economic reform after the decadelong Cultural Revolution ended in 1976 (Gittings 2005). In the 1980s, the Chinese government encouraged Chinese from overseas to return to their homeland to visit or conduct business (van Kemenade 1997). In the early 1990s, many PRC nationals began to go abroad, either as legal or illegal migrants, and settled in various parts of the world (Chin 1999). As China began to flex its economic muscle in the new millennium, large numbers of PRC nationals can be observed as either business entrepreneurs or tourists in almost every corner of the world. The intermingling between Chinese diasporas living overseas for many generations and the newly arrived PRC nationals in the various major urban centers of Asia, Europe, and North America enables the current generation of ethnic Chinese to revitalize old, and establish new, "Chinatowns" in these urban centers and allows them to position themselves to be competitive in transnational business activities. The networks among businesspeople in Hong Kong, Taiwan,

Singapore, China, the United States, and other parts of the world have successfully utilized China as the center of production and the various urban centers around the globe as the satellite branches for marketing the commodities produced in China.

It is against this backdrop that we must understand the emergence of a new generation of Chinese who are involved in transnational crime such as drug trafficking, human smuggling, and money laundering. These transnational criminal activities can be easily carried out by a network of overseas Chinese and PRC nationals, very often with the help of, or cooperation with, non-Chinese local people in the host countries. The existence of a rapidly expanding global Chinese business network, the ease in traveling back and forth between China and the various host societies, and the trust and secrecy based on a common dialect or hometown allow the Chinese in the global village to circumvent the laws and regulations of the host communities. Most of these networks are based on family or district, and they are not set up to commit crime, but to use an existing network to occasionally become involved in crime whenever and wherever there is an opportunity. The people who are involved in transnational crime are not professional criminals with prior criminal records, but are otherwise legitimate businesspeople who are also opportunists and risk takers.

These emerging Chinese crime networks are horizontally structured, fluid, and opportunistic. These networks can take cover in the various Chinatowns of the world community, which are often also bustling commercial centers dotted with legitimate business establishments. Because these networks do not have a turf, a name, a leader, or sworn members, it is extremely difficult for local law enforcement authorities to understand or penetrate these networks. As a result, for convenience's sake, the local authorities simply lump all these networks together and call them the "Chinese mafia," the "Chinese triad," or the "Chinese crime syndicate." The problem is, there are actually many well-established Chinese crime groups that have been in existence for many years, and confusing the newly established Chinese crime networks with the traditional Chinese organized crime syndicates impedes our understanding of the problem and hinders our ability to effectively deal with transnational crime involving ethnic Chinese.

The changing patterns of drug production and drug trafficking in the Wa area and other special regions in the Shan State of Burma are also closely tied to the political economy of China and the development of a global Chinese business network involving ethnic Chinese from around the world. The Wa region is a remote area controlled by an armed insurgent group and located within an undeveloped country that is under the grip of a military regime. As a result, well-established Chinese business enterprises in Beijing, Shanghai, Hong Kong, or Taiwan are highly unlikely to be interested in doing business in the Wa area. These enterprises have the entire world to conquer—why should they be concerned about going to the Wa area? Nevertheless, as the Chinese economy began to expand, there were also many entrepreneurs from the provinces of Yunnan and Sichuan who ventured into northeastern Burma to try their luck. Most of them do not go to the Wa area with the intention of entering the drug business, but after their own businesses fail or when they find out that the drug business is the only way to make money in the area, some of them may join in. They then can play vital roles in enabling the Wa leaders to become involved in the production of new drugs, and in the transportation and marketing of the drugs to the outside world. When I was doing fieldwork in the Wa Hills, I met many business entrepreneurs from China. The few lucky ones came and made a quick buck and returned to China, but the majority of them were stuck in an environment they did not understand and were just hustling to get by and waiting for an opportunity to strike gold. Many of them may end up in the drug business.

For the leaders of the various special regions in the Shan State of Burma, their only chance to improve themselves and their people is to look eastward to China, not westward to Burma. Unfortunately, the Chinese entrepreneurs who come knocking at the door are not the ones from Beijing, Shanghai, or Guangzhou, but the significantly less capable, and rather opportunistic, individuals from nearby provinces such as Yunnan, Sichuan, and Hunan. When these so-called businessmen talk, the Wa leaders listen. With the arrival of these Chinese entrepreneurs, the various special regions of the Shan State did modernize considerably over the past fifteen years. However, these Chinese entrepreneurs also brought a culture of lawlessness with them and turned these areas into centers of vice where drugs, gambling, and prostitution flourished.

The Wa leaders are determined to develop the Wa State into a modern society not that different from nearby Chinese cities such as Menglian, Simao, or even Kunming. However, because of the Chinese entrepreneurs who are now active in the Wa Hills, it is questionable whether the Wa leaders will ever be able to achieve their goal. What the world community should do is help the Wa leaders learn how to make money in a legitimate way. Legitimate and enduring opportunities to make money must be developed, so that individuals can prosper and share in the building of a modern state. The world must not stand by and watch the area be exploited by a group of unscrupulous outsiders. Calling the Wa leaders evil or greedy drug lords and indicting them is not going to solve the problem.

The assumption that Wa leaders, Burmese authorities, and traditional organized crime groups all work together to promote the drug trade in the Golden Triangle fails to provide us with an objective and nuanced understanding of the problem. There are many other groups in Burma that are involved in the drug business (for example, the Kokang, Mengla, Kachin, and Shan), Burmese authorities are unfairly accused of major participation in the drug trade, while organized crime groups do not play a dominant role in the Southeast Asian illicit drug industry.

In the Wa area and other special regions of Burma, there are a number of state builders who are leaders of various armed groups and in control of vast areas of land. These state builders were very concerned about maintaining their autonomy even after the cease-fire agreements were signed; these leaders are well aware that they need a strong army to back up their claims of independence. And to support an army, one needs plenty of money. Besides supporting an army, these leaders also need money to build roads, power plants, bridges, and other public works projects to improve the infrastructure of their societies and thus legitimize their leadership. Taxing opium farmers and drug entrepreneurs is one way for these leaders to secure funds for state building. However, the opium tax and the so-called (heroin or methamphetamine) manufacturing fee may not be enough to finance the many ambitious projects. As a result, these leaders and their family members entered the drug business themselves, and in the process not only were able to secure enough funds for state building but also to accumulate personal or family wealth. Eventually, the difference between a state builder and a drug kingpin, between benevolence and greed, and between public funds and personal wealth become all the more difficult to delineate, especially if we move from opium to heroin and then to methamphetamine. After these leaders had accumulated enough money, and given that the local infrastructure had improved and there were more opportunities to interact with the outside world, they tried to venture into legitimate businesses to reduce their reliance on the drug business.

The Politics of Drugs

As Alfred McCoy (1972, 1991), Chao-Tzang Yawnghwe (1993, 2005), and other observers of the Golden Triangle have suggested, the drug trade is almost always tied to politics; it follows that the rise and fall of any drug trade cannot be fully understood if we do not take into consideration its political backdrop. The same is true with the development and implementation of law enforcement or military measures to fight against drugs. More often than not, drug enforcement operations are shaped by the local political climate or international political alliances.

The Wa leaders remain convinced that they have been unfairly—and mistakenly—characterized by the West as one of the most powerful drug trafficking organizations in the world. The Wa believe this is because of their unwillingness to act as a tool in the joint Thai-U.S. efforts to undermine the Burmese government. A Wa official with the Wa Office in Rangoon said that

> the Wa were blamed for the whole drug problem in Southeast Asia even though they were not the main culprits. That's because the Thai government wanted to demonize the Wa after the Wa refused to be their ally in their war against the Burmese government. If we tell the Thai that we are willing to be their puppets, then even if we really are the main drug producers, the Thai would not treat us like this. It's really not about drugs, it's mostly politics.[9]

The development of the drug trade along the Thai-Burma border area was also tied to the political alliance and tensions between the Burmese and the Wa, on the one hand, and the Thai and the Shan, on the other. Very often, the Wa and the Shan were used as buffers by the Burmese and the Thai authorities and the fighting between the former was often the manifestation of the hostilities between the latter. In the long history of the animosities between the Burmese and the Thai, drug production and drug trafficking among the Wa and the Shan were often overlooked or exaggerated by the authorities in Rangoon and Bangkok to make a political statement or to achieve a political goal.

For the authorities in Rangoon, political factors also seemed to play an important role in their decisions about what to do about the drug trade in their border areas and the armed groups that were involved in it. After fighting the insurgent groups for more than four decades, Burmese authorities abruptly signed cease-fire agreements with seventeen of these groups in 1989 because of the rise of Aung San Suu Kyi and her democratic movement in the heartland of Burma. For the military regime in Rangoon, Suu Kyi and her followers became a more serious threat to their survival than the insurgent groups in the border areas. And if these insurgent groups must, after the cease-fire agreements, rely on the drug trade to survive, to the Burmese authorities this concern could not outweigh their concern for their own survival. As the secretary general of the ONCB said in 1998, "For the Burmese government political stability is the priority, drug control comes later. If the two can go hand in hand, then fine but if a choice is to be made, it will be political stability" (Thaitawat 1998, 2).

The level of cooperation between Burmese and Western authorities was also significantly affected by politics. Some drug experts in the West did not want to work with the Burmese military regime because they saw it as a brutal totalitarian government, even though they were aware that the Burmese officials did not have the means and resources to cope with the drug problem on their own. On the other hand, a significant number of Western officials were willing to put politics aside so that they could work closely with the Burmese authorities on drug enforcement. These officials were convinced that Burma should not be left alone; economic sanctions would only further punish ordinary Burmese citizens, and engagement was a better approach. In 2001, Luo Xinghan, the former King of Opium, described the mentality of the Burmese authorities:

The Burmese government is *qiongao* (poor and arrogant). They don't like people telling them what to do, even though they are desperate for outside help. As a result, foreign governments dealing with Burma must offer the Burmese something (because they are poor) while at the same time be sensitive in dealing with them (because they are arrogant). The bottom line is this: the Burmese generals work very hard to improve their country, but they just don't have the technical know-how or the financial support to bring about change. That's the sad part.[10]

Besides the issue of whether it is appropriate to work with a military junta with a poor human rights record, there is also the big question of how best to tackle the drug problem in Burma. Many experts believe that the drug problem in Burma cannot be solved until the political issues, especially the unstable relationship between the majority Burmans and the minority ethnic groups in the border areas, are solved first:

The explosion of the drug trade in the Golden Triangle . . . is the inevitable consequence of the decades-long Burmese tragedy: the inability of successive governments in Rangoon to come to terms with the country's ethnic minorities and the refusal of post-1962 military-dominated regimes to permit an open, pluralistic society. . . .

No anti-drug policy in Burma has any chance of success unless it is linked to a real political solution to the civil war and a meaningful democratic process in Rangoon. The alternative is a continuing strife—which will keep the heroin flowing. (Lintner 1994b, 331–35)

Gibson and Haseman (2003, 1) write that, "the issue must be approached as an economic and social problem rather than a political or military one. The approaches must be multinational and multi-discipline, taking into account the economic, commercial, political, and social issues that force the cultivation of the opium poppy and the production of illegal drugs in the Shan State."

Chao-Tzang Yawnghwe summed up the Burma problem as follows:

What exists now in Burma is what could be called a nation-state formation that does not have a constitution; a country without a properly functioning legal system, where the rule of law is a fiction; where regulations are neither rational nor predictable; where the economy is anarchic, decayed, and broken down; where money is no longer capital but a medium of exchange as in the middle ages; where infrastructures are but hollow shells, and all service structures and systems (for example, in the sphere of health and education) are nonfunctioning; and where the social fabric is torn and in tatters. . . . It is not merely being idealistic, nor is it wishy-washy liberalism, to say that Burma's drug problem and its solution require measures that will restore a functional relationship between the state and broader society in Burma. (2005, 31–32)

Like other drug-producing countries such as Colombia and Afghanistan, the drug problem in Burma is very much related to the country's politics. In these countries, it is true that many poor farmers must rely on poppy or coca plants to survive, but the deeply embedded political conflicts provide a social and political context for drug production because the people in power, be they the ruling authorities or the insurgent groups, often rely on drug money to achieve their political goals. Moreover, political conflicts in these countries also impede the development of effective social and educational programs for drug prevention and law enforcement measures for drug suppression.

It is also true that the Wa area was deeply affected by China's economic reform and open door policy. After the Cultural Revolution in 1976, the Gang of Four, led by Mao Zedong's wife, Jiang Qing, was purged, and

Deng Xiaoping reemerged. Deng then went on to implement a market economy and adopt an open door policy. He also claimed that "To get rich is glorious," "Poverty is not socialism," "Development is the overriding principle," and "Whether a cat is black or white makes no difference. As long as it catches mice, it is a good cat." Deng essentially was instructing his people to get rich by all means through economic development and not to be bothered anymore with class struggle, revolution, and Marxist ideology. It was during Deng's time that China decided not to continue to support the Communist Party of Burma, which was one of the most important factors causing Kokang and Wa leaders to dissociate themselves from the CPB (Lintner 1990; Kramer 2007). After that, Kokang and Wa leaders simply took Deng's instructions to heart and tried mightily to develop their societies and, in the process, to get rich by any and all means. If the drug business is a black cat that catches mice, it is a good cat. Economic development and getting rich became the "superstructure" of the Wa, Kokang, and Mengla leadership, and this "superstructure" came to dictate the relations of production, the productive forces, and the modes of production (Friedman 1975). Leaders of the insurgent groups who were once specialists in armed struggle and ideological debate quickly transformed themselves into state builders, business entrepreneurs, and drug lords.

It is also imperative to understand that the transformation from insurgents to state builders and drug entrepreneurs was deeply affected by the external geopolitical ecosystem. There was the volatile relationship between the Wa Central Authority and local authorities throughout the Wa State, as well as the delicate relationship between Bao Youxiang's Northern Wa area and Wei Xuegang's Southern Wa area. The amount of opium cultivated and taxed, the amount of heroin refined, and the amount of methamphetamine produced, all depend on the nature of these relationships. Moreover, the relationship between the Wa and neighboring regions such as Kokang, Mengla, and Kachin in northern Shan State and the communities located west of Salween River in the Burmese-controlled territories also affect the drug trade as displacement and diffusion occur when drug activities in a particular region increase or decrease dramatically.

In addition to the relationships between central and local authorities in the Wa area and between the Wa area and neighboring regions, there is also the relationship between the Wa and China's Yunnan Province and the provinces in northern Thailand. The drug business in the Wa area is heavily influenced by events in Yunnan and northern Thailand because people in these border provinces are economically, socially, and culturally closely linked to people in the Wa area. These provinces are, on the one hand, devastated by rampant drug use and drug trafficking activities in their jurisdictions and, on the other hand, heavily indebted to the many business opportunities presented to them by the newly rich special regions in Burma. As a result, these border provinces are often ambivalent about their relationships to the drug-producing special regions in Burma, yet they often clash with the central governments in Beijing and Bangkok when the central governments try to take a harsher approach toward these special regions.

In my opinion, the most critical factor in determining the fate of the drug trade in the Wa area and other regions in the Golden Triangle is the Sino-U.S. relationship because this, in turn, dictates the relationships between China, Burma, and Thailand. The movement of chemical precursors, machinery, technology, capital, people, drugs, and the development of drug markets across international borders all very much depend on the political atmosphere in the border areas; this atmosphere is ultimately predicated on the Sino-U.S. relationship. If the governments in Washington, D.C., and Beijing can work together not only to suppress the drug trade but also to improve the economic condition and political stability of the region, then there is a good chance that the area's drug scourge can be eliminated once and for all. In sum, sociopolitical formations and economic choices made in the Wa area are a part of global economic and power structures that have deep effects and dictate conditions in the local setting.

The Need for International Engagement

In his book *The River of Lost Footsteps*, Thant Myint-U (2006, 342) criticized the current policy adopted by the West in dealing with Burma as counterproductive and dangerous:

> The paradigm is one of regime change, and the assumption is that sanctions, boycotts, more isolation will somehow pressure those in charge to mend their ways. The assumption is that Burma's military government couldn't survive further isolation when precisely the opposite is true: Much more than any other part of Burmese society, the army will weather another forty years of isolation just fine.

One of the consequences of this policy is that, without investments from Western countries and Japan, the Burmese economy will continue to be penetrated by former or current drug entrepreneurs, as many of them become the owners of banks, airlines, hotels, and other major business establishments in Rangoon and Mandalay. The participation of these drug entrepreneurs in the mainstream Burmese economy not only allows them to launder their drug money but also provides them with a legitimate front to cover or facilitate their drug activities. The other consequence is that Burma will continue to cling to China for survival, mainly in the form of cross-border trade or economic or military aid. According to Toshihiro Kudo, a Japanese economist, cross-border trade with China is detrimental to the development of a healthy economy in Burma because Burma's exports to China consist mostly of wood in the form of logs or roughly squared ones rather than products from a technologically developed lumber or other industry. He concluded that "Myanmar's trade with China has failed to have a substantial impact on its broad-based economic and industrial development. China's economic cooperation apparently supports the present regime, but its effects on the whole economy will be limited with an unfavorable macroeconomic environment and distorted incentives structure" (Kudo 2006, 1).

Not long after I completed this Wa study, I conducted another study with a colleague on the changing patterns of cross-border drug trafficking between Burma and China. In that study, we concluded that it would be unwise for the United States to stand by and do nothing about the drug problem in Southeast Asia:

> The U.S. cessation of involvement in Myanmar's anti-narcotics efforts should be reexamined. . . . The absence of any involvement in Myanmar's anti-narcotics efforts only tarnishes the U.S. image as playing politics at the expense of legitimate law enforcement cooperation, which only further diminishes the American influence in the region. . . . The greater influx of consumer products from China and other Asian countries to North America will inevitably increase the flow of illicit goods and services. The global economy and increasingly fragmented drug production and trafficking systems will ensure a convergence of drug distribution networks between Western countries and Asia. It behooves the United States not only to remain engaged but also to play an active leadership role in bringing together regional efforts in combating the production and trafficking of illicit drugs in Southeast Asia. (Chin and Zhang 2007, 82–83)

In the final analysis, the warning by Jelsma, Kramer, and Vervest (2005, xiii) in their edited volume on the drug problem in Burma is well taken here:

Without adequate resources, the long-term sustainability of "quick solutions" is highly questionable. Since local authorities are eager to comply with promises made, law enforcement repression is likely to increase, with human rights' abuses and more displacement a potential outcome. The only viable and humane option lies in a simultaneous easing of drug control deadline pressures while increasing international humanitarian aid efforts. Both require stronger international engagement of a different kind from what we have seen this far.

It is not clear what will happen to the Wa area in the near future, especially after the ban in opium cultivation went into effect in 2005. A key informant in Bangkang made the following comments when asked in April 2005 about the future of the Wa:

Frankly, I don't see how the Wa government can keep drug production out of its area. What is going to happen is that the Wa government in and of itself will avoid direct involvement in the drug business, and all the drug activities will become a lot more discreet and secretive—just like what is going on in the Kokang and the Mengla areas. There are still many people in those two areas who continue to be involved in drug production and trafficking, but the activities are all hidden. I think this is going to be the case in the Wa area after June 2005. Regardless, the drug business is going to shrink somewhat after June 2005.[11]

When I was writing this in June 2006, I called someone in Bangkang who had worked for me on this project and asked her whether the opium ban had been carried out as planned:

The opium ban was a success. I just got back from a trip to the north, and I did not see any poppy plants. The Wa authorities were very strict in enforcing the ban, and they watched the farmers closely. There were also large numbers of Wa militia in the hills, and they patrolled their area to see if anyone was growing opium clandestinely. If they discovered anyone planting opium, they destroyed the poppy plants and fined the violator. I would say the majority of the Wa people are not growing opium anymore. Of course, this ban has had a major impact on the people. Luckily, the World Food Program delivered free rice to the farmers, even though the amount was extremely limited. Many

Wa farmers are now eating vegetables growing in the wild because they do not have the cash from opium anymore.[12]

When I was in Taipei in May 2008, I met a man who had just returned from the Wa area after spending some time following the lives of five Wa families. He said he had wanted to see the impact of the opium ban in 2005 on the livelihoods of the opium farmers. In his opinion, the opium ban is not going to last because neither the farmers nor the leaders can survive without money from the opium trade. Moreover, he said that opium cultivation in the Wa area is prohibited only in the areas along the main roads; opium is still cultivated in places far away from roads and from the view of outsiders. His observation confirmed the prediction of the key informant in Bangkang cited above. Instead of being eliminated, the opium trade in the Wa area simply went underground and became more difficult for outsiders to monitor. This development is troubling news for the world community.

NAMES IN PINYIN ROMANIZATION
AND OTHER SPELLINGS

Aicheng: Siku, Aiceen, Ai Chun, Aik Chaing

Bangkang: Panghsang, Pang Kham, Pan Kham, Pangsang
Bao Huaqiang: Pao Hua Chiang
Bao Youhua: Pao Yu Hua
Bao Youliang: Pao Yu Liang
Bao Youxiang: Bao You Chang, Pao Yu-chang, Pao Yo Chang, Pao Yu
    Hsiang, Pu Yu Chen, Pu Yucheen, Pauk Yu Chan
Bao Yuoyi: Pao Yu Yi
Bo Laikang: Bao Lai Kham

Hedao: Ho Tao, Hawtaw, Ho Taung

Kentung: Kyaintong, Kyaington
Kokang: Kokant
Kunma: Khunma, Hkwin Ma

Laukkai: Laukai
Lin Mingxian: Lin Min-shing
Longtan: Lon Htan
Luo Xinghan: Lo Hsing-han

Menga: Mon Ah
Mengbo: Mong Pawk, Mong Paw, Mengpawk, Mengpaw
Mengla: Mongla, Mainglun
Mengmao: Mengmaw, Mong Mao, Mong Maw
Mengga: Mengkax, Mong Kar
Mengping: Menghpin, Mong Phen
Mong Yawn: Meng Yawn

Nandeng: Namten, Nam Teek, Nam Tit, Nam Tip
Nankangwu: Nam Kham Wu, Nam Khan Wo

Panglong: Panglung
Peng Jiasheng: Pheung Kya-shin

Shaopa: Shaopha, Sau Pha

Tachilek: Tachileik

United Wa State Party: Wa Unity Party

Wei Xuegang: Wei Hsueh Kang
Wei Xuelong: Wei Hsueh Lung, Wei Hsueh Long
Wei Xueyun: Wei Hsueh Ying
Wengao: Venkaw, Venaw, Wein Kao, Wein Kaung

Yingpan: Yong Pean, Yinphan, Yin Pang, Yin Pant

Zhao Nilai: Chao Ngi Lai, Zhao Nyi Lai

Notes

Introduction: Into the Thick of It

1. I use the word "Burma" throughout this book, even though the official name of the country is now "Union of Myanmar," because most people in the English-speaking world are still not familiar with the new name and because many who regard the military junta as illegitimate continue to call the country "Burma."

2. Officially known as the Number 2 Special Region.

3. As the text mainly deals with inhabitants from Burma, I will use the word "Shan" to refer to this ethnic group. The word "Shan" is a corruption of "Siam," the old name for Thailand, and a name given to them by the Burmans (Elliott 1999). This ethnic group is referred to as the "Dai" in China, so I will use the word "Dai" when I discuss this group of people in China. This group is also called the "Tai" or the "Dtai."

4. Pinyin romanization is used for most of the names of the persons and places mentioned in this book. See the appendix for the other spellings of these names that are in widespread use.

5. Della Porta and Vannucci (1999) have provided a detailed analysis of the triangular relationship between the Mafia, tycoons, and politicians in southern Italy, where these three groups of people are heavily engaged in what the authors called "corrupt exchanges."

6. The Rangoon government called an area a special region to imply that, even though the area was still controlled by an independent armed group, it had nevertheless signed a cease-fire agreement with the authority in Rangoon and was working toward full reunification.

7. To ensure the confidentiality and safety of the participants in this study, all the names of the people in this book, with the exception of law enforcement officials, high-ranking armed group leaders, and well-known drug traffickers, have been changed. Other names, including cities, towns, and organizations, have not been altered.

8. People who trusted me the most were my research assistants and interviewers, even though they too at first wondered what my real motives were. It was only after they learned to conduct the interviews, actively participated in the arduous process of conducting the interviews in the remote Wa Hills, then cleaned, coded, and entered the data, did they come to believe that I was a legitimate researcher. The three Wa women who conducted fieldwork in a Wa village for three months were able to build a trustful relationship with their subjects quite easily. My relationship with the subjects in the Thai-Burma border areas was also relatively solid because of my contacts in the town of Mae Sai. I had no doubt that these subjects were candid in their answers.

Chapter 1. The Golden Triangle and Burma

1. It might be confusing when an area within a state (Shan State) is also called a state (Wa State). Because Wa people prefer to use the word "Wa State" to characterize their territory, I will do so also. Shan State was once called the Federated Shan States and the Wa region was called the Wa States (Maule 1992).

2. The CPB was formed in Rangoon in 1939 by a group of young Burmese intellectuals. In 1948, it went underground after it decided to launch an armed struggle against the Burmese government (Lintner 1990).

3. All the figures related to opium cultivation and yields are estimates only.

4. Interview with a childhood friend, Rangoon, July 19, 2002.

5. In the early 1970s, the exchange rate was 8 kyat = $1. The kyat began to depreciate in the 1980s and its value continued to drop substantially in the late 1990s. In 2006, the Burmese government offered a tenfold salary increase to all its employees, and the kyat immediately devalued to 1,330 kyat to a dollar.

6. No one knows how many people were actually killed by the military junta; there are unconfirmed reports that the number of casualties was much higher.

7. The Association of Southeast Asian Nations is composed of Brunei, Indonesia, Laos, Malaysia, Myanmar (Burma), the Philippines, Singapore, Thailand, Vietnam, and Cambodia.

Chapter 2. The Wa

1. In May 2005, the Wa authorities were planning to hold an international event to mark the start of the ban on opium cultivation in their territory. After the letters of invitation had been sent out to various participants both inside and outside of Burma, the Burmese authorities informed the Wa that the ceremony had to be postponed. According to a Wa leader, one of the reasons the Burmese government cited was that the Wa authorities had used the words "Wa State" in the invitation letters, and that was not considered appropriate because the Burmese government always has used Wa Special Region. Under the British, the Wa area was referred to as the Wa State.

2. According to the Burmese government, seventeen armed groups "have returned to the legal community to bring about peace" since 1989 (Yan Nyien Aye 2000, 5).

3. Interview with Bo Laikang, deputy commander of the UWSA and minister of the Construction Bureau, Bangkang, April 30, 2001.

4. Interview with Sun Chengde, minister of the Health Bureau, Bangkang, May 4, 2001.

5. Interview with a Wa man, Kunma, August 19, 2002.

6. Interview with a Wa woman, Kunma, August 19, 2002.

7. Interview with a Wa man, Kunma, September 30, 2002.

8. Interview with a Wa woman, Kunma, August 19, 2002.

9. Interview with Sun Chengde, minister of the Health Bureau, Bangkang, May 4, 2001.

10. Interview with Bao Aimen, mayor of Bangkang Special District, Bangkang, April 25, 2001.

11. Interview with Zho Dafu, deputy director, Wa Central Authority, Bangkang, February 13, 2001.

12. Interview with Chen Longsheng, director, Wa Central Authority, Bangkang, February 18, 2001.

13. Ibid.

14. Interview with Luo Xinghan, Rangoon, July 20, 2002.

15. Ibid.

16. Interview with Zho Dafu, deputy director, Wa Central Authority, Bangkang, May 13, 2001.

17. In 1998, it was 27 baht to a dollar but three years later in 2001 it was 40 baht to a dollar.

18. One of the major concessions the Rangoon government made after the cease-fire agreement was permitting the Wa leaders to become involved in the gem business. The Wa government later formed the Kang Xiang (Good Health) Jewelry Company to take advantage of this opportunity. Established in March 1998 with an investment of 10 million yuan ($1.2 million), the company has its own gem mines in Mongsu and Moko, two Burmese towns famous for their precious stones. The company is run by Bao Youxiang's brother-in-law.

19. According to a Wa government document (United Wa State Party 2001c), between 1990 and 2000 the Wa received 5 billion kyat in financial aid from the Burmese government.

20. Interview with Xiao Mingliang, deputy commander, United Wa State Army, Bangkang, May 13, 2001.

21. Interview with a veteran Wa army officer, Bangkang, April 23, 2001.

22. In the Wa Hills, every town has a so-called market day or street day every five days (Daw Tin Yee 2004). The market day may vary from town to town. For the ordinary Wa people, market day is the day when they go to the market to sell their opium, farm products, or anything they can sell and buy food, clothes, and household items. People from remote villages may have to walk three hours or more to the market located in a nearby town. The markets are also open on nonmarket days, but very few people shop during these days.

23. Interview with a Chinese businessman, Bangkang, May 13, 2001.

24. Interview with a jewelry store owner, Bangkang, February 17, 2001.

25. Interview with Ting Xiao, Bangkang, February 19, 2001.

26. Interview with a man working for Bao Youxiang, Bangkok, Thailand, December 14, 2001.

27. Interview with a Wa woman, Kunma, October 2, 2002.

28. Interview with Bao Aimen, mayor of Bangkang Special District, Bangkang, April 25, 2001.

29. Interview with Aiguo, chief of police of Bangkang, Lancang, China, April 9, 2005.

30. Interview with a Wa man, Kunma, August 19, 2002.

31. Interview with a Chinese man, Bangkang, February 20, 2001.

32. Interview with Aiguo, chief of police of Bangkang, Bangkang, April 13, 2005.

33. Interview with Wei Xiang, Bangkang, May 13, 2001.

34. Interview with a Wa woman, Kunma, August 24, 2002.

35. Interview with a Wa woman, Kunma, October 8, 2002.

36. Interview with a Wa woman, Kunma, August 27, 2007.

37. Interview with a female teacher from China, Xindifang, March 12, 2001.

38. Interview with Ailun, commander of Division 468, Bangkang, May 9, 2001.

Chapter 3. The Opium Trade

1. Interview with a male opium grower, Mengmao, March 12, 2001.

2. Interview with a female opium farmer, Aicheng, March 24, 2001.

3. Interview with a Wa woman, Kunma, October 5, 2002.

4. Interview with a Wa woman, Kunma, August 27, 2002.

5. Interview with a Wa man, Kunma, October 14, 2002.

6. Interview with Zhou Dafu, deputy director, Wa Central Authority, Bangkang, February 13, 2001.

7. In India, thousands of small landowners are licensed to grow opium. Every year, Indian officials collect about 1,350 tons of opium from the farmers and export most of it to the United States, England, France, and Japan, to be used as medicine.

8. Most Wa are Buddhist, animist, or atheist (Luo 1995). This subject is probably a Christian. According to Daw Tin Yee (2004, 181), the Christian missionaries "converted Wah [Wa] national into Brothers and Sisters of the Christian faith and sent them abroad on scholarships. Thus, the Christian missionaries saved the Wa national from animism. Buddhist missionaries reached the Wah region only at a much later time." Daw Tin Yee estimated that there are three thousand Baptists and ten thousand Catholics among the Wa.

9. Interview with a local official, Longtan, March 11, 2001.

10. Interview with a local official, Kunma, March 10, 2001.

11. Interview with Zhou Dafu, deputy director, Wa Central Authority, Bangkang, April 11, 2005.

12. One *joi* or viss equals 10 *kang*, 100 *qie*, 3.3 *jin*, 3.5 pounds, or 1.6 kilogram. One *jin* equals 10 *liang*.

13. Interview with a Wa man, Kunma, August 19, 2002.

14. Interview with Chen Longsheng, director, Wa Central Authority, Bangkang, February 18, 2001.

15. According to the 2005 U.S. Department of State's International Narcotics Control Strategy Report, none of the regions is truly opium-free.

16. Interview with a female opium farmer, Aicheng, March 24, 2001.

17. Interview with a male opium grower, Denge, March 25, 2001.

18. Interview with a male opium grower, Aicheng, March 24, 2001.

19. Interview with a male opium farmer, Shaopa, March 23, 2001.

20. Interview with a male opium grower, Shaopa, March 23, 2001.

21. Interview with a male opium cultivator, Yingpan, March 8, 2001.

22. Interview with a male opium grower, Wengao, April 10, 2001.

23. Interview with a male opium grower, Kunma, March 10, 2001.

24. Interview with a male opium farmer, Yingpan, March 8, 2001.

25. Interview with a male opium cultivator, Nankangwu, March 7, 2001.

26. Interview with a female opium cultivator, Shaopa, March 23, 2001.

27. Interview with a female opium grower, Kunma, March 9, 2001.

28. Interview with a male opium grower, Longtan, March 11, 2001.

29. Interview with a male opium cultivator, Mengmao, March 12, 2001.

30. Interview with a male opium farmer, Wengao, April 10, 2001.

31. Interview with Zhou Dafu, deputy director, Wa Central Authority, Bangkang, April 15, 2005.

32. Interview with a Wa woman, Kunma, November 30, 2002.

33. Interview with a female opium trader, Bangkang, March 31, 2001.

34. Interview with a Chinese businessman, Bangkang, February 16, 2001.

35. Interview with a female opium trader, Bangkang, February 27, 2001.

36. Interview with a male opium trader, Bangkang, March 31, 2001.

37. Interview with a female opium trader, Bangkang, March 31, 2001.

38. Interview with a male opium trader, Bangkang, April 15, 2001.

39. Interview with a female opium trader, Bangkang, February 27, 2001.

40. Interview with two female opium traders, Bangkang, March 4, 2001.

41. Interview with a female opium trader, Bangkang, February 27, 2001.

42. Interview with two female opium traders, Bangkang, March 4, 2001.

43. Interview with one of my interviewers, Bangkang, April 2, 2001.

44. Interview with a male opium trader, Bangkang, April 15, 2001.

45. Interview with a Chinese businessman, Bangkang, February 16, 2001.

46. Interview with Col. Hkam Awng, Central Committee for Drug Abuse Control, Rangoon, July 22, 2002.

47. Interview with a female opium trader, Bangkang, February 27, 2001.

48. Interview with Zhou Dafu, deputy director, Wa Central Authority, Bangkang, February 13, 2001.

49. Interview with Bao Aimen, mayor of Bangkang Special District, Bangkang, April 25, 2001.

50. Interview with Zhou Dafu, deputy director, Wa Central Authority, Bangkang, February 13, 2001.

51. Interview with a Chinese businessman, Bangkang, February 16, 2001.

52. Interview with Ailun, commander, Division 468, Bangkang, May 9, 2001.

53. Interview with a Wa army officer, Bangkang, May 15, 2001.

54. Interview with Zhou Dafu, deputy director, Wa Central Authority, Bangkang, February 13, 2001.

Chapter 4. Heroin Production and Trafficking

1. The Wa Basic Law, passed and implemented in 1993 and revised in December 2003, is the basic, and only, law of the Wa State. The law is divided into civil, criminal, marriage, transportation, fire, investment, military, exit and entry, land, forestry, mine, electricity, drug, public safety, and artifact sections.

2. Interview with a Wa woman, Bangkang, April 2, 2001.

3. A typical unit (or *jian*) of Southeast Asian heroin is produced in a compressed brick form. A 700-gram brick is approximately six inches long, four inches wide, and one inch thick; it is white in color, and is very hard. In the 1990s, a half-unit (350 grams) of Southeast Asian heroin, wrapped in the same manner, was introduced into the heroin trade, and has now become the preferred size. In contrast, South American, Mexican, and Southwest Asian heroin traffickers traffic in kilogram quantities (see U.S. Drug Enforcement Administration 2001).

4. Interview with a heroin producer, Bangkang, April 2, 2001.

5. Interview with a Burmese drug enforcer, Muse, October 29, 2004.

6. Interview with a heroin producer, Bangkang, April 2, 2001.

7. Ibid.

8. Interview with Ting Xiao, director, Investment and Tourism Bureau, Bangkang, February 19, 2001.

9. Interview with a Chinese businessman, Bangkang, February 19, 2001.

10. Interview with Ting Xiao, director, Investment and Tourism Bureau, Bangkang, February 19, 2001.

11. Interview with Wang Keqiang, minister, Investment and Tourism Bureau, Bangkang, April 29, 2001.

12. Interview with Ting Xiao, director, Investment and Tourism Bureau, Bangkang, February 19, 2001.

13. Interview with an imprisoned heroin trafficker, Bangkang, April 13, 2005.

14. Interview with a Chinese businessman, Bangkang, April 21, 2001.

15. Interview with a Chinese businessman, Bangkang, April 10, 2005.

16. Interview with Dong Sheng, deputy director, Yunnan Provincial Anti-Narcotics Bureau, Kunming, January 15, 2005.

17. Interview with a businesswoman, Mae Sai, December 17, 2001.

18. Organized crime bosses in Thailand are called *jao pho* (godfather). According to Phongpaichit and Piriyarangsan (1994, 59), "the term is traditionally used to refer to a god, or to a spirit residing in a place." *Jao pho* are mostly ethnic Chinese based in the provinces who have business interests in both legitimate and criminal activities. Moreover, they have groups of associates and followers, are closely allied with powerful bureaucrats, policemen, and military figures, occupy official positions in local administrations, and play a key role in parliamentary elections. There are *jao pho* groups in thirty-nine of Thailand's seventy-six provinces.

19. Interview with a businesswoman, Mae Sai, December 21, 2001.

20. Interview with a businesswoman, Mae Sai, December 18, 2001.

21. Interview with a former heroin dealer, Mae Sai, December 19, 2001.

22. Ibid.

23. Ibid.

24. Interview with the mother of an imprisoned heroin dealer, Ban Yang, December 18, 2001.

25. Interview with a businesswoman, Mae Sai, December 22, 2001.

26. Interview with Ting Xiao, director, Investment and Tourism Bureau, Bangkang, February 19, 2001.

27. According to a drug enforcer I talked to in China, right after the Wa signed a cease-fire with the Burmese government in 1989 and transformed itself into a special region, Chinese policy toward the Wa was called the "three no principle": no political acknowledgement, no military support, and no economic aid. Since then, authorities in Beijing, and especially in Yunnan Province, had become more and more cordial to the Wa.

28. Interview with a drug dealer, Kunming, June 22, 2005.

29. Heroin is translated from English into *haileyin* in Chinese. Heroin users in China use a variety of names when they refer to heroin, just to protect themselves from the law enforcement authorities. Among these terms is *haichan* (seafood), because the first word *hai* is the same as the first word of *haileyin*. Often, heroin is simply called *dongxi*, the "thing."

30. Interview with a drug dealer, Kunming, June 22, 2005.

31. In China, trafficking fifty grams or more of heroin can result in the death penalty.

32. The Green Gang or Qing Bang was a secret society formed in the late seventeenth century in China by sailors and laborers. Later, the society was transformed from a political group to a criminal group. The group reached its peak from 1920 through 1950, a period when China was divided by political parties, warlords, and foreign powers. The gang virtually controlled Shanghai and the French and British concessions there (Seagrave 1985; Wakeman 1995). Using their close connections with local leaders and the colonialists, Green Gang leaders dominated the opium smuggling, gambling, and prostitution rackets in the city (Martin 1996).

Chapter 5. The Methamphetamine Business

1. Interview with Chartchai Suthiklom, deputy secretary-general, Office of Narcotics Control Board (ONCB) of Thailand, Bangkok, July 15, 2002.

2. Interview with Wang Keqiang, minister, Investment and Tourism Bureau, Bangkang, April 29, 2001.

3. A subject in Bangkang suggested that the Wa leaders during that time period collected significantly much more money from methamphetamine producers than they would like to admit.

4. Methamphetamine tablets produced in Burma are stamped with the number 99 or the symbol *wy*, with the *y* having a longer tail. The trademark is widely recognized in the drug market as marking Wa products.

5. Interview with Zhou Dafu, deputy director, Wa Central Authority, Bangkang, February 13, 2001.

6. Interview with Col. Hkam Awng, Central Committee for Drug Abuse Control, Rangoon, July 22, 2002.

7. Interview with Zhou Dafu, deputy director, Wa Central Authority, Bangkang, February 13, 2001.

8. Interview with a businesswoman, Mae Sai, December 18, 2001.

9. Ibid.

10. Interview with a female methamphetamine retailer, Bangkang, May 11, 2001.

11. Interview with a female methamphetamine wholesaler, Bangkang, May 12, 2001.

12. Interview with a male methamphetamine producer, Bangkang, May 11, 2001.

13. Ibid.

14. Methamphetamine producers in Burma and methamphetamine distributors in Thailand often engaged in barter deals and a lot of methamphetamine pills were brought into Thailand in exchange for stolen cars. According to one source, it was estimated that about five hundred stolen cars were smuggled into Thailand from Malaysia every year by Thai-Malaysian gangs, with the help of corrupt officials in both countries who were also profiting from the racket (Charoenpo 2001).

15. Interview with a female methamphetamine producer, Bangkang, May 11, 2001.

16. Interview with a Chinese businessman, February 16, 2001.

17. Ibid.

18. Interview with a male methamphetamine retailer, Bangkang, May 14, 2001.

19. Interview with a Chinese businessman, Bangkang, May 13, 2001.

20. Ibid.

21. Interview with a Wa female, Bangkang, April 2, 2001.

22. Bao Youhua died in 2007.

23. Interview with a Chinese businessman, Hedao, April 5, 2001.

24. Interview with Zhou Dafu, deputy director, Wa Central Authority, Bangkang, February 13, 2001.

25. Interview with Bao Youxiang, Bangkang, May 7, 2001.

26. Interview with a Hui (Muslim) businessperson, Mae Sai, December 17, 2001.

27. Interview with a person close to the Wa leadership, Bangkok, July 11, 2002.

28. Interview with Bao Aimen, mayor of Bangkang Special District, Bangkang, April 25, 2001.

29. Interview with Li Zulie, representative, Rangoon Office, Rangoon, July 20, 2002.

30. Interview with Ai Xiaoshi, a former Wa leader, Bangkang, May 3, 2001.

31. Interview with Chen Longsheng, former director of the Wa Central Authority, Bangkang, April 17, 2005.

32. Interview with Bao Youxiang, Bangkang, May 7, 2001.

33. Interview with Maung Maung Kyaw, a military intelligence officer, Rangoon, July 22, 2002.

34. Interview with Chartchai Suthiklom, deputy secretary-general of the Office of Narcotics Control Board of Thailand, Bangkok, July 15, 2002.

35. Interview with Luo Xinghan, Rangoon, July 20, 2002.

36. Interview with a businesswoman, Mae Sai, December 16, 2001.

37. Interview with Zhou Dafu, deputy director, Wa Central Authority, February 13, 2001.

38. Interview with Chen Longsheng, director, Wa Central Authority, Bangkang, February 18, 2001.

39. Ibid.

40. Thailand has been deeply affected by the massive production of methamphetamine tablets in Burma. Of course, many young people in Bangkang and other parts of Burma are also involved in methamphetamine use. Besides, methamphetamine from Burma is also exported to many countries for Thai labor consumption. The destination countries are Switzerland, Japan, Denmark, Germany, Singapore, Indonesia, Brunei, Malaysia, and South Korea (Office of Narcotics Control Board 2000). Neither the United States nor China is a major market for methamphetamine produced in Burma.

41. Interview with Chartchai Suthiklom, deputy secretary-general of the Office of Narcotics Control Board of Thailand, Bangkok, July 15, 2002.

42. Interview with Mr. Lee, Bangkok, December 14, 2001.

43. According to various sources (Jinakul and Charasdamrong 2001), a methamphetamine tablet costs less than two cents to produce. Its wholesale price at factories in Burma is between twenty and thirty cents. At the Thai-Burma border, the price is between thirty-five and forty cents. Inside Thailand, the tablets sell wholesale from eighty cents to $1.50, and retail from two to five dollars.

44. Interview with a businesswoman, Mae Sai, December 16, 2001.

45. Interview with a resident, Ban Yang, December 17, 2001.

46. Interview with a businesswoman, Mae Sai, December 16, 2001.

47. Interview with a businesswoman, Mae Sai, December 18, 2001.

48. Interview with a businesswoman, Mae Sai, December 17, 2001.

49. Ibid.

50. Interview with a male resident, Mae Sai, December 21, 2001.

51. Interview with a businesswoman, Mae Sai, December 22, 2001.

52. Methamphetamine tablets could also be transported into Thailand by boat. For example, in June 2001, Burmese security forces seized nine million methamphetamine pills from a Chinese vessel on its way down the Mekong River to Chiang Rai's Chiang Saen port. The boat, loaded with agricultural products from China, was searched while it was moored at Mueng Pong in Burma, opposite Mueng Mom in Laos (Kasitipradit, Nanuam, and Kamtida 2001). Moreover, the tablets could be smuggled across the border by drug caravans escorted by armed forces.

53. Interview with Chen Longsheng, former director of the Wa Central Authority, April 17, 2005.

Chapter 6. Drug Use

1. In this chapter, the discussion of opium use in the Wa area refers only to the present situation. Patterns of drug use in the Wa area in the past may not necessarily be similar to the present.

2. Interview with Sun Chengde, minister of the Health Bureau, Bangkang, May 4, 2001.

3. Interview with a female opium user, Bangkang, April 18, 2001.

4. Interview with a female opium user, Bangkang, April 19, 2001.

5. Interview with a male opium user, Bangkang, April 19, 2001.

6. Interview with a female opium user, Bangkang, April 19, 2001.

7. Interview with a male opium user, Bangkang, April 18, 2001.

8. Interview with a female opium user, Bangkang, April 18, 2001.

9. Interview with a male opium user, Bangkang, April 19, 2001.

10. Interview with a male opium user, Bangkang, April 21, 2001.

11. Interview with a female opium user, Bangkang, April 19, 2001.

12. Interview with a male opium user, Bangkang, April 19, 2001.

13. Interview with a female opium user, Bangkang, April 20, 2001.

14. Interview with a male opium user, Bangkang, April 20, 2001.

15. Interview with a male opium user, Bangkang, April 20, 2001.

16. Interview with a female opium user, Bangkang, April 18, 2001.

17. Interview with a male opium user, Bangkang, April 22, 2001.

18. Interview with a male opium user, Bangkang, April 21, 2001.

19. Interview with a male opium user, Bangkang, April 20, 2001.

20. Interview with a female opium user, Bangkang, May 5, 2001.

21. Interview with a female opium user, Bangkang, April 19, 2001.

22. Interview with a female opium user, Bangkang, April 19, 2001.

23. The mother of the baby, herself a methamphetamine user, was also interviewed. Her case will be discussed later in this chapter on the section on methamphetamine use. Her elder sister, also a speed pill user, also participated in this study.

24. Cangyuan County is one of the two Wa autonomous areas located in Yunnan Province. The other is Ximeng (Luo 1995; Fiskesjo 2000). In Yunnan Province, there are a large number of autonomous areas populated by various minority groups. In these autonomous areas, minority groups are given more administrative and political power, like having a minority person serve as the mayor (Gao 2001).

25. Interview with a male heroin user, Bangkang, April 20, 2001.

26. Interview with a male heroin user, Bangkang, May 4, 2001.

27. Interview with a Chinese businessman, Bangkang, February 16, 2001.

28. Ibid.

29. Interview with two interviewers, Bangkang, April 20, 2001.

30. Interview with a female methamphetamine user, Bangkang, April 28, 2001.

31. Interview with a male methamphetamine user, Bangkang, May 5, 2001.

32. Interview with a male methamphetamine user, Bangkang, May 3, 2001.

33. Interview with a male methamphetamine user, Bangkang, May 4, 2001.

34. Interview with a female methamphetamine user, Bangkang, April 28, 2001.

35. Interview with a male methamphetamine user, Bangkang, May 10, 2001.

36. Interview with a female methamphetamine user, Bangkang, April 28, 2001.

37. Interview with a female methamphetamine user, Bangkang, April 29, 2001.

38. Interview with a female methamphetamine user, Bangkang, May 2, 2001.

39. Interview with a female methamphetamine user, Bangkang, May 6, 2001.

40. Interview with a female methamphetamine user, Bangkang, April 29, 2001.

41. Interview with a female methamphetamine user, Bangkang, May 1, 2001.

42. Interview with a male methamphetamine user, Bangkang, May 1, 2001.

43. Interview with a female methamphetamine user, Bangkang, May 1, 2001.

44. Interview with a male methamphetamine user, Bangkang, May 1, 2001.

45. Interview with a male methamphetamine user, Bangkang, May 5, 2001.

46. Interview with a female methamphetamine user, Bangkang, April 21, 2001.

47. Interview with a female methamphetamine user, Bangkang, April 28, 2001.

48. Interview with a male methamphetamine user, Bangkang, May 3, 2001.

49. Interview with a female methamphetamine user, Bangkang, May 6, 2001.

50. Interview with a female methamphetamine user, Bangkang, April 21, 2001.

51. Interview with a female methamphetamine user, Bangkang, April 27, 2001.

52. Interview with a female methamphetamine user, Bangkang, May 13, 2001.

53. Interview with Zhou Dafu, deputy director, Wa Central Authority, Bangkang, February 19, 2001.

54. Interview with Bao Youxiang, Bangkang, May 7, 2001.

55. Interview with Sun Chengde, minister, Health Bureau, May 4, 2001.

56. Interview with a businessman, Bangkang, April 10, 2005.

57. Interview with a friend, Rangoon, July 19, 2002.

58. Ibid.

59. Interview with Chartchai Suthiklom, deputy secretary-general, Office of Narcotics Control Board of Thailand, Bangkok, July 15, 2002.

60. Interview with a businesswoman, Mae Sai, December 16, 2001.

61. Interview with a male heroin user, Kunming, January 6, 2005.

62. Interview with a male heroin user, Kunming, January 6, 2005

63. Interview with a male heroin user, Kunming, January 7, 2005.

64. Interview with a male heroin user, Kunming, January 12, 2005.

65. Interview with a male heroin user, Kunming, October 19, 2004.

66. Interview with a male heroin user, Kunming, November 1, 2004.

67. Interview with a male heroin user, Kunming, January 6, 2005.

68. Interview with a male heroin user, Kunming, January 7, 2005.

69. Interview with a male heroin user, Kunming, January 12, 2005.

70. Interview with a male heroin user, Kunming, November 1, 2004.

71. Ibid.

72. Interview with a male heroin user, Kunming, October 19, 2004.

73. Ibid.

74. In China, people accused of involvement in minor offenses such as burglary and fraud are not prosecuted in the criminal court but referred to a *laojiao* institution by local law enforcement authorities without a court hearing. This type of punishment, normally for one to three years, is considered an executive or administrative punishment. A person released from a *laojiao* institution is not viewed as an ex-convict, and he or she may have little difficulty in reintegrating into his or her community. Criminal offenders are sent to *laogia* (reform through labor) prisons.

75. Interview with a male heroin user, Kunming, January 6, 2005.

76. Interview with a male heroin user, Kunming, November 1, 2004.

77. Interview with a male heroin user, Kunming, January 7, 2005.

78. Interview with a male heroin user, Kunming, November 1, 2004.

79. Interview with a male heroin user, Kunming, January 12, 2005.

80. Interview with a male heroin user, Kunming, January 13, 2005.

81. Interview with a male heroin user, Kunming, October 19, 2004.

82. Interview with a male heroin user, Kunming, January 6, 2005.

83. Interview with a male heroin user, Kunming, January 6, 2005.

Chapter 7. Drug Control

1. Interview with a Wa woman, Kunma, August 28, 2002.

2. Interview with Zhao Aina, minister, Public Relation Bureau, Bangkang, April 30, 2001.

3. Opium cultivation, use, and trade were widespread in the Shan, Kachin, and Wa regions in precolonial Burma (Maule 1992). However, after Burma was colonized by the British, the British observed a laissez-faire policy toward opium cultivation and distribution in the trans-Salween Shan States due to "political expediency, the incapacity of State police to halt smuggling activities, the lack of alternative crops available to cultivators, the absence of a permanent British administrative presence in Kokang and the Wa States, and the fact that opium production in China tended to be uncontrolled" (Maule 1992, 15).

4. Interview with Zhou Dafu, deputy director, Wa Central Authority, Bangkang, February 13, 2001.

5. Interview with Li Ziru, deputy commander, United Wa State Army, Bangkang, May 18, 2001.

6. The law did not say anything about the weight of a unit, and it could be 700 grams (a big unit) or 350 grams (a small or half unit). Small or half unit packaging has become popular only recently.

7. Interview with Aiguo, chief of Police, Bangkang, April 12, 2005.

8. The Political Legal Bureau was basically a law enforcement agency; after police departments were established in 2003, the bureau was dissolved.

9. Interview with Xiao Mingliang, deputy commander, United Wa State Army, Bangkang, May 13, 2001.

10. Interview with Li Xueming, general manager, Wa State Tobacco Company, Bangkang, February 21, 2001.

11. Interview with a military intelligence officer, Rangoon, July 22, 2002.

12. Interview with Col. Hkam Awng, Central Committee for Drugs Abuse Control, Rangoon, July 22, 2002.

13. Ibid.

14. Interview with a businesswoman, Mae Sai, December 21, 2001.

15. Blacklisted drug pushers are drug dealers who are known to the police. It was not clear how the 25 percent of blacklisted drug pushers should be "reduced."

16. Interview with a subject close to the Wa leadership, Taipei, August 25, 2003.

17. Interview with a drug enforcement officer, Luxi, China, March 21, 2005.

18. Interview with a drug enforcement officer, Ruili, China, March 22, 2005.

19. Interview with a drug enforcement officer, Ruili, China, October 31, 2004.

20. Ibid.

21. Ibid.

22. Interview with Liang Jingyun, professor, Yunnan Police Academy, Kunming, August 14, 2003.

23. Interview with Zhou Yunlong, professor, Yunnan Police Academy, May 23, 2001.

24. Interview with Wang Yong, professor, Fujian Police Academy, Chengdu, May 29, 2005.

25. Interview with Xia Hung, professor, Guizhou Police Academy, June 2, 2005.

26. Controlled delivery means the technique of allowing prohibited substances or prohibited articles to pass from, toward, or through the territory of one or more jurisdictions with the knowledge and under the supervision of the competent authorities with a view to identify persons involved in the commission of prescribed offences.

27. Interview with Tang Jianhua, professor, Guangxi Police Academy, June 5, 2005.

28. The four cities are directly under the control of the central government because they do not belong to any provinces.

29. Interview with a drug enforcement officer, Chongqing, May 31, 2005.

30. Interview with Dong Sheng, deputy director, Yunnan Provincial Anti-Narcotics Bureau, January 12, 2005.

31. Interview with a DEA agent, New York office, New York, May 30, 2006.

32. Ibid.

33. Interview with Chartchai Suthiklom, deputy secretary-general, Office of Narcotics Control Board of Thailand, Bangkok, July 15, 2002.

34. Interview with Ting Xiao, director, Investment and Tourism Bureau, Bangkang, February 19, 2001.

35. Interview with Zhou Dafu, deputy director, Wa Central Authority, Bangkang, April 11, 2005.

Chapter 8. The Business and Politics of Drugs

1. Interview with a subject close to the Wa leadership, Bangkang, February 20, 2001.

2. Interview with Luo Xinghan, Rangoon, July 20, 2002.

3. Ibid.

4. Interview with a former KMT drug trafficker, Rangoon, July 18, 2002.

5. Interview with a schoolmate, Rangoon, July 19, 2002.

6. Interview with a Burmese military intelligence officer, Rangoon, July 22, 2002.

7. According to Chinese authorities, the most powerful and best organized criminal organizations in China have not yet reached the status of underworld organizations like the Italian Mafia, the Japanese yakuza, or the Hong Kong triad. As a result, Chinese authorities described the most advanced criminal organizations in China as "organizations with an underworld nature" (or characteristics), to differentiate them from other loosely knit and less influential criminal organizations such as criminal gangs and crime groups (He 2003).

8. Interview with a drug enforcement officer, Chongqing, June 2, 2005.

9. Interview with Li Zulie, Wa representative of Rangoon Office, Rangoon, July 20, 2002.

10. Interview with Luo Xinghan, Rangoon, July 20, 2002.

11. Interview with a businessman, Bangkang, April 11, 2005.

12. A phone conversation with a Wa woman in Bangkang, June 15, 2005.

Bibliography

In English

ALTSEAN-Burma. 2004. *A Failing Grade: Burma's Drug Eradication Efforts.* Bangkok: Alternative ASEAN Network on Burma.

Ashayagachat, Achara. 2001. "Rangoon Envoy Given Protest Note." *Bangkok Post,* February 13.

Assavanonda, Anjira. 2001. "Black Magic Invoked against Traffickers: Suphan Buri Fights an Uphill Battle." *Bangkok Post,* July 26.

Australian Crime Commission. 2007. *Illicit Drug Data Report 2005–06.* Canberra.

Ball, Desmond. 1999. *Burma and Drugs: The Regime's Complicity in the Global Drug Trade.* Working Paper No. 336. Canberra: Strategic and Defense Studies Centre of the Australian National University.

Bangkok Post. 1999. Editorial. "Burma's Dangerous Message on Drugs." November 7.

———. 2000. Editorial. "Burma Plan Puts People at Risk." January 18.

———. 2000. Editorial. "Good Neighbors Help One Another." April 14.

———. 2000. "400m Pills to Flood Streets of Thailand: Labourers Hooked, Says Research Center." April 17.

———. 2000. "Senator Backs Legal Speed Sale: Pills at a Baht Each to End Black Market." October 28.

————. 2000. "Five Burmese Troops Killed in Clash with Shan Fighters: Soldiers Slain While Delivering Speed Pills." November 14.

————. 2000. "Wa Link to Triads Confirmed, Shipment Seized in Transit to Australia." December 22.

————. 2001. "Mae Sai Evacuated as Shells Hit Town: Army Retaliates after Mortar Fire Kills Two." February 12.

————. 2002. Editorial. "Drugs—A Problem That Won't Go Away." March 2.

————. 2002. Editorial. "Rangoon Refuses to Keep Promises." October 9.

————. 2003. "Dealers to Face Lethal Government Action, Wan Nor Warns: Death May Await." January 25.

————. 2003. "Three-Month Crusade Launched: PM Declares Role as Commanding General." February 1.

————. 2003. "Killings Mar Launch of 3-Month Campaign: Suspected Traffickers Shot Dead in Bangkok." February 2.

————. 2003. Editorial. "No Lasting Solace Exists in Drug World." *Bangkok Post*, March 1.

————. 2003. "Campaign Hailed as a Huge Success: Gunmen, Influential Figures Next Targets." May 1.

————. 2003. "PM to Tackle Dark Influence." May 9.

————. 2003. "Police Hit-List Has 800 Targets." May 15.

————. 2003. Editorial. "Justice Isn't Found at the End of a Gun." August 21.

————. 2003. "US Official Declares War on Drugs a Success." November 27.

————. 2005. "Crime/Drug Bust: Boat Seized Off Trat with 546kg Heroin." March 21.

Belanger, Francis. 1989. *Drugs, the United States, and Khun Sa*. Bangkok: Editions Duang Kamol.

Belenko, Steven. 1993. *Crack and the Evolution of Drug Policy*. Westport, Conn.: Greenwood Press.

Black, David. 1992. *Triad Takeover: A Terrifying Account of the Spread of Triad Crime in the West*. London: Sidgwick and Jackson.

Booth, Martin. 1997. *Opium: A History*. London: Pocket Books.

————. 1999. *The Dragon Syndicates: The Global Phenomenon of the Triads*. New York: Carroll and Graf.

Boucaud, Andre, and Louis Boucaud. 1992. *Burma's Golden Triangle: On the Trail of the Opium Warlords*. Hong Kong: Asia 2000.

————. 1998. "Burma Goes for Extreme Solutions: Repression and Drug Trafficking." *Le Monde Diplomatique*. November.

Bourgois, Philippe. 1996. *In Search of Respect: Selling Crack in El Barrio*. New York: Cambridge University Press.

Bresler, Fenton. 1981. *The Chinese Mafia*. New York: Stein and Day.

Brookes, Stephen. 1990. "The Perilous Swim in Heroin's Stream." *Insight*, February 5: 8–17.

Bryant, Robert. 1990. "Chinese Organized Crime Making Major Inroads in Smuggling Heroin to U.S." *Organized Crime Digest* 11, no. 17: 1–6.

Callahan, Mary. 2003. *Making Enemies: War and State Building in Burma*. Ithaca: Cornell University Press.

Central Committee for Drug Abuse Control. 2000. *Myanmar's Efforts for the Eradication of Narcotic Drugs*. Rangoon: Central Committee for Drug Abuse Control.

———. 2001. *The War on Drugs: Myanmar's Efforts for the Eradication of Narcotic Drugs*. Rangoon: Central Committee for Drug Abuse Control.

Chalk, Peter. 2000. "Southeast Asia and the Golden Triangle's Heroin Trade: Threat and Response." *Studies in Conflict and Terrorism* 23: 89–106.

Charoenpo, Anucha. 2001. "Wa Taking Smuggled Cars in Barter Deals with Local Help." *Bangkok Post*, August 24.

———. 2002. "Wei's Frozen Assets Now Reach B270m: Relatives, Aides Ran Laundering Dens." *Bangkok Post*, February 25.

———. 2003. "Price of Pills Rises Five-Fold as Traffickers Beat Hasty Retreat: Police Try to Locate Buried Consignments." *Bangkok Post*, March 14.

Chepesiuk, Ron. 2003. *The Bullet or the Bribe: Taking Down Colombia's Cali Drug Cartel*. Westport, Conn.: Praeger.

Chin, Ko-lin. 1990. *Chinese Subculture and Criminality: Non-traditional Crime Groups in America*. Westport, Conn.: Greenwood Pres.

———. 1996. *Chinatown Gangs: Extortion, Enterprise, and Ethnicity*. New York: Oxford University Press.

———. 1999. *Smuggled Chinese: Clandestine Immigration to the United States*. Philadelphia: Temple University Press.

———. 2003. *Heijin: Organized Crime, Business, and Politics in Taiwan*. Armonk, N.Y.: M. E. Sharpe.

Chin, Ko-lin, and Sheldon Zhang. 2007. *The Chinese Connection: Cross-Border Drug Trafficking between Myanmar and China*. A final report submitted to the U.S. National Institute of Justice.

Choe, Sang-hun. 2007. "On Quiet Streets of Myanmar Fear Is a Constant Companion." *New York Times*, October 21: A1.

Chouvy, Pierre-Arnaud, and Joel Meissonnier. 2004. *Yaa Baa: Production, Traffic and Consumption of Methamphetamine in Mainland Southeast Asia*. Singapore: Singapore University Press.

Chu, Yiu-kong. 2002. *Triads as Business*. London: Routledge.

Collignon, Stefan. 2001. "Human Rights and the Economy in Burma." In *Burma: Political Economy under Military Rule*, edited by Robert Taylor. New York: Palgrave.

Cowell, Adrian. 2005. "Opium Anarchy in the Shan State of Burma." In *Trouble in the Triangle: Opium and Conflict in Burma*, edited by Martin Jelsma, Tom Kramer, and Pietje Vervest. Chiang Mai: Silkworm Books.

Davis, Anthony, and Bruce Hawke. 1998. "Burma: The Country That Won't Kick the Habit." *Jane's Intelligence Review* 10, no. 3: 26–31.

Dawson, Alan. 2002. "Wa Drug Cartel in US Sights." *Bangkok Post*, March 18.

Daw Tin Yee. 2004. *The Socio-Economic Life of the Wah National*. Rangoon: National Centre for Human Resource Development.

Della Porta, Donatella, and Alberto Vannucci. 1999. *Corrupt Exchanges: Actors, Resources, and Mechanisms of Political Corruption*. New York: Aldine De Gruyer.

DeStefano, Anthony. 1988. "The Asian Connection: A New Main Line to U.S." *New York Newsday*, February 14: 5.

DeStefano, Anthony, and Richard Esposito. 1987. "Asian Gangs Move into Drugs." *New York Newsday*, September 16: 7.

Dikotter, Frank, Lars Laamann, and Zhou Xun. 2004. *Narcotic Culture: A History of Drugs in China*. Chicago: University of Chicago Press.

Dobinson, Ian. 1993. "Pinning a Tail on the Dragon: The Chinese and the International Heroin Trade." *Crime & Delinquency* 39, no. 3: 373–84.

Dubro, James. 1992. *Dragons of Crime: Inside the Asian Underworld*. Markham, Ontario: Octopus Publishing Group.

Dupont, Alan. 1999. "Transnational Crime, Drugs, and Security in East Asia." *Asian Survey* 39, no. 3: 433–55.

———. 2001. *East Asia Imperiled: Transnational Challenges to Security*. Cambridge: Cambridge University Press.

Eads, Brian. 2002. "Lords of Addiction." *Reader's Digest* (May): 55–61.

Ekachai, Sanitsuda. 2002. Commentary. "Peace Is Not Built on Oppression." *Bangkok Post*, June 13.

Elliott, Patricia. 1999. *The White Umbrella*. Bangkok: Post Books.

Emery, James. 2003. "War on Drugs Is Not All about Killing." *Bangkok Post*, February 26.

Erlanger, Steven. 1990. "Southeast Asia Is Now No. 1 Source of U.S. Heroin." *New York Times*, February 11: A26.

Esposito, Richard, and Sheryl McCarthy. 1988. "Record Heroin Bust Sends Agent Searching in NY." *New York Newsday*, February 14: 5.

Evans, Grant, Christopher Hutton, and Kuah Khun Eng, eds. 2000. *Where China Meets Southeast Asia*. New York: St. Martin's Press.

Fabre, Guilhem. 2005. "The Black Hole of 'China White.'" In *Trouble in the Triangle: Opium and Conflict in Burma*, edited by Martin Jelsma, Tom Kramer, and Pietje Vervest. Chiang Mai: Silkworm Books.

Finckenauer, James, and Ko-lin Chin. 2006. "Asian Transnational Organized Crime and Its Impact on the United States: Developing a Transnational Crime Research Agenda." *Trends in Organized Crime* 10, no. 2: 18–107.

Fink, Christina. 2001. *Living Silence: Burma under Military Rule*. Bangkok: White Lotus.

Fiskesjo, Nils Magnus Geir. 2000. "The Fate of Sacrifice and the Making of Wa History." Ph.D. diss., University of Chicago, Chicago.

Forero, Juan, and Tim Weiner. 2003. "Latin American Poppy Fields Undermine U.S. Drug Battle." *New York Times*, June 8: N1.

Friedman, Jonathan. 1975. "Tribes, States, and Transformation." In *Marxist Analyses and Social Anthropology*, edited by Maurice Bloch. London: Malaby Press.

———. 1987. "Generalized Exchange, Theocracy and the Opium Trade." *Critique of Anthropology* 7, no. 1: 15–31.

———. 1998 [1979]. *System, Structure, and Contradiction: The Evolution of "Asiatic" Social Formation*. Walnut Creek, Calif.: AltaMira Press.

Fuller, Thomas. 2007. "For Myanmar's Neighbors, Mutual Needs Trump Qualms." *New York Times*, October 2: A8.

Gaylord, Mark. 1997. "City of Secrets: Drugs, Money and the Law in Hong Kong." *Crime, Law and Social Change* 28: 91–110.

Gelbard, Robert. 1998. "Burma: The Booming Drug Trade." In *Burma: Prospects for a Democratic Future*, edited by Robert Rotberg. Washington, D.C.: Brookings Institution.

Gibson, Richard, and John Haseman. 2003. "Prospects for Controlling Narcotics Production and Trafficking in Myanmar." *Contemporary Southeast Asia* 25, no. 1: 1–19.

Gittings, John. 2005. *The Changing Face of China: From Mao to Market*. New York: Oxford University Press.

Godson, Roy, ed. 2003. *Menace to Society: Political-Criminal Collaboration around the World*. New Brunswick, N.J.: Transaction Publishers.

Gould, Terry. 2004. *Paper Fan: The Hunt for Triad Gangster Steven Wong*. Toronto: Random House.

Greenfeld, Karl Taro. 2001. "Need for Speed." *Time Asia* 157, no. 9: March 5.

Greenhouse, Steven. 1995. "Heroin from Burmese Surges as U.S. Debates Strategy." *New York Times*, February 12: 3.

Haq, M. Emdad-ul. 2000. *Drugs in South Asia: From the Opium Trade to the Present Day*. New York: St. Martin's Press.

Hawke, Bruce. 1998. "Burma's Cease-fire Agreements in Danger of Unraveling." *Jane's Intelligence Review* (November 1): 23–27.

Hkam Awng. 2002. "Changing Trends in Narcotic Crime in Myanmar." In *Bridging the Gap: A Global Alliance Perspective on Transnational Organized Crime*, edited by Roderic Broadhurst. Hong Kong: Hong Kong Police Force.

Hla Min. 2000. *Political Situation of Myanmar and Its Role in the Region*. Yangon: Ministry of Defense.

Hutasingh, Onnucha, and Mongkoi Bangprapa. 2003. "Rights Abuse Fears as Death Toll Rises: Government Slammed over Shoot-to-Kill Policy." *Bangkok Post*, February 14.

Jacobs, Bruce. 1999. *Dealing Crack: The Social World of Streetcorner Selling*. Boston: Northeastern University Press.

Jagan, Larry. 2004. "Burma Warlord Appeals for Understanding." *Bangkok Post Sunday Perspective*, October 17.

Jelsma, Martin. 2005. "Burma in the Global Drug Market." In *Trouble in the Triangle: Opium and Conflict in Burma*, edited by Martin Jelsma, Tom Kramer, and Pietje Vervest. Chiang Mai: Silkworm Books.

Jelsma, Martin, Tom Kramer, and Pietje Vervest, eds. 2005. *Trouble in the Triangle: Opium and Conflict in Burma*. Chiang Mai: Silkworm Books.

Jinakul, Surath. 2005. "The Chase Is on for International Drug Lords." *Bangkok Post Sunday Perspective*, March 27.

Jinakul, Surath, and Prasong Charasdamrong. 2001. "Advantage Drug Lords." *Bangkok Post*, March 4.

Johnson, Bruce, Paul Goldstein, Edward Preble, James Schmeidler, Douglas Lipton, Barry Spunt, and Thomas Miller. 1985. *Taking Care of Business*. Lexington, Mass.: Lexington Books.

Kasitipradit, Sermsuk, and Wassana Nanuam. 1999a. "Rangoon's Troops Active in Drug Trade." *Bangkok Post*, July 25.

———. 1999b. "Third Army Wants to Lead Drive: Special Threat Needs Firm Actions, It Says." *Bangkok Post*, December 25.

Kasitipradit, Sermsuk, Wassana Nanuam, and Teerawat Kamtida. 2001. "Burmese Raid River Boat, Seize 9m Pills." *Bangkok Post*, June 14.

Khamthita, Theerawat. 2002. "Thai Merchants Stranded, Prices of Goods Soaring." *Bangkok Post*, May 24.

Khuenkaew, Subin. 1999a. "Drug Gangs Targeted in Joint Sweep." *Bangkok Post*, July 15.

———. 1999b. "Army Nets Huge Haul after Clash: Gunships Called in to Oust Intruders." *Bangkok Post*, July 30.

Khuenkaew, Subin, and Wassana Nanuam. 2000. "Rangoon-Backed Wa Army Moves into Shan Region: Five Battalions Enter Area Rich with Opium." *Bangkok Post*, December 3.

———. 2002. "Army Angered by Pull-Back: Chavalit Orders Early End to Troop Exercise." *Bangkok Post*, May 24.

Kinkead, Gwen. 1992. *Chinatown*. New York: HarperCollins.

Koziol, Ronald. 1988. "Multimillionaire Charged in Heroin Case." *San Francisco Examiner*, April 27: A7.

Kramer, Tom. 2005. "Ethnic Conflict and Dilemmas for International Engagement." In *Trouble in the Triangle: Opium and Conflict in Burma*, edited by Martin Jelsma, Tom Kramer, and Pietje Vervest. Chiang Mai: Silkworm Books.

———. 2007. *The United Wa State Party: Narco-Army or Ethnic Nationalist Party?* Washington, D.C.: East-West Center.

Kuah, Khun Eng. 2000. "Negotiating Central, Provincial, and County Policies: Border Trading in South China." In *Where China Meets Southeast Asia: Social and Cultural Change in the Border Regions*, edited by Grant Evans, Christopher Hutton, and Kuah Khun Eng. New York: St. Martin's Press.

Kudo, Toshihiro. 2006. *Myanmar's Economic Relations with China: Can China Support the Myanmar Economy?* Discussion Paper no. 65. Chiba, Japan: Institute of Developing Economies, Japan External Trade Organization.

Kumtita, Teerawat, and Yuwadee Tunyasiri. 2002. "Thaksin Says Matters Will Be Resolved Soon: Checkpoint Closures Push Fuel Prices Up." *Bangkok Post*, May 26.

Labrousse, Alain. 2005. "Drugs: The Major Obstacle to Afghan Reconstruction?" In *Trouble in the Triangle: Opium and Conflict in Burma*, edited by Martin Jelsma, Tom Kramer, and Pietje Vervest. Chiang Mai: Silkworm Books.

Lay, Richard, and Chris Dobson. 1993. "Rise and Fall of Machine Gun Johnny." *South China Morning Post Spectrum*, March 14: 4.

Leach, Edmund. 1954. *Political Systems of Highland Burma: A Study of Kachin Social Structure*. London: London School of Economics and Political Science.

Lintner, Bertil. 1990. "Roads from Mandalay." *Far Eastern Economic Review*, June 28: 27.

———. 1993a. "Tracing New Tracks." *Far Eastern Economic Review*, March 18: 25.

———. 1993b. "The Politics of the Drug Trade in Burma." In *Narcotics in Burma, Conference Report*. Washington, D.C.: United States Department of State.

———. 1994a. "The Volatile Yunnan Frontier." *Jane's Intelligence Review*, February: 84–92.

———. 1994b. *Burma in Revolt: Opium and Insurgency since 1948*. Boulder, Colo.: Westview Press.

———. 1998a. "Drugs and Economic Growth: Ethnicity and Exports." In *Burma: Prospects for a Democratic Future*, edited by Robert Rotberg. Washington, D.C.: Brookings Institution.

———. 1998b. "Global Reach: Drug Money in the Asia Pacific." *Current History* 97 (April): 179–82.

———. 1990. *The Rise and Fall of the Communist Party of Burma (CPB)*. Ithaca: Cornell University, Southeast Asia Program.

———. 2003. *Blood Brothers: The Criminal Underworld of Asia*. New York: Palgrave Macmillan.

Lo, T. Wing. 1993. *Corruption and Politics in Hong Kong and China*. Buckingham: Open University Press.

Mark, Gregory Yee. 1992. "From Jung Gwok to Gam Saan: Wah Kiu and Yen Shee." Paper presented at the Luodi-Shenggen Conference on Overseas Chinese, San Francisco, November.

Marriott, Michael. 1989. "Heroin Seizure at 3 Queens Sites Is Called Biggest U.S. Drug Raid." *New York Times*, February 22: B5.

Marshall, Andrew. 2002. *The Trouser People: A Story of Burma in the Shadow of the Empire*. Washington, D.C.: Counterpoint.

Marshall, Andrew, and Anthony Davis. 2002. "Soldiers of Fortune." *Time Asia*, December 16: 16–24.

Martin, Brian. 1996. *The Shanghai Green Gang*. Berkeley: University of California Press.

Maule, Robert. 1992. "The Opium Question in the Federated Shan States, 1931–1936: British Policy Discussions and Scandal." *Journal of Southeast Asian Studies* 23, no. 1: 14–36.

———. 2002. "British Policy Discussions on the Opium Question in the Federated Shan States, 1937–1948." *Journal of Southeast Asian Studies* 33, no. 2: 203–24.

Maung Pho Shoke. 1999. *Why Did U Khun Sa's MTA Exchange Arms for Peace?* Yangon: U Aung Zaw.

McLeod, Alexander. 1947. *Pigtails and Gold Dust*. Caldwell, Ida.: Caxton Printers.

McCoy, Alfred. 1972. *The Politics of Heroin in Southeast Asia*. New York: Harper Colophon Books.

———. 1991. *The Politics of Heroin: CIA Complicity in the Global Drug Trade*. New York: Lawrence Hill Books.

———. 1992. "Heroin as a Global Commodity: A History of Southeast Asia's Opium Trade." In *War on Drugs: Studies in the Failure of U.S. Narcotics Policy*, edited by Alfred McCoy and Alan Block. Boulder, Colo.: Westview Press.

———. 1999a. "Requiem for a Drug Lord: State and Commodity in the Career of Khun Sa." In *States and Illegal Practices*, edited by Josiah McC. Heyman. Oxford: Berg.

———. 1999b. "Lord of Drug Lords: One Life as Lesson for US Drug Policy." *Crime, Law and Social Change* 30: 301–31.

Meyer, Kathryn, and Terry Parssinen. 1998. *Webs of Smoke: Smugglers, Warlords, Spies, and the History of the International Drug Trade*. Lanham, Md.: Rowman and Littlefield.

Milsom, Jeremy. 2005. "The Long Hard Road Out of Drugs: The Case of the Wa." In *Trouble in the Triangle: Opium and Conflict in Burma*, edited by Martin Jelsma, Tom Kramer, and Pietje Vervest. Chiang Mai: Silkworm Books.

Ministry of Information, Union of Myanmar. 2002. *Myanmar: Facts and Figures, 2002*. Yangon: Printing and Publishing Enterprise.

Ministry of Justice Investigation Bureau. 2003. *Drug Crime Prevention Work Yearbook, 2002*. Taipei: Investigation Bureau.

Morain, Dan, and Philip Hager. 1991. "Officials Call Heroin Seizures a Major Victory." *Los Angeles Times*, June 22: A24.

Murphy, Dan. 2002. "A Drug Craze Sweeps Thailand." *Christian Science Monitor*, May 29.

Mydans, Seth. 2007a. "Monks' Protest Is Challenging Burmese Junta." *New York Times*, September 24: A1.

———. 2007b. "More Deaths in Myanmar, and Defiance." *New York Times*, September 27: A1.

Nanuam, Wassana. 2002. "Klong Toey to Face Daily Raid." *Bangkok Post*, February 28.

National Narcotics Control Commission. 1999. *1998 Annual Report on Drug Control in China*. Beijing: Office of the National Narcotics Control Commission.

———. 2001. *2000 Annual Report on Drug Control in China*. Beijing: Office of the National Narcotics Control Commission.

———. 2003. *2002 Annual Report on Drug Control in China*. Beijing: Office of the National Narcotics Control Commission.

National Security Council. 2000. *International Crime Threat Assessment*. Washington, D.C.

New York Times. 1998. "Colombian Heroin Dominates U.S. Market, Government Says." January 1: A19.

Ngamkham, Wassayos. 2003. "Police Admit to 57 Drug War Killings from the 1,320 Killed." *Bangkok Post*, December 20.

Nugent, David. 1982. "Closed Systems and Contradiction: The Kachin In and Out of History." *Man* 17: 508–27.

Office of Narcotics Control Board. 1999. *Thailand Narcotics Annual Report 1998– 1999*. Bangkok: Office of the Prime Minister.

———. 2002. *Thailand Narcotics Annual Report 2001*. Bangkok: Office of the Prime Minister.

Pathan, Don. 2005. "Thailand's War on Drugs." In *Trouble in the Triangle: Opium and Conflict in Burma*, edited by Martin Jelsma, Tom Kramer, and Pietje Vervest. Chiang Mai: Silkworm Books.

Penn, Stanley. 1990. "Asian Connection: Chinese Gangsters Fill a Narcotics Gap Left by U.S. Drive on Mafia." *Wall Street Journal*, March 22: A1.

Phongpaichit, Pasuk, and Chris Baker. 2003. "Slaughter in the Name of a Drug War." *New York Times*, May 24: A15.

Phongpaichit, Pasuk, and Sungsidh Piriyarangsan. 1994. *Corruption and Democracy in Thailand*. Chiang Mai: Silkworm Books.

Phongpaichit, Pasuk, Sungsidh Piriyarangsan, and Nualnoi Teerat. 1998. *Guns, Girls, Gambling, Ganja: Thailand's Illegal Economy and Public Policy*. Chiang Mai: Silkworm Books.

Posner, Gerald. 1988. *Warlords of Crime*. New York: McGraw-Hill.

Powell, Michael. 1989. "Tong Influence in Chinatown Turns to Drugs." *New York Newsday*, February 27: 7.

President's Commission on Organized Crime. 1984. *Organized Crime of Asian Origin: Record of Hearing III—October 23–25, 1984, New York, N.Y.* Washington, D.C.: Government Printing Office.

Renard, Ronald. 1996. *The Burmese Connection: Illegal Drugs and the Making of the Golden Triangle*. Boulder, Colo.: Lynne Rienner.

Ruangdit, Pradit. 2003. "PM 'Guilty of Emotional Blackmail': Opposition, Activists Take Thaksin to Task." *Bangkok Post*, March 2.

Sack, John. 2001. *The Dragonheads*. New York: Crown.

Santimetaneedol, Ampa. 2003a. "Probe Urged into All Violent 'Drug' Deaths: Critics Query Police Claim of Innocence." *Bangkok Post*, February 11.

———. 2003b. "Real Mafia Members 'Not Being Identified': Police Being Paid B20bn Bribes a Year." *Bangkok Post*, May 16.

Schalks, Toon. 1991. *Chinese Organized Crime in the Netherlands*. The Hague: National Criminal Intelligence Service, NCB Interpol.

Seagrave, Sterling. 1985. *The Soong Dynasty*. New York: Harper and Row.

Selth, Andrew. 2001. *Burma's Armed Forces: Power without Glory*. Norwalk, Conn.: EastBridge.

Seper, Jerry. 1986. "Chinese Gangs and Heroin Cast Lawless Shadow." *Washington Times*, January 28: A1.

Seper, Jerry, and Glenn Emery. 1986. "Opium Daze and Pink Knights Herald the Age of the Dragon." *Insight*, February 17: 20–24.

Shelley, Louise. 1997. *Policing Soviet Society*. London: Routledge.

Sheng, Lijun. 2006. "China-Asean Cooperation against Illicit Drugs from the Golden Triangle." *Asian Perspective* 30, no. 2: 97–126.

Skidmore, Monique. 2004. *Karaoke Fascism: Burma and the Politics of Fear.* Philadelphia: University of Pennsylvania Press.

———. ed. 2005. *Burma at the Turn of the 21st Century.* Honolulu: University of Hawaii Press.

Smith, Martin. 1999. *Burma: Insurgency and the Politics of Ethnicity.* Revised and updated edition. Bangkok: White Lotus.

Southeast Asian Information Network. 1998. *Out of Control 2: The HIV/AIDS Epidemic in Burma.* Bangkok: SAIN.

Spence, Jonathan. 1990. *The Search for Modern China.* New York: W. W. Norton.

Steinberg, David. 2001. *Burma: The State of Myanmar.* Washington, D.C.: Georgetown University Press.

———. 2006. *Turmoil in Burma: Contested Legitimacies in Myanmar.* Norwalk, Conn.: EastBridge.

Stille, Alexander. 1995. *Excellent Cadavers.* New York: Vintage Books.

Stutman, Robert. 1987 "Emerging Criminal Groups in Heroin Trafficking." Statement before the Select Committee on Narcotics Abuse and Control, U.S. House of Representatives, July 10.

Suksamram, Nauvarat. 2005. "Drug Village Exploits Its Culture Roots." *Bangkok Post,* October 25.

Takano, Hideyuki. 2002. *The Shore beyond Good and Evil: A Report from Inside Burma's Opium Kingdom.* Reno, Nev.: Kotan Publishing.

Tasker, Rodney, and Bertil Lintner. 2001. "No Quick Fix for the Junta." *Far Eastern Economic Review,* November 29: 29–30.

Taylor, Robert, ed., 2001. *Burma: Political Economy under Military Rule.* New York: Palgrave.

Thaitawat, Nusara. 1998. "Burma Likely to Escape the Bricks." *Bangkok Post,* June 8.

Thant Myint-U. 2001. *The Making of Modern Burma.* Cambridge: Cambridge University Press.

———. 2006. *The River of Lost Footsteps: Histories of Burma.* New York: Farrar, Straus and Giroux.

Thayer, Nate. 1993. "Diverted Traffic." *Far Eastern Economic Review,* March 18: 24–25.

Thoumi, Francesco. 1995. *Political Economy and Illegal Drugs in Colombia.* Boulder, Colo.: Lynne Reinner.

Ting, Chang. 2004. *China Always Says "No" to Narcotics.* Beijing: Foreign Languages Press.

Transnational Institute. 2003. "Drugs and Conflict in Burma (Myanmar): Dilemmas for Policy Response." Drugs and Conflict Debate Papers no. 9. Amsterdam: Transnational Institute.

———. 2005. "Downward Spiral: Banning Opium in Afghanistan and Burma." Drugs and Conflict Debate Papers no. 12. Amsterdam: Transnational Institute.

———. 2006. "HIV/AIDS and Drug Use in Burma/Myanmar." Drug Policy Briefing no. 17. Amsterdam: Transnational Institute.

Treaster, Joseph. 1991. "U.S. Officials Seize Huge Heroin Cache." *New York Times*, June 22: A10.

Tunyasiri, Yuwadee, and Achara Ashayagachat. 2003. "Death Toll Irrelevant, Says PM: Says Children Should Come before Dealers." *Bangkok Post*, March 2.

Tunyasiri, Yuwadee, and Anucha Charoenpo. 2003. "All-Out War Declared on Traffickers: PM Sets Three-Month Deadline, 'Or Else . . .' " *Bangkok Post*, January 15.

Tunyasiri, Yuwadee, and Wassayos Ngarmkham. 2003. "Chavalit Backs Special Drugs Court: Crackdown by Police Likely to Limit Supplies." *Bangkok Post*, February 8.

Tunyasiri, Yuwadee, and Temsak Traisophon. 2003. "Sights Now Targeting Big Players: State Officials, Major Dealers to Feel Heat." *Bangkok Post*, March 4.

U Win Naing. 2001. "No Opium without Takers." *Bangkok Post*, July 16.

———. 2004. "Will the New PM Make a Difference?" *Bangkok Post*, October 31.

United Nations International Drug Control Programme. 1997. *World Drug Report*. New York: Oxford University Press.

United Nations Office on Drugs and Crime. 2005a. *Myanmar Opium Survey 2005*.

———. 2005b. *Patterns and Trends of Amphetamine-Type Stimulants (ATS) and Other Drugs of Abuse in East Asia and the Pacific 2005*.

———. 2006. *Opium Poppy Cultivation in the Golden Triangle: Lao PDR, Myanmar, Thailand*.

———. 2007. *Opium Poppy Cultivation in South East Asia: Lao PDR, Myanmar, Thailand*.

U.S. Department of State. 1993. *International Narcotics Control Strategy Report*. Washington D.C.: U.S. Government Printing Office.

———. 1994. *International Narcotics Control Strategy Report*. Washington D.C.: U.S. Government Printing Office.

———. 1995. *International Narcotics Control Strategy Report*. Washington D.C.: U.S. Government Printing Office.

———. 1996. *International Narcotics Control Strategy Report*. Washington D.C.: U.S. Government Printing Office.

———. 1998. *International Narcotics Control Strategy Report*. Washington D.C.: U.S. Government Printing Office.

———. 2000. *International Narcotics Control Strategy Report*. Washington D.C.: U.S. Government Printing Office.

———. 2001. *International Narcotics Control Strategy Report*. Washington D.C.: U.S. Government Printing Office.

———. 2002. *International Narcotics Control Strategy Report*. Washington D.C.: U.S. Government Printing Office.

———. 2003. *International Narcotics Control Strategy Report*. Washington D.C.: U.S. Government Printing Office.

———. 2004. *International Narcotics Control Strategy Report*. Washington D.C.: U.S. Government Printing Office.

———. 2005. *International Narcotics Control Strategy Report*. Washington D.C.: U.S. Government Printing Office.

———. 2006. *International Narcotics Control Strategy Report*. Washington D.C.: U.S. Government Printing Office.

U.S. District Court, Eastern District of New York. 2005. *United States vs. Wei Hsueh Kang, Wei Hsueh Lung, Wei Hsueh Ying, Pao Yu Hsiang, Pao Hua Chiang, Pao Yu Yi, Pao Yu Liang, Pao Yu Hua*.

U.S. Drug Enforcement Administration. 2001. "The Price Dynamics of Southeast Asian Heroin." *Drug Intelligence Brief*. February.

———. 2002. *Burma Country Brief. Drug Intelligence Brief*. May.

U.S. General Accounting Office. 1989. *Drug Control: Enforcement Efforts in Burma Are Not Effective*. Washington, D.C.: U.S. General Accounting Office.

———. 1996. *Drug Control: U.S. Heroin Program Encounters Many Obstacles in Southeast Asia*. Washington, D.C.: U.S. General Accounting Office.

U.S. House of Representatives. 1987. *Hearing on Emerging Criminal Groups Involved in Heroin Trafficking in New York*. Select Committee on Narcotics Abuse and Control, Kennedy International Airport.

U.S. Senate. 1978 [1877]. *Report of the Joint Special Committee to Investigate Chinese Immigration*. Reprint. New York: Arno Press.

———. 1986. *Emerging Criminal Groups*. Hearings before the Permanent Subcommittee on Investigations of the Committee on Governmental Affairs. Washington, D.C.: U.S. Government Printing Office.

———. 1992. *Asian Organized Crime*. Hearing before the Permanent Subcommittee on Investigations of the Committee on Governmental Affairs. Washington, D.C.: Government Printing Office.

van Kemenade, Willem. 1997. *China, Hong Kong, Taiwan, Inc.* New York: Alfred A. Knopf.

Wakeman, Frederic. 1995. *Policing Shanghai, 1927–1937*. Berkeley: University of California Press.

Wa State Government. 2001. "The Peaceful Economic Construction of Special Region II (Wa State) 1990–2000." Unpublished.

Westermeyer, Joseph. 1982. *Poppies, Pipes, and the People: Opium and Its Use in Laos*. Berkeley: University of California Press.

Williams, Terry. 1989. *The Cocaine Kids: The Inside Story of a Teenage Drug Ring*. Reading, Mass.: Addison-Wesley.

Witkin, Gordon. 1994. "The New Opium Wars." *U.S. News & World Report*, October 10: 39–44.

Worobec, Stephen. 1984. "International Narcotics Control in the Golden Triangle of Southeast Asia." Ph.D. diss., Claremont Graduate School, Claremont, Calif.

Yan Nyien Aye. 2000. *Endeavours of the Myanmar Armed Forces Government for National Reconsolidation*. Yangon: U Aung Zaw.

Yawnghwe, Chao-Tzang. 1993. "The Political Economy of the Opium Trade: Implications for Shan State." *Journal of Contemporary Asia* 23, no. 3: 306–26.

————. 1998. "Burma's 'Minorities' and Drugs: Hamburger Flippers and the Mc-Donald's Empire." *BurmaNet News*, October 21.

————. 2005. "Shan State Politics: The Opium-Heroin Factor." In *Trouble in the Triangle: Opium and Conflict in Burma*, edited by Martin Jelsma, Tom Kramer, and Pietje Vervest. Chiang Mai: Silkworm Books.

Yunnan Province Narcotics Control Committee. 2003. *Brilliant Efforts: Yunnan's Drug Control 1998–2003*. Kunming: Yunnan Nationalities Publishing House.

Zaitch, Damian. 2002. *Trafficking Cocaine: Colombian Drug Entrepreneurs in the Netherlands*. The Hague: Kluwer Law International.

Zhang, Sheldon, and Ko-lin Chin. 2003. "The Declining Significance of Triad Societies in Transnational Illegal Activities." *British Journal of Criminology* 43, no. 3: 469–88.

In Chinese

Bo, Yang. 1987. *Jin San Jiao: Huang Cheng* [Golden Triangle: Frontier and Wilderness]. Hong Kong: Joint Publishing Company.

Chen, Beidi. 2006. *Zhong Guo Xi Du Diao Cha* [Drug Use in China]. Beijing: Xinhua Publishers.

Chou, Kerting. 1993. *Niu Yue Hua Fu De Gu Ling Jing Guai* [Ghosts and Spirits in New York City's Chinatown]. New York: People and Events Publisher.

Chu, Ping. 2004. *Du Xiao* [Drug Baron]. Hong Kong: Sheffield Press.

Cui, Min. 1999. *Du Pin Fan Zui* [Drug Crime]. Beijing: Police Officers Education Publisher.

Deng, Xian. 2000. *Liu Lang Jin San Jiao* [Wandering in the Golden Triangle]. Beijing: People's Literature Publisher.

Gao, Fayuan. 2001. *Yun Nan Min Zu Cun Zhai Diao Cha: Wa Zu* [Surveys of Minority Villages in Yunnan Province: The Wa]. Kunming: Yunnan University Press.

Guizhou Police College. 2004. *Gui Zhou Jin Du Mou Lue* [Drug Prohibition Strategy in Guizhou]. A research report supported by the 2002 Guizhou Province Philosophy and Social Sciences Planned Research.

Han, Yunfeng. 2004. *Ya Pian De Xiao Xiang* [Portraits of Opium]. Beijing: China Youth Publisher.

He, Bingsong. 2003. *Hei She Hui Fan Zui Jie Du* [Understanding Organized Crime Activities]. Beijing: China Judicial Press.

Hu, Yue, and Xianhui Li. 2005. *Nu Ji Zhe Yu Da Du Xiao Liu Zhao Hua Mian Dui Mian* [Face-to-Face between Female Journalist and Drug Kingpin Liu Zhaohua]. Beijing: China Youth Publisher.

Huang, Yuanling. 1988. *Ba Qi Nian Niu Yue Hua Ren Fan Du An Da Zeng* [The Number of Chinese Heroin Cases Increased Dramatically in 1987]. *World Journal*, January 6: 36.

Jin, Ma. 2003. *Guo Men Bei Huan: Jin San Jiao Yu Zhogn Guo Mi Jing Pi Lian Di Ji Shi* [Joy and Tears at the Country's Gate]. Beijing: Tungxin Publisher.

Li, Rentang. 2000. *Bei Jin San Jiao Tan Mi: Wo Yu Da Du Xiao De Yi Bai Ge Ri Ri Ye Ye* [Exploring the Northern Golden Triangle: My 100 Days and Nights with Drug Warlords]. Beijing: Qunzhong Publication.

Luo, Bingsen, and Jinyun Liang, eds. 1999. *Yun Nan Jin Du Yan Jiu Lun Wen Ji* [Essays on the Suppression of Drugs in Yunnan]. Beijing: Qunzhong Publication.

Luo, Bingsen, Jinyun Liang, and Hongping Yang, eds. 2004. *Jin Du Wen Ti Yan Jiu* [Studies on Drug Prevention]. Beijing: Public Security University Press.

Luo, Zhiji. 1995. *Wa Zu She Hui De Li Shi Yu Wen Hua* [The History and Culture of Wa Society]. Beijing: Central Ethnology University Press.

Ma, Minai. 1999. *Wo Guo Du Pin Fan Zui De Xin Te Dian* [New Trends in Drug Trafficking in China]. In *Essays on the Suppression of Drugs in Yunnan*, edited by Luo Bingsen and Liang Jinyun. Beijing: Qunzhong Publication.

Ma, Mojen. 1994. *Du Pin Zai Zhong Guo* [Drugs in China]. Taipei: Kerning Publications.

Ma, Wenyuan, and Kejin Ren. 1999. *Guang Zhou Du Pin Wen Ti Yan Jiu* [The Drug Problem in Guangzhou]. Beijing: Police Officers Education Publication.

Shi, Anda. 1996. *Ru He Jia Qiang Guo Ji He Zuo Fa Zhan Ti Dai Jing Ji Chan Chu Du Yuan: Lai Zi Mian Dian Shan Bang Di Er Te Qu De Jin Du Bao Gao* [Enhancing International Cooperation to Develop Crop-Substitution Programs to Eliminate Drug Source: A Research Report on Drug Prevention in the Burma Shan State Number 2 Special Zone (Wa State)]. August 1. Unpublished.

Sun, Dahong. 2001. *Jin Du Feng Yun Lu* [Drug Prevention in China]. Kunming: Yunnan Arts Publisher.

Ting, Xiao. 2001. *Guan Yu Zhi Chi He Yuan Zhu Mian Dian Di Er Te Qu (Wa Bang) Kai Zhan Jin Du Gong Zuo De Kao Cha Bao Gao* [A Report on the Support and Assistance of Burma Special Zone No. 2 (Wa State) to Develop Drug Eradication Plans]. Kunming: Yunnan Province Business Association.

Ting, Yihe. 2005. *Zhong Guo Da Jin Du* [Drug Prohibition in China]. Beijing: China City Publication.

United Wa State Party. 1991. *Tong Ling* [General Announcement]. Political Legal Department. November 26.

———. 1996. *Guan Yu Zhao San Mu Li Si Zi Pi Zhun Bei Wa Yong Bang She Li Du Pin Jia Gong Chang De Chu Li Jue Ding* [A Decision on the Punishment of Zhao Sanmuli for Privately Allowing the Establishment of a Heroin Refinery in Yongbang, Northern Wa County]. August 2.

———. 1999a. *Zhong Yang Dui Jing Wei Tuan 906 Sji Jian Zhu Fan Ai Tai, Jie Bei, Ying Xiang San Ren Chu Fen Jue Ding De Tong Bao* [An Announcement of the Decision of the Headquarters Regarding the Punishment of Key Offenders, Aitai, Jiebei, and Yingxiang, in the Jinweituan 906 incident]. October 8.

———. 1999b. *He Ping Yu Fa Zhan: Mian Dian Di Er Te Qu (Wa Bang) Gai Kuang* [Peace and Development: The Current State of Myanmar's Special Region II (Wa State)]. Unpublished.

———. 2001a. *Wa Bang 2000 Nian Du Gong Zuo Ren Wu* [A 2000 Summary Report of Government Work in the Wa State]. February 10. Unpublished.

————. 2001b. *Wa Bang 2001 Nian Gong Zuo Ren Wu* [Work Plan for 2001]. February 17. Unpublished.

————. 2001c. *Mian Dian Di Er Te Qu (Wa Bang) 1990 Nian–2000 Nian He Ping Jing Ji Jian She Gai Kuang* [Burma No. 2 Special Region (Wa State), 1990–2000, Peaceful Economic Construction Report]. March. Classified. Provided to the author by a Wa leader.

————. 2001d. *Bi Er Ke Li Si Xian Sheng (Mei Guo) Cai Fang Mian Dian Di Er Te Qu (Wa Bang) Zheng Fu Zhu Xi Bao You Xiang* [Mr. Bill Curtis (USA) Interviewing Burma Special Region 2 (Wa State) Chairman Bao Youxiang]. March 24. Classified. Provided to the author by a Wa leader.

————. 2001e. *Zheng Fa Bu Chen Xi Bang Zhang Zai Wa Bang Jin Du Gong Zuo Hui Shang De Jiang Hua* [A Speech by Chen Xibang, Director of Political Legal Bureau, at a Drug Eradication Workshop]. Unpublished.

————. 2004. *Wa Bang Ji Ben Fa* [Wa Basic Law].

————. 2005a. *Wa Bang Di Si Ge Wu Nian Ji Hua Gang Yao (2005 Nian–2009 Nian)* [Outline for the Fourth Five-Year Plan of the Wa State (2005–2009)]. Unpublished.

————. 2005b. *Guan Yu Mei Guo Mo Zhou Fa Yuan Kong Gao Wa Bang Ling Dao Ren Yi Shi De Yan Zheng Sheng Ming* [An Announcement Regarding the Indictment of Wa Leaders by a State Court in the United States]. February 8. Unpublished.

Xiao, Shu. 2005. *Jin San Jiao De Nu Ren* [Women of the Golden Triangle]. Beijing: Writers' Press.

Yang, Jiafu. 2005. *Jin Du Feng Bao: Zhong Guo Da Ji Bian Jing Du Bo Zhan Dou Ji Shi* [Gambling Prohibition: China Declares War on Gambling in the Border Areas]. Beijing: Chaohua Publication.

Zhao, Shilung, and Shuya Ke. 2003. *Jie Du Jin San Jiao: Zhong Guo Ji Zhe Kua Guo Cai Fang Shou Ji* [Golden Triangle: A Future without Heroin?] Beijing: Economic Daily Publisher.

Zhu, Ling. 2004. *Ying Su Hua Kai* [Poppy Ablooming]. Beijing: China Prosecutorial Publisher.

Index

acetic anhydride, 221
Afghanistan, 1, 9, 53
Ahka, 106, 108, 109, 147
Aicheng, 21, 57, 64, 156
Ailun, 43, 80
amphetamine, 96
amphetamine-type stimulant (ATS). *See*
    methamphetamine
Anti-Money Laundering Office, 214
Asian Forum for Human Rights and
    Development, 202
Asian Heroin Task Force, 214, 215
Association of Southeast Asian Nations
    (ASEA), 16, 246n7
Aung San, 10, 14
Aung San Suu Kyi, 3, 14, 15, 16, 24, 213,
    235
Australian Crime Commission, 86

Baker, Chris, 203
Ball, Desmond, 225
Bangkang, 21, 22, 26, 27–30, 36, 38, 58
Bangkok, 105, 111, 197, 216
Bangsai, 208
Ban Yang, 109, 199
bao (bag), 132–33

Bao Aimen, 22, 37
Bao Huaqiang, 36, 214
Baoshan, 96, 180, 208
Bao Youhua, 36, 139, 214
Bao Youliang, 31, 36, 214
Bao Youxiang, 21, 24, 31, 32, 36, 38, 62, 145,
    238; businesses owned by, 29; and the
    drug trade, 45, 89, 90, 99, 222; indictment
    of, 26, 214; relationship with Wei
    Xuegang, 141; words of, 101, 113, 139, 172,
    188–89, 190, 223
Bao Youyi, 32–33, 36, 102, 113, 214
Bay of Bengal, 3
Belanger, Francis, 87, 105, 111
Belenko, Steven, 177
Black, David, 87, 122, 228
Bo Laikang, 18
Booth, Martin, 82, 87, 118, 177, 228
Boucaud, Andre, 87, 187
Boucaud, Louis, 87, 187
Bourgois, Philippe, 131, 177
Bresler, Fenton, 118, 228
Brookes, Stephen, 228
Bryant, Robert, 120, 122
buffer state, 3, 235
Bureau of International Narcotics Matters, 53

Burma, 245n1; 1962 coup in, 12–14; anti-
  Chinese movement in, 13; armed conflict
  in, 12, 14; colonization of, 10; economy of,
  13, 15; ethnic minorities in, 10; location
  of, 10
Burman, 3, 10
Burma Socialist Programme Party (BSPP), 12
Burmese Way to Socialism, 12

caffeine, 221
Callahan, Mary, 11, 16
Cangyuan, 1, 208, 254n24
cease-fire agreements, 9, 14, 15, 24, 88, 129,
  195, 214
Chalk, Peter, 111
Chang Chi-fu. *See* Khun Sa
Chartchai Suthiklom, 127, 143, 144, 146, 176,
  203
Chengdu, 210
Chen Longsheng, 22, 23, 59
Chepesiuk, Ron, 2
Chiang Mai, 216
Chiang Rai, 216
Chin, 10
Chin, Ko-lin, 2, 86, 87, 118, 119, 187, 229, 231,
  240
China-Burma border, 4, 111–12
Chinese businessmen: in the drug trade, 2,
  43, 46, 83–84, 94–95, 124, 152–53, 230–33;
  in the Wa area, 27, 192–93
Chiu Chau, 105, 114
Chongqing, 96, 211–12
Chouvy, Pierre-Arnaud, 8, 10, 86, 148, 187
Chu, Yiu-kong, 86, 87, 118, 231
Collignon, Stefan, 13
Colombian drug cartels, 122–23
Communist Party of Burma (CPB), 246n2;
  collapse of, 9, 14, 23–24, 44, 77, 88–89,
  189, 238; insurgency of, 3, 12–13; in the
  Wa area, 21–23
controlled delivery, 210, 257n26
corrupt exchanges, 2–3, 6, 126, 245n5
Cowell, Adrian, 12, 14, 23
crack cocaine, 131, 186
crop-substitution program, 191
Cultural Revolution, 13, 112, 237

Dai. *See* Shan
Dali, 208, 209
Davis, Anthony, 87, 88, 99, 152, 190, 222
Dehong, 206
Denge, 30, 52, 57, 64, 156
Deng Xiaoping, 238

detoxification center, 182–83
Dikotter, Frank, 177, 205
Diqing, 96
Dobinson, Ian, 111, 122
Dongcheng, 97
Dong Sheng, 104, 213
drug: and the Burmese government,
  225–27; businesspeople, 5; as commodity,
  216–17, 218–19; courier, 115; demand, 220;
  enforcers, 5; and organized crime, 227–31;
  politics of, 3, 7, 234–39; supply, 220;
  trade, 45, 206–7, 221, 224. *See also* heroin;
  methamphetamine; opium
drug control: 2003 drug war, 200–204;
  in Burma, 194–97; in China, 204–13;
  in Thailand, 198–200; in the Wa area,
  188–93; international cooperation, 212–13;
  U.S. role, 213–15
Drug Control Bureau, 212
Drug Prevention through Migration. *See*
  forced migration
drug use: in China, 114, 207; in the Golden
  Triangle, 185–86; in Thailand, 176. *See
  also* heroin use; methamphetamine use;
  opium use
Dubro, James 122, 228
Dupont, Alan, 10, 88, 195, 225

Eads, Brian, 78
Elliott, Patricia, 10
ephedrine, 127, 145, 151, 210, 221
ethnic conflict, 217
Evans, Grant, 112

Fabre, Guilhem, 114, 217
Finckenauer, James, 118, 119, 187
Fink, Christina, 13, 14, 15, 24
Fiskesjo, Nils Magnus Geir, 20
forced migration, 32, 33–34, 193
Foreign Narcotics Kingpin Designation Act,
  214
Friedman, Jonathan, 83, 238
Friendship Bridge, 199
Fusan, 103
Fuzhou, 213, 216

gambling, 26, 29, 129
Gaylord, Mark, 118
Gelbard, Robert, 8, 24, 78, 87, 90, 99
general election, 14–15
Gengma, 1
Gibson, Richard, 213, 227, 237
Gittings, John, 231

Godson, Roy, 2
Golden Triangle, 8
Goldfish Case, 212–13
Gould, Terry, 228
Greenfeld, Karl Taro, 146
Green Gang, 118, 251n32
Group 41. *See* Asian Heroin Task Force
Guangdong, 117, 210
Guangxi, 210, 211
Guangzhou, 93, 96, 112, 117, 210, 211
guerrilla groups, 21
Guiyang, 210
Guizhou, 210, 211
gumlao, 83
gumsa, 83

Hani, 52
Haq, M. Emdad-ul, 82, 86, 105
Haseman, John, 213, 227, 237
Hawke, Bruce, 78, 88
Hayward, 118, 122
head-hunting, 19–21
Hedao, 31, 52, 56, 57, 64, 138, 156, 166
Hedao Incident, 138
heroin: Chinese route, 111–17; as a
  commodity, 124–26; in Hong Kong,
  117–18; in Kokang, 101–3; in Mengla,
  103–4; producers, 76, 91, 94; production,
  4, 8, 77–78, 87–89, 100; retail, 100,
  116–17; seizure, 33, 92–93, 96, 112–13,
  118; tax, 87, 94, 99–100; Thai route,
  105–11; trade, 98; traffickers, 92, 95–97,
  102–3; trafficking, 100, 107; in the
  United States, 8, 86, 120–24; wholesale,
  115–16
heroin use: addiction, 179–81; in Burma,
  173–75; cessation, 182–84; changing
  patterns of, 181–82; impact of, 184;
  initiation into, 178–79; in the Wa area,
  163–64
Hkam Awng, 77, 218
Ho Mong, 90
Hong Kong, 111
Hong Pang Group, 215
Huai Khrai, 199
Hunan, 233
Hushuang, 21
Hutton, Christopher, 112

Independence Commission Against
  Corruption (ICAC), 118
Independent Regiment (*dulituan*), 33
international engagement, 239

International Law Enforcement Academy
  (ILEA), 216
International Narcotics Control Strategy
  Report (INCSR), 53, 54, 86, 112, 128, 129,
  175, 195, 196, 226

Jacobs, Bruce, 131
Jagan, Larry, 188
jao pho, 106, 126, 250n18
Jelsma, Martin, 9, 62, 78, 86, 123, 187, 194, 240
jian (unit), 91, 92, 133, 250n3
Jinghong, 209
Johnson, Bruce, 184
joint venture, 191–92

Kachin, 3, 10, 83
Ka Kwe Ye (KKY), 13–14
kamnan. See *jao pho*
Kang Xiang Jewelry Company, 29, 247n18
Karen, 10
Kayah, 10
Kentung, 12, 18
Khin Nyunt, 14, 15–16, 26, 97, 196, 225
Khun Sa, 29, 99, 128, 140, 187, 197, 216; the
  surrender of, 4, 9, 24–25, 32, 33, 44, 78, 87,
  88, 89, 125, 129, 142, 198, 223
Kinkead, Gwen, 122
Klong Toey, 105, 176, 200, 202
Kokang, 3, 13, 17, 30, 39, 60, 77, 82, 90, 105, 129,
  166, 223, 238, 241
Kramer, Tom, 10, 23, 34, 60, 62, 78, 152, 187,
  194, 238, 240
Kuah, Khun Eng, 111, 112
Kudo, Toshihiro, 112, 240
Kunma, 21, 31, 36, 38, 42, 64
Kunming, 96, 180, 209, 233
Kuomintang (KMT), 106, 187, 204, 226; and
  the opium trade, 12; in the Wa area, 18, 21
Kyaw Thein, 214

Laamann, Lars, 177, 205
labor camp, 183, 255n74
Labrousse, Alain, 9, 53
Lahu, 1, 27, 30, 106, 147
Lancang, 1
Laos, 200
Laukkai, 26, 31, 97, 115
Leach, Edmund, 83
Liangshan, 210
Li Guoting, 112
Li Laoer, 33
Li Mi, 12
Lincang, 27, 208–9

Lin Mingxian, 90, 225
Lintner, Bertil, 3, 8, 9, 12, 14, 16, 23, 24, 78, 83, 87, 88, 89, 90, 105, 187, 237, 238
Lishu, 106, 147
Liu Ming, 96–97, 196
Liu Shuanyueh, 113
Li Ziru, 33, 36, 89, 90, 99, 113, 189
Lo, T. Wing, 118
Longling, 208
Longtan, 27, 31, 57, 58, 64, 156, 193
Luoping, 114
Luo Xinghan, 14, 23–24, 89, 99, 144, 187, 197, 223, 224, 236
Luxi, 206, 208

Mae Sai, 91, 106, 107, 108, 109, 110, 148, 197, 199. *See also* methamphetamine, trade centers of
Mandalay, 5, 103
Mark, Gregory Yee, 120
market day, 27, 64, 70, 247n22
Marshall, Andrew, 13, 87, 99, 130, 152, 190, 222
Maule, Robert, 173
Maung Aye, 16
Maung Pho Shoke, 89, 90
McCoy, Alfred, 82, 87, 89, 111, 117, 118, 122, 187, 217, 221, 234
McLeod, Alexander, 120
Meissonnier, Joel, 8, 10, 86, 148, 187
Mekong, 3
Mengbo, 27, 31, 194
Mengga, 27, 31
Mengla, 13, 17, 26, 60, 82, 90, 129, 209, 223, 225, 238, 241
Menglian, 233
Mengmao, 18, 21, 27, 30, 31, 64, 103
Mengping, 27, 31
methamphetamine: in Kokang, 143–44; participants in, 153–54; production of, 4, 9–10, 127–32, 135–36, 151; retail, 132–33, 137; smuggled into Thailand, 146–49; tax, 128, 144–45, 152; trade centers of, 149–51; transportation of, 136; wholesale, 133–35
methamphetamine use: addiction, 168–69; in Bangkang, 164–66; in Burma, 175; cessation, 168–70; among drug traders, 173; impact of, 170–72; initiation into, 166–67; reactions to, 167–68; in Thailand, 176–77; Wa leaders' responses to, 172–73
Meyer, Kathryn, 82, 177
Milsom, Jeremy, 34, 77, 143, 152, 190, 193, 230
Ministry of Public Security, 212
Mon, 10

Mong Tai Army (MTA), 89–90
Mong Yawn, 107, 140, 142, 146
Murphy, Dan, 176
Muse, 5, 16, 95, 96, 206, 208
Myanmar. *See* Burma

Nandeng, 6, 27, 52, 56, 57, 64, 78, 87, 103, 156
Nankangwu, 57, 64, 156
Narcotics Suppression Bureau, 214
National League for Democracy (NLD), 3, 14–15, 24, 213
National Narcotics Control Commission (NNCC), 212
National Narcotics Operation Centre, 225
National Unity Party, 14
Naypyidaw, 10
Ne Win, 12, 13, 14, 24
New York, 216
Nixon, Richard, 217
Nu, U, 12, 18
Nugent, David, 83

Office of Narcotics Control Board (ONCB), 146, 149, 176, 214, 216, 236
open door policy, 112
Operation Tiger Trap, 90, 122, 216
Operation Warlord, 214
Operation White Mare, 121
opium: ban, 22, 26, 60–62, 129, 190–91, 217, 241–42; converting, into heroin, 60; cultivation, 1, 8–9, 50–56, 256n3; economy, 82–83; income, 57; in Kokang, 77; licit, 248n7; price, 87; problems in trading, 76–77; reasons for growing, 48–50; seeding, 56; survey, 54–55; tax, 22–23, 43, 48, 50, 53, 58–60, 81–82; trade, 59, 64–66, 68–76; weight, 248n12; yield, 55–57
opium use, 49–50; addiction, 158–59; in Burma, 173; cessation, 159–61; in China, 177; impact of, 161–63; initiation into, 156–57; in the Wa area, 156

Panglong Agreement, 10
Parssinen, Terry, 82, 177
Pathan, Don, 25, 147
Peng Jiafu, 197
Peng Jiasheng, 23–24, 88, 90, 196, 197
Phongpaichit, Pasuk, 8, 86, 87, 105, 106, 187
Pingyuan, 209
Piriyarangsan, Sungsidh, 8, 86, 87, 105, 106, 187
political-military actors, 224
Posner, Gerald, 86, 87, 118, 228

precursor chemicals, 4, 218–19, 221
President's Commission on Organized
    Crime, 120, 228

Rakhine, 10
Rangoon, 5
Renard, Ronald, 89, 173, 175, 187
research methods, 4–6
Revolutionary Council, 12–13
Royal Thai Police, 214
Ruili, 16, 95, 206, 208

Sack, John, 87, 228
Salween River, 223, 238
San Mulu, 33
Schalks, Toon, 122
Security Regiment (*jingweituan*), 31, 138–39
Selth, Andrew, 16
Shan, 1, 3, 10, 20, 27, 98, 245n3
Shan State, 1, 2, 3, 8–9, 57, 104, 114, 144, 226,
    233
Shan State Army (SSA), 89, 144, 198, 200, 201
Shan United Army (SUA), 32
Shaopa, 21, 64, 156
Shelley, Louise, 2
Shenzhen, 93
Skidmore, Monique, 16
Sichuan, 210, 211, 233
Simao, 27, 33, 113, 209
Smith, Martin, 9, 12, 82
Snipes, William J., 203
Soe Win, 16
Southern Military Region (SMR). *See* Wa
    State: Southern
South Vietnam, 117
special region, 245n6
speed pills. *See* methamphetamine
Spence, Jonathan, 112
State Law and Order Restoration Council
    (SLORC), 14–15, 24, 216, 225
State Peace and Development Council
    (SPDC), 15, 16, 214, 225
Steinberg, David, 9, 14, 16, 33, 193, 214
Stille, Alexander, 2
street demonstrations, 14, 16
Sun Chengde, 19, 21

Tachilek, 91, 106, 107, 136, 146. *See also*
    methamphetamine, trade centers of
Taiwanese, 119
Takano, Hideyuki, 33, 37, 60, 87, 99, 187
Tan Xiaolin, 95–96
Tasker, Rodney, 16
tatmadaw, 15, 16, 194, 214

Taylor, Robert, 15
Teerat, Nualnoi, 8, 86, 87, 105, 106, 187
Tenchong, 208
Thai-Burma border, 10, 22; clashes and
    closures, 25, 30, 113–14, 198–200; drug
    trade in, 89, 90, 105–6, 109, 235
Thaksin Sinawatra, 25, 186, 200, 201, 202, 204
Than Shwe, 16
Thant Myint-U, 10, 12, 13, 16, 195, 239
Thayer, Nate, 111
Thoumi, Francesco, 2
Ting, Chang, 33, 65, 86, 93, 95, 96, 97, 114, 177,
    187, 205, 209, 210, 211, 212
tongs, 227–31
Transnational Institute, 26, 174, 214
triads, 118, 227–32
tribal warfare, 18, 21

Unit 51, 22
United Wa State Army (UWSA), 16, 31,
    34–36, 78, 80, 88–89, 90, 99, 100, 128, 152,
    187, 192, 198, 200, 214, 221–22, 225. *See
    also* Independent Regiment; Security
    Regiment
United Wa State Party (UWSP), 24, 34–35, 92
United Nations Drug Control Program
    (UNDCP), 31, 192
United Nations Office on Drugs and Crime
    (UNODC), 8, 9, 55, 57, 77, 156, 176, 194
United States Department of State, 53, 227
United States Drug Enforcement
    Administration (DEA), 32, 114, 129, 212,
    214, 215, 216, 222, 227

van Kemenade, Willem, 231
Vervest, Pietje, 62, 78, 187, 194, 240

Wa administration, 34–37
Wa Alternative Development Project
    (WADP), 31, 57, 194
Wa Basic Law, 87, 156, 160, 250n1
Wa Central Authority (WCA), 22, 32, 34–35,
    44–45, 84, 136, 138, 154, 238
Wa government. *See* Wa administration; Wa
    Central Authority
Wa leaders: as businessmen, 44–45; as drug
    entrepreneurs, 43, 75, 78–81, 87–88,
    100–101, 106, 124, 137–40, 151–52, 222–24;
    as insurgents, 13; multiple roles of, 84–85;
    as organized crime, 38–39; relationship
    with Burmese authorities, 37; as state
    builders, 2–3, 7, 234; U.S. indictment of,
    36, 44, 214–15. *See also* Bao Youxiang; Wei
    Xuegang; Zhou Dafu

Wa National Army (WNA), 88
Wanding, 208
Wang Jianzhang, 123–24, 216
Wang Keqiang, 102, 127
Wa people: children, 42–43; farmers, 5,
    39–40; population, 1, 30; reactions to
    outside criticism, 62–63; religion, 248n8;
    women, 41–42
Wa Special Region. *See* Wa State
Wa State, 17, 246n1; drug ban in, 4; economy
    of, 25, 29–30; education in, 42; modern
    history of, 18–26; Northern, 1, 27;
    principles of, 34; social inequality in, 37;
    Southern, 1, 6, 27, 32–34
Wa State Tobacco Company, 192
Wei Saitang, 33, 34
Weishan, 209
Wei Xuegang, 88, 99, 187, 199, 238; as drug
    lord, 140–41, 214; indictment of, 26, 154; as
    philanthropist, 141–43; in Southern Wa,
    32–33; U.S. reward for, 90, 140
Wei Xuelong, 36, 88, 141, 214
Wei Xueyun, 36, 88, 141, 214
Wengao, 22, 27, 31, 57, 64
Wenshan, 209
Westermeyer, Joseph, 82
Williams, Terry, 131
Win Naing, U, 16, 221
World Food Program, 194, 241
Worobec, Stephen, 105

Xiao Mingliang, 25, 191
Xichang, 210
Ximeng, 1
Xindifang, 31, 103
Xishuangbanna, 27, 209

yaba. See methamphetamine
Yang Guodong, 95
Yang Maoliang, 112
Yang Maoxian, 112
Yao, 147
Yawd Serk, 198
Yawnghwe, Chao-Tzang, 24, 221, 223, 224,
    230, 234, 237
Yingpan, 21, 31, 52, 57, 64, 74, 150, 156
Yongbang, 92
Yunnan, 1, 27, 114, 117, 206, 209, 211, 233,
    238
Yunnan Provincial Anti-Narcotics Bureau,
    213
yuntu (Yunnan opium), 177

Zaitch, Damian, 2
Zhang, Sheldon, 231, 240
Zhao Nilai, 21, 24, 92, 93
Zhao Sunmuli, 92–93
Zhenkang, 208
Zhou Dafu, 22, 25, 55, 65, 128, 172
Zhou Enlai, 18
Zhou Xun, 177, 205